SAILING TO THE REEFS

Also by Bernard Moitessier

Cape Horn: The Logical Route
The Long Way
Tamata and the Alliance
A Sea Vagabond's World

BERNARD MOITESSIER

Sailing
to the Reefs

Translated from the French by
RENÉ HAGUE

with postscripts by
K. ADLARD COLES AND
MICHAEL RICHEY

SHERIDAN HOUSE

This edition first published 2001 by
Sheridan House Inc.
145 Palisade Street
Dobbs Ferry, New York 10522
www.sheridanhouse.com

First published in France under the title
Un Vagabond des Mers du Sud by Flammarion

*A Cataloging-in-Publication record for this book is available from the
Library of Congress, Washington, DC.*

Printed in the United States of America

ISBN 1-57409-120-4

Introduction

I don't imagine I am the only English-speaking reader who has swallowed the bulk of Moitessier's work at nearly one bolt. He, of all those who have written on the subject, fought most doggedly to give voice to that which is effervescent in the sport of ocean sailing. If you have ever spent a starlit night alone at sea divining philosophy in the phosphorescent vapor trails of fish and fellow mammals (or hope to), you will have appreciated what the man was trying to say. You will have set your sights on any title with his name appended, will have read it greedily, will have prowled for the next. And eventually you'll have read them all, except for this one.

*

My own entrée into the curious phenomenon that is Moitessier was through his second book, *Cape Horn: The Logical Route* (*Cap Horn à la Voile*). Here, already, he was a legend in the making. A penniless shipwrecked castaway on a beach in Trinidad, he wheels and deals and dreams (his most inspired scheme involves the building of a composite paper boat) and is quickly afloat again in a steel boat called *Joshua*, in which he cruises from Europe to Tahiti with his new bride. To save himself the bother of a circumnavigation, he then returns to Europe via Cape Horn, sailing 14,216 miles non-stop. Along the way he pioneers a new active storm-management technique, cutting away his warps in a brilliant flash of intuition during a fierce gale in high southern latitudes. He hand steers down breaking seas for days on end, and revels in it.

In the sequel, of course, *The Long Way (La Longue Route)*, the legend runneth over. Moitessier's decision in mid-passage in the South Atlantic to quit the London *Sunday Times'* vaunted Golden Globe singlehanded non-stop round-the-world race, and the message he flung so characteristically via slingshot on to the deck of a passing freighter—"I am continuing on to save my soul . . ."—were

i

determinative in the sport's history. It was here, irrevocably, that ocean racing and bluewater cruising became distinct avocations. And it was here, too, that the French passion for singlehanded ocean sailing (in both its permutations), having been forged in the heat of Eric Tabarly's early racing victories, was tempered and honed to such a fine edge.

The true magnitude of the achievement documented in *The Long Way*—a non-stop passage of 37,455 miles, one-and-a-half circuits around the globe in high latitudes—is glaringly apparent only when one troubles to read the other contemporaneous volumes in the trilogy of books describing the battle for the Golden Globe. The most dramatic, of course, is *The Strange Last Voyage of Donald Crowhurst* (by the *Sunday Times'* Nicholas Tomalin and Ron Hall), in which we see how the pressures of preparing a boat for the event, and an abiding fear of the Southern Ocean, led the highstrung Crowhurst to panic and report false positions while circling aimlessly for months off Brazil. His insane deception finally ended with his tragic suicide in mid-ocean and led Nigel Tetley, who believed Crowhurst was hard on his heels, to push his own boat so hard that it disintegrated just 1,200 miles from the finish. Meanwhile, Robin Knox-Johnston, in *A World of My Own,* at least tells a tale with a happy ending—he was, after all, the eventual victor in the event—but his own passage through the Southern Ocean was by no means a pleasure cruise. Having lost his self-steering gear early in the race, Knox-Johnston's voyage quickly turned into an excruciating test of endurance.

Compare these miserable experiences with Moitessier's, and one can easily savor the genius of the man. Where others suffer, kill themselves, endure endless misery, Moitessier's voyage is one of sheer exaltation. He communes with the open ocean and its inhabitants and eventually becomes a sort of sea-creature himself. His passage is at once effortless and flawless—the only significant problem being a collision with a freighter, which results in a bent bowsprit that he ingeniously straightens at sea using a sheet winch and a multi-part tackle. In the end, we find in *The Long Way* a document unique in the annals of yachting; it is, in fact, nothing less than a description of an intense ten-month-long bluewater epiphany.

Having absorbed all this, an incredulous reader may at last think to wonder how it was this seemingly superhuman sailor ended up shipwrecked and penniless on that beach in Trinidad in the first place. This is the story told in Moitessier's very first book, *Sailing to the Reefs (Un Vagabond des Mers du Sud)*.

I searched for this book for a long time before finally finding a copy. First published in France in 1960, it was immediately a success there, and, of course, it was the fact of this success that made it possible for Moitessier to build *Joshua* and embark on the voyages that established his international reputation. A translation in English did not appear until 1971, in the wake of his quixotic Golden Globe bid, and it seems those who purchased it at that time have been loathe to part with it. In more than ten years of methodical scrounging through the shelves of used-book stores, I never found a single copy for sale. It wasn't until the advent of the Internet (and the very excellent Advanced Book Exchange website at www.abebooks.com) that I at last achieved success. So that those of you purchasing this new edition in paperback may now appreciate the fine bargain you are receiving, I will confess I had to pay $100 (the asking price was $200!) for the old hardcover copy I finally located online.

*

Like myself, then, you likely will be coming at Moitessier all backwards, having read his later books before this first one. There is something deliciously appropriate in this, for Moitessier, after all, seems to have come at us (particularly us American readers) in exactly the same manner. In part this is because he was French, but more specifically it is because he was colonial French. One of the great ironies of his life, and of his relationship with the whole of late twentieth-century Western political culture, is that while we were all rushing towards and in some way personalizing the tragedy that was the conflict in Vietnam, Moitessier from the beginning was actively fleeing it and deliberately putting it behind him.

For we must remember that this man, who more than any other personified the "hippy" spirit in ocean sailing in the mid- and late-60's (and, indeed, personifies it to this day), was in fact a fierce partisan and active combatant in the early fighting against Vietnamese nationalists after World War II. As related in his very last book, *Tamata and the Alliance (Tamata et l'Alliance)*, Moitessier became disillusioned with the civil war that eventually split Vietnam into north and south, but never because he lost faith in his cause. He always thought of Indochina as his country; he was born and raised there and felt a deep connection to its land and people. The problem, rather, was that he perceived early on that his cause could not prevail. Moitessier's original purpose in fashioning himself a bluewater sailor was emigration plain and simple.

But Moitessier swam more than just a contrary course against the current of modern history. In the end, his was a trajectory that cut against the whole of animal evolution. From the beginning he seems to have sensed that the sea was where he truly belonged and that his emigration was complete as soon as he had boarded a boat and cast off his lines. Even as Westerners were coming to the East, Moitessier was, in effect, an Easterner coming to the West, and in that sense he was moving toward us and meeting us halfway. But more significantly, he was a land creature returning to the sea, and in this sense he was moving away from everyone and everything and was a singularity on to himself.

The Moitessier we find here then in *Sailing to the Reefs* is Moitessier the apprentice, a man who has grasped that he is at last in his element and is learning how to flourish in it. The book does not cover his very first voyages, but does allude to them. His initial attempt to leave Vietnam (described in *Tamata and the Alliance*) was aboard a decrepit Malaysian proa named *Snark*, which he sailed with a partner, Pierre Deshumeurs, as far as Indonesia. Their plan was to emigrate to Australia, but Indonesian authorities, concerned about the patent unseaworthiness of their vessel, sent them packing back to Singapore. Amazingly, though *Snark* was taking on an estimated two tons of water a day, they succeeded in returning all the way to Saigon. Deshumeurs went back to his job, but Moitessier immediately sold his stock in his father's import business and invested the proceeds in another boat, a gaff-rigged Siamese junk, which he named *Marie-Thérèse*, after a fiancée he had recently jilted.

Sailing to the Reefs picks up the story shortly after *Marie-Thérèse* has cleared Singapore and the Straits of Malacca and, after a monumental battle with the contrary monsoon, has finally reached the tradewind belt in the Indian Ocean. Though Moitessier does not remark upon it here, this is in fact a very significant moment in his life, for here at last he had permanently broken his bond with Southeast Asia to emerge in what he later termed that "nation of wind, light, and peace [where] there is no ruler but the sea." That he had a lot to learn on board *Marie-Thérèse* is immediately evident in the fact that this is the story of not one, but two shipwrecks. In all, Moitessier wrecked three boats in his life, if one includes his loss of *Joshua* on a beach in Baja California after a freak blow at Cabo San Lucas in 1982. (The boat was sold on the spot for $20, and she was subsequently refit by others.) All three losses, it must be noted, resulted from proximity to land, and in this respect Moitessier's career is a vivid illustration of the old saw about sailors being safest at sea. In even the most delapidated craft, it seems nothing could touch him as long as he was far enough offshore.

As a writer Moitessier was no great stylist, but his later work is blisteringly genuine in its effort to express that which is perforce inexpressible. The essence of his voice at its best is an ineffable mix of prosaic practical advice and metaphysical exaltation. At times, however, he seems much too self-conscious in his role as an evangelist promoting a religion of his own devising. In *Sailing to the Reefs* there is none of this self-consciousness. His voice here is delightfully naïve and unaffected and focussed wholly on the tutorials of his daily existence as a bluewater vagabond.

In this sense, I think, *Sailing to the Reefs* may be Moitessier's strongest work. For though he has not yet overtly developed his "spiritual" side here—indeed, this wasn't really to happen until his transcendent experience in *The Long Way*—we see it inchoate in the incredible energy he displays and in the amazingly creative solutions he devises to the day-to-day problems that confront him. His writing reflects his youthful enthusiasm, his energy, and his creativity and never fails to carry us along into the ups and downs of the happy maelstrom that is his life.

True, the events of this drama are not writ as large as those in his later books. But, still, the challenges he faces are every bit as daunting, and the fact that they are often born of his own blunders and stupidity, and that he freely confesses this and chastises himself without mercy, will seem both amusing and refreshingly familiar to any novice sailor who has likewise learned his lessons the hard way. In this respect, we may identify with Moitessier much more than when we followed him on his record-breaking passages through the Southern Ocean. By the same token, however, we can't help but be awestruck by the breadth of his resourcefulness.

In the end, perhaps, this is what is truly most interesting about this book, and why our appreciation of it is enhanced by our coming to it last. The seeds of Moitessier's future accomplishments are very evident here. Yes, this is the story of a man careless enough to lose his boat on a charted reef through a gross error in navigation. But it is also the story of a man who contrives to build himself a new boat from scratch, without any plan to work from, without any power tools, and without any appreciable financial resources, in just nine months. Here is a man who feeds himself hunting cormorants and penguins with a slingshot, who dives on wrecks and reefs for fish with an ingenious homemade underwater breathing apparatus, who makes his own rope from nylon scraps found on the quay, builds his own galvanized steel water tanks, constructs his own self-steering gear, sews his own sails.

Moitessier is able to do all this not because he is possessed of omnipotent skill or encyclopedic knowledge, but rather because he is simply willing to start a job and learn it along the way by trial and error, however long it takes. Obviously, this is often a painful process. Indeed, some of the mistakes we see Moitessier making here are truly monumental. But in the last analysis, there can be no doubt that it was this uncanny autodidactic ability, combined with an unquenchable optimism that permitted him—again and again—to rebuild from nothing, that made him one of the greatest bluewater sailors of the twentieth century.

Charles J. Doane
Rockland, Maine
September 2000

SAILING TO THE REEFS

CONTENTS

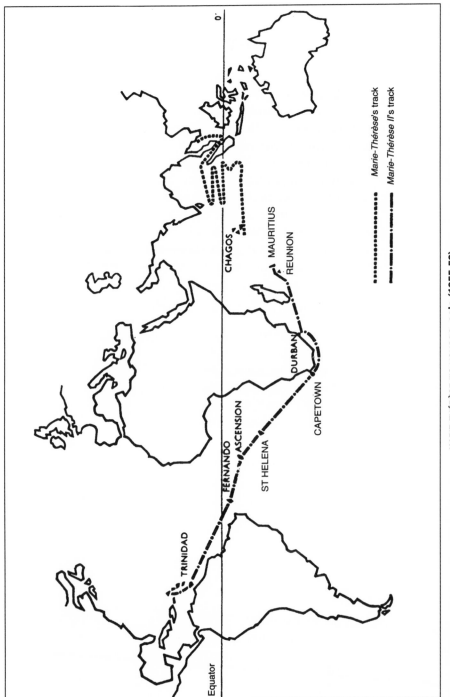

MARIE-THÉRÈSE II's voyage, solo (1955-58)

Equator

TRINIDAD

FERNANDO

ASCENSION

ST HELENA

CAPETOWN

DURBAN

REUNION

MAURITIUS

CHAGOS

0°

Marie-Thérèse's track

Marie-Thérèse II's track

DIAGRAMS

TRACK CHARTS

Drawn by M. A. Verity

CHAPTER 1

In the Indian Ocean

The date in the log-book that day was September 4th, 1952. It was our eighty-fifth day since leaving Singapore. I say 'our', because there were two of us: *Marie-Thérèse* and myself. We were in fact only one person, just as the body and the spirit which dwells in it are one.

This integration of man and boat had been effected in progressive stages: at our first meeting I had quite simply fallen in love with this beautiful junk from the gulf of Siam, with her bold and sturdy lines, fragrant with natural oil, the stem of her bows thrusting forward in a graceful continuation of her pronounced sheer—a finger pointing both to the sky and the horizon, and the lands that lie far beyond the horizon.

But this total fusion of boat and man would never, I believe, have come about without the monsoon in the Indian Ocean, into which we had wandered, frankly, at random—just to see whether all the tales were true, taking it almost as a game.

It was true enough: and there was nothing playful about the monsoon. Together, we had then beaten up against this inferno of headwinds, finally succeeding in emerging from it in six weeks of tirelessly tacking to and fro. For that south-west monsoon was indeed pure hell for the unit which we already constituted: a hell inside which the mind could not even entertain the idea that anything else existed outside it.

It was an eternity of headwinds and squalls, punctuated by dead calms which were too brief to allow the seas to subside: and all this under the grey sky of the rainy season, which banished the seaman's fairest deity, the sun.

At the end of our first week in the Indian Ocean I could hardly have been completely a human being: I had become some sort of aquatic animal, governed by an instinct: for as soon as I came up against this wall of wind, as we emerged from the Malacca Strait, intelligence ceased to be of any practical use; and with intelligence there went all the feelings which normally inspire the human mind. The mind had then jettisoned everything that might prove harmful to it, since a thing that is of no use can only be harmful. Only the animal instinct which remains hidden deep inside each one of us had risen to the surface, there to exaggerate its dimensions, take complete possession of the boat-man unit, and impose on it the only order that then made sense: to hang on, whatever happens—hang on, without attempting to understand, keep the head as close to the wind as possible, giving a wide berth to land and rocks, and, above all, live in the present, shutting the mind to everything else.

In the end, we got through the monsoon: how and why, I have no idea, for once we reached the zone of the following trade winds, the animal who a few days earlier was still in control had, in its turn, become of no use; it was then a source of danger, and the numbed mind woke up again. The human in me reasserted itself, but the man could neither judge nor understand the animal which for six weeks he had become. That however, did not matter, because we had got through and the monsoon, now lying in our wake, belonged to a time that was no more.

*

It was on June 12th that I had left the little island of Porto-Angska, our last call in the Malacca Strait. Since then, a more or less uneventful passage had brought us to the entry into the Indian Ocean, which we reached on July 3rd.

Then came the monsoon—best forgotten now—and finally the trade wind, which we came up with about August 12th: a trade wind in the Indian Ocean! We call the trades by the same name wherever they occur, but the way in which they behave is often a very different story. However, this was indeed the trade wind, in spite of its changing moods and the disturbed seas it produced; and, compared with what we had just been through, it was like Paradise.

Once *Marie-Thérèse* reached the fair-wind zone, she headed west, towards the Seychelles. All that I had in the way of navigational instruments was a compass and a sextant, just enough, that is, to work out my noon latitude. For the last two months I had to rely on an estimated longitude, since I had no chronometer on board, nor even a log, let alone a dry-battery receiver to pick up time-signals, which would have enabled me, if need be, to use my alarm-clock as a chronometer and so obtain a longitude approximate enough for making the Seychelles, after rounding the big Chagos Bank which lay between *Marie-Thérèse* and her destination.

Lacking the necessary means for working out an exact position, I thought I could rely on the famous seamen's 'nose' for land, which can divine its proximity by a number of signs—floating sea-weed, the increase in the number of flying fish, and barely perceptible changes in the behaviour of the sea, whose normal rhythm may be disturbed by currents; finally, there is the presence in the sky of frigate-birds, small sea-birds, which are never found more than forty miles or so from the coast. A friend in Singapore who had lived in a number of different islands in the Indian Ocean, had often spoken to me about these.

However, none of these signs was apparent as yet. Perhaps my senses had not yet become sufficiently attuned to pick them up. And so *Marie-Thérèse* sailed on, the helm lashed, with the wind aft for weeks on end.

At noon on September 4th, my reckoning put us five or six hundred miles east of Diego-Garcia, the most southerly of the Chagos atolls.

My first objective was to pass about ten miles north of this atoll, before heading north as far as the latitude of Mahe in the Seychelles; then to make a ninety-degree turn and sail west towards the Seychelles. Coming under the lee of Diego-Garcia, with the trades blowing, in the southern hemisphere, from the south-east, I could not fail to note a difference in the behaviour of the seas. At the same time, even though my reckoning put me five or six hundred miles east of Diego-Garcia, my instinct warned me to keep my eyes open, for I might well be much nearer than I thought. For the last three days it had been repeating this warning.

For all my alertness, I could detect no sign of land: no sea-weed, no fish, no sea-birds except the bo'sun-birds and petrels which had been my companions ever since I emerged from the Malacca Strait. The sea's behaviour, in this squally trade wind, had been constantly unpredictable. It wore that slightly menacing poker face which it can assume when it has made up its mind not to give itself away. Although I was not really worried, something inside me still kept up this insistent warning.

*

The sun would soon be setting. A glance round the horizon, with particular attention: forward nothing to be seen in the sky, no bo'sun-bird. Then I should have my normal night's rest: one hour's sleep, followed by a turn on deck, with an eye on the horizon ahead. Still nothing to be seen. Or rather, nothing but the eternal sea, with the vague blur of the horizon, more clearly defined when a stronger swell than its fellows heaved *Marie-Thérèse* up on its crest, silvered by the rays of the moon still hanging low in the sky.

On deck, the caress of the trade wind was soft on my bare skin. For five days it had been blowing strongly, without too many squalls, driving, along with my boat, great cloud masses interspersed with stretches of clear sky in which the hot sun shone by day and the stars by night.

This infinity of sea, wind, clouds, sun and stars would be ours for some weeks still to come, until the anchor gripped the coral of a palm-bordered island in the Seychelles.

It was now that one appreciated the freshness of the night. A glance at the compass—heading correct: I corrected it at noon, after working up the latitude, which placed us some miles south of the line drawn on the chart. This southerly current, of some strength, had been apparent for the last week, and could only be caused by the Equatorial Current being diverted by the Chagos Bank.

A moment's hesitation: should I leave the helm as it is, or give it a touch to port, in order to bring the heading a couple of degrees north? Best, however, to leave well alone. The noon adjustment must be correct. And *Marie-Thérèse* carried on, with the wind aft, the mainsail against the starboard rigging, staysail sheeted home along the fore and aft axis of the boat.

I am really proud of this boat, because, from all the accounts I have read, only Slocum's *Spray* kept her course with the helm lashed in a following wind under working canvas, and with no need for twin staysails. *Marie-Thérèse* had been doing this for weeks (with the mizzen lowered, of course). It may have been a fluke, but that did not make me any less proud of my boat.

*

The moon had just begun to dip down towards the west when a sudden violent lurch threw me against the starboard bulkhead of the cabin. In a split second I was on deck, grabbing the mizzen mast in order not to be carried away by the solid wall of water which had just swept the boat from stem to stern with all the fury of a breaker flinging itself against the shore. *Marie-Thérèse* was heeling over, under the impact of the wave which was dragging her beam-on along the reef, covered by a metre of water, half a cable's length off the Diego-Garcia Atoll. At the same time there was a musty smell of crushed coral coming up, mixed with sea-weed.

A third sea of terrifying strength came crashing down on the hull, now heeled well over, in a cloud of wind-blown spray. There was a long groan from the woodwork as the coral on which *Marie-Thérèse* was dragged bit into her. It would be a brief death-agony for my poor boat, I thought, in this sea of white foam.

There followed a succession of violent waves, and then hope returned. *Marie-Thérèse* had been carried some twenty yards away from the coral edge. There the ocean swell had lost some of its force after its first breaking on the escarpment of the reef. The coral shelf lies almost a foot deeper and the hull seemed to be suffering less than at first.

After half an hour of violent bumping and lurching my boat was almost on the beach, still heeling over on her side and driven by the waves. I then put out the two anchors so that there would be no danger of the boat's being carried along by the strong current of the falling tide—that southerly current, again. Her poor hull had already taken some death-blows, and the damage was still going on. The water had poured in through the gaps in the caulking and filled the bilges; this added to her weight, her inertia resisting the force of the waves—but how much more of this could she take, I wondered.

The moon, meanwhile, had dropped ten degrees towards the west. If the tide had not already begun to fall, it soon would be. All along the bottom there were pitiful sounds of cracking. Hull and man suffered together; I felt it in my guts every time the planking screamed as it was flung against the merciless coral.

The rudder-blade was broken. The wooden fastenings, which take the place of nails in the planking of most Asiatic craft, were loosened. The water had now come into the cabin. And still the tide had not begun to fall. Lord of sky and sea, I prayed, make that ebb come soon, and then, perhaps, with your help and that of the inhabitants of Diego-Garcia I shall save *Marie-Thérèse*.

The level of water was still rising inside the hull, and I hastily threw some of my possessions into a metal container, which I then, not without a good deal of difficulty, stuffed under a bush on the beach. This was in case any light-fingered persons should find *Marie-Thérèse* while I was away looking for help. I made two further journeys to the beach, where I hid a suitcase of clothing, the sextant, and my thin Cambodian mattress. Everything was soaking wet, but that was no matter.

Still the tide did not seem to be turning, and the hull was already disintegrating. Nothing short of a miracle would save her now, I thought.

I had crossed the atoll's fringe of coconut-palms, looking for the path marked on the map. I had then turned south, running in the moonlight which filtered through the clumps of palms. The moon was half-way to the horizon when at last, in a stillness that was almost unreal, I saw the palm-covered roofs silhouetted in the clear night, at the edge of the peaceful lagoon.

I hammered at the first door I came to. Inside I could hear yawns and stretchings. Finally an old negress opened the door, only to slam it in my face with a startled exclamation. With my bushy beard, my tousled hair, tan leather shorts, shirtless and bare-footed, she might well have taken me for an apparition. After a while the door of the next straw-hut opened, to reveal a big negro whom I led out into the yard of white sand, bathed in moonlight. He seemed completely drunk and answered in monosyllables, or rather grunts, the questions I asked him in English, Italian, Spanish, Vietnamese and Malayan: not in French, for how could he possibly know French?

Two more negroes then came on the scene, attracted by the noise or fetched by the old woman I had so terrified a few minutes earlier. These were followed by three more. They were bright enough, and willing, but my command of languages was exhausted and I did not know their dialect. Fortunately, we have the international language of gestures and pictures. I drew a sailing vessel in the sand on which we stood, and then put down in front of it a lump of coral with a gesture that indicated 'Boum!'

'*Mo compends.*'

I thought I must be dreaming. Could it be possible? But no, it would be too much of a coincidence.

'*Tu comprends?*'—'Can you understand me?'

'*Bien su, mo compends.*'

I can hardly reproduce, in English, the curious dialogue that followed: but it was no dream. These negroes spoke French, or at least a dialect derived from French, and I had got it across to them that my boat had been driven onto the reef; they asked me in which direction she lay. I thought it only prudent to point in the opposite direction and spare *Marie-Thérèse* a premature visit from these good fellows, who might occupy their leisure moments with a little pilfering.

I asked where the headman could be found, and I was soon standing in front of the 'great house'. It was a fine, big, building, with a wide verandah running around it.

'Captain! Captain!' shouted the blacks, crowding round the garden fence.

Roars came from inside the house, and then there appeared the awesome figure of Captain Lasnier, grasping a cudgel in his fist, and ready to subdue the rebellion, if that was what the negroes were after. Scram!

After the initial surprise, I was installed in a comfortable chair in the sitting-room, with a glass of cognac in my hand, given me by Mme Lasnier. Captain Lasnier is old wooden-ship man. In his sixties he left the big sailing ship of which he was master, to take up the position of manager for the Mauritian company which handles the copra on Diego-Garcia. A bluff character, blunt and straight-forward, with a heart of gold.

'You did well,' her husband told me, 'to give those black fellows the wrong direction. And now, let's get going.' We set off in the captain's jeep to look for *Marie-Thérèse*, whom, in spite of the moonlight, we failed to find.

'No need to worry,' Captain Lasnier assured me. 'It is practically low water and the sea is no longer breaking on the beach. In two hours it will be dawn and we will come back with a truck and all the able-bodied men in the village, and drag your boat out of reach of the sea. Then we can take our time bringing it to the edge of the lagoon, and get on with the repairs. Meanwhile, consider yourself our guest; food and shelter are no problem. You can sleep in the guest-house and have your meals with us.'

'But do you think, captain, that we shall really be able to move that heavy junk of mine across the atoll?'

'Not a doubt of it! There are over six hundred inhabitants on Diego-Garcia. A hundred will do it easily enough, with a block and tackle, if necessary, for the difficult parts. And if there's a palm-tree in the way—all right, we'll cut it down. And you needn't worry about repairs either, my lad: I have three excellent shipwrights, and they're real workers.'

Dear Captain Lasnier! I fear he will never know with what brilliance the moon shone for me when I heard those words spoken in that gruff voice of his, which yet was full of simple warmth and kindness.

Daybreak found us at the spot where the boat was lying, on the coral and clear of the water. A brief gesture from the old seaman checked my companions and me as we moved towards the beach. *Marie-Thérèse* was dead. The keel had gone; the floor-frames and the whole bottom were shattered. In the deck itself, forced up by the hammer blows of the sea which had poured into the fractured hull, there was a gaping wound.

For my own part, leaning my cheek against her lovely bows, lifeless now, but still with its fragrance of salt and wood oil and adventure, I wept.

I wept for my memories, for my books, for the loss of this boundless world, made up of dreams and action, of which I had become so integral a part that I could not now imagine that any other world existed.

But above all, I wept for my boat.

The next tide was to carry her off into the rock-free ocean of the sailors' Paradise. Twelve hours after the wreck, there was no trace of *Marie-Thérèse*: not even a plank, not a frame, not even a fragment of the keel. The southerly current had carried it all away.

CHAPTER 2

Mauritius:
the friendly island

I shall not write at length about the six weeks I spent on Diego-Garcia. This is a memory which I should prefer to keep to myself. The joy, the release from anxiety and the peace which those days brought me made it into one of the most treasured periods of my life, and this in spite of the fact that the loss of my boat was still so recent.

Words, moreover, would be far too clumsy an instrument to express my feelings for the friends who received me on their atoll as they would have done a member of their own family. The Diego-Garcia Atoll is run by families from Mauritius and the Seychelles, and you need to have lived among these people to understand what the words 'family' and 'hospitality' mean to them, and to realize how impossible it would be to try to translate them into a European language.

Two months after the wreck, the British corvette *Loch Glendhu*, after putting in at Diego-Garcia, dropped me at the island of Mauritius. A new leaf was turned over, and a new chapter opened.

I went immediately to call on the French consul, and enquire from him about the prospects of working a passage home in one of the Messageries Maritimes ships. M. Hector Paturau, who belongs to one of the great Mauritian families, was not a complete stranger to me before my visit to him. My friends on Diego-Garcia had told me that he was a man of great practical energy; the owner of a guano island in the Mozambique Channel; and extremely fond of underwater exploration and fishing. After a few minutes' conversation, I was to realize that this French consul, restrained in his gestures but a forceful man and with a mind of uncommon quality, was what we call in French a '*chic type*'—a thoroughly good fellow. The first thing he did was to urge me not to leave Mauritius

17

before getting to know the country better. 'Take my word for it, and don't hurry anything. Plenty of time to leave when you feel like doing so.'

'True—but how am I going to earn a living meanwhile, on an island that's already over-populated?'

'Don't worry about that. You don't have a brass farthing at the moment, do you? Well, I'll take care of your immediate needs.'

The next day a relation of the consul's, Mme Labat, offered me hospitality in her big house in Curepipe.

I was not long in making many friends. And first among these were the d'Unienvilles and the de Sornays, relations of the Labats and the Paturaux.

Noel d'Unienville, editor of the daily newspaper *Le Cernéen* suggested that I gave some lectures on the adventures which had led me to the Chagos. It would be a quick way of putting me on my feet again until I could find some regular work, and at the same time would interest the islanders. Pierre de Sornay, too, would see about the publication of the meagre log-book I had kept in the Indian Ocean. The sale of this booklet, whose production (thanks to the generosity of a group of friends) would cost me nothing, would be a welcome assistance. The lecturing went very well, with large and sympathetic audiences, although I felt somewhat nervous at the beginning of each talk.

Shortly afterwards my hostess's eldest son, Emile Labat, took me in charge, with an invitation: 'Curepipe is not the right sort of place for you. It's ten miles from the sea. Come and stay in my place at Riambelle on the south coast.'

The next day I arrived at *Port d'attache* ('Home port')—what a delightful name for a house! And what a delightful house! The walls were built from blocks of raw coral laid on top of one another and bonded with a lime mortar. The thatch which originally covered the whole building had been replaced, after a terrible cyclone which devastated the island a few years earlier, by a more resistant flat roof. In *Port d'attache*, shaded by a ring of ancient baobabs, lived Emile, with his wife Amy, his sister-in-law Denise, and his daughter Marguerite-Blanche, an adorable twelve-year-old slip of mischief, who ran bare-foot over the rolling beaches, fought with her cousins, and swam like a fish. And it was in *Port d'attache* that I found a second family.

However, the time had come when I had to find myself some

work. Mauritius is essentially an agricultural country. Ninety-nine per cent of its industry is centred on the cultivation of sugar-cane, its processing, and the export of sugar. A long way behind this comes food-production, tea planting, and, finally fishing along the reefs and coral banks which lie to the north of the island.

I was not much attracted by agriculture. Moreover, the island is so over-populated that it would be difficult to get work on a sugar plantation. On the other hand, there is an abundance of fish at the edge of the reefs, chiefly off the savannah coasts: these are seldom visited by the underwater sportsmen, since the majority of the camps are built on the leeward side of the island. Now, some fishes will not take a line and, as a result, they increase peacefully in number and size. Emile was not greatly taken by this idea of underwater fishing. 'There are plenty of fish, I agree, but to make up for that it's infested with sharks. There are hardly any to the north of the island, but down here I've caught very large ones, both out to sea and at the edge of the reefs. You'd do better to make charcoal in my lime-kiln. It's fetching a good price just now.' I should explain that when Emile was not busy with his fishing-lines or with *Chimaera* (the boat he kept for pleasure-fishing) he used to make lime by a most ingenious system of his own. It consisted in burning coral sand inside a horizontal cylinder which revolved on its axis. The sand went in at one side, through a tall chimney, and came out at the other end as a continuous stream of quick-lime.

The next day we went off together to deliver some lime to the owner of a sugar plantation; the lime is used to purify the sugar during the processing. Two days later, a cylindrical iron tank, nine feet high and six feet in diameter, arrived in the yard on a lorry. The manager of the plantation had been interested in the charcoal scheme and offered me 'this old tank that's cluttering up the place'— it was taking up too much room on some waste ground behind the factory. There are, indeed, some uncommonly obliging people in Mauritius.

And so I became a charcoal-burner. It is as easy as pie. You load the tank with wood, from the top, and fit the lid. Then you light it from the bottom, blowing to make the wood catch. You adjust the flue, keeping it wide open the first day, a little less wide the second day, and almost closing it on the third. When the smoke becomes light blue, you close the vent at the bottom and then wait quietly for a couple of days until the charcoal has cooled. All you have to do then is to put it into sacks, and start the operation again.

The trouble with this delightful occupation is that wood is pretty expensive, and charcoal is pretty cheap. The profits, accordingly, remain modest, to put it mildly. Moreover there is something rather tedious about sitting on your backside and watching a charcoal-kiln cooling. The logically-minded will perhaps suggest that with three or four more kilns I would have had a full-time occupation. True—but nought multiplied by three or even four still makes nought. (The nought represents 'profits'.) Further, I was not anxious to force down the price of charcoal by flooding the market with my possibly inferior product. After devoting much thought to the immutable laws of supply and demand, I went in to Port Louis, the commercial capital; and there, with good ringing, sound, rupees, I bought a 'Champion' underwater spear-gun, with four springs, an extra spear, a spring balance, and the indispensable diving-mask— no flippers, to save money.

A worthy negro was then taken on to blow the fire (you never know—the price of charcoal might go up, at the same time as the price of wood went down) while I was going to play the human fish among the rainbow-hued parrots which crowd the edges of the reefs, swarming with life, lovely with all the shades of blue the coral depths take on as the touch of a tropical sun filters down to them.

My word! What a wealth of fish! A real underwater goldmine. In three days the equipment was paid for, and a month later I was trying to decide whether or not to buy a second-hand Renault 4CV which had taken my fancy. An average catch was 80 to 100 lb. of fish, and the record was 145lb. in one morning. With a selling price of a rupee a pound, my bank balance was looking healthier.

*

'Here, look at the paper.' And the pretty little nurse who had taken me into the operating theatre the evening before handed me *Le Cernéen* for January 23rd, 1953, in which she had ringed the following passage:

'Bernard Moitessier, the single-handed sailor who arrived here some months ago after being wrecked on the Chagos, is well known as a keen underwater sportsman. An exceptionally fine swimmer, he practises, somewhat rashly perhaps, the art of fishing with an underwater spear-gun, obtaining astonishing results.

'Yesterday morning he was at work off the savannah coast when he fired at a carp which escaped. The smell of blood attracted a very small shark; he fired at this and hit it. Turning round, he found that he was held in the jaws of a huge shark. Far from losing his presence of mind, he struck it with the butt of his spear-gun, at the same time endeavouring to get back to the surface. In the end he succeeded in freeing himself and with the help of some fishermen managed to haul himself into a boat. Losing blood rapidly, he was rushed to the hospital in Souillac, where he received first aid.

'He was operated on yesterday at the Ferrière clinic, in Curepipe, by Dr. Dufourmentel. He has one foot badly torn, with the tendons severed, but it is hoped that his accident will not have permanently damaging effects. We beg him to accept our most cordial wishes for a speedy recovery.'

So that was that: again I had escaped by the skin of my teeth, though with some nasty scratches! A close shave, and I need hardly say how grateful I am to Gérard Dufourmentel.

Here are the details of the story. I was working a few hundred yards from the shore, on a rocky bottom, in about thirty feet of water. The configuration down there consisted of large clumps of coral (frequented by shoals of carp) overhanging small underwater gullies. I had shot about eighty pounds of fish, chiefly carp of five to six pounds, which two native sailors were loading into a pirogue. At that moment I noticed a small shark (about four feet) which had been attracted by the smell of blood and the commotion among the fish I had speared. I decided to tempt the shark with a wounded carp, still flapping. Accordingly, I detached the carp from my spear and released it, while standing a short distance away. Although the shark was suspicious, it came close enough for me to fire and hit it at a range of about six feet from the muzzle of my spear-gun—which is quite a long range. (The four-spring 'Champion' is robust, simple, moderate in price, and requires practically no maintenance. When the duralumin frame becomes too worn, it can be replaced by a broom-handle, and the gun will still float.) Although it was hit in one of the gills, it was still full of vigour and would soon have dragged me down to the bottom, since (for convenience and because I had no reel) my line was not even eight feet long. After only a few seconds' struggle, I found myself towed into one of those underwater trenches, overhung by large blocks of coral which they call a 'couline' in Mauritius. It was then that the line—already worn where it is attached to the sleeve—parted. The shark was free and made off.

At that moment I was lying obliquely, my head down, both hands holding the spear-gun and my feet beating the water to counter the pull of the shark. As soon as the latter was free, I took hold of the gun by the middle, in my right hand, as one normally does, and attempted to regain the surface.

It was then that a violent pain in my right foot, which felt as though it were being crushed in a vice, made me quite lose control of the situation. However, I had not let go of my gun, and, fortunately, it was only a moment before I recovered by presence of mind. A shark as big as myself, or perhaps a little bigger, had hold of me by one foot; by a reflex action which probably saved me from worse disaster, I struck him a violent blow on the head with the butt. He immediately let go of me!

I was then at a depth of some twenty feet and lost no time in surfacing; the shark, now thoroughly excited, was whirling around me, while I was ready to beat off as best I could any attack he might decide to make. In fact, however, his belligerence decreased as I approached the surface, and I was able to cover the ten or fifteen yards which still separated me from the pirogue without impediment.

Readers of Hans Hass's *Diving to Adventure* will wonder why I did not shout to scare the shark. This is sometimes an effective method and I have often used it myself, *though with very variable results;* I was afraid, however, of running out of breath and was saving up this life-saver as my last trump card.

I have gone into the details of this incident only because it enables me to draw a number of practical conclusions from what I have described, and this one cannot do without the exact facts. Moreover, what I am recording here is a piece of evidence which, if it is to be worth serious consideration, cannot afford to omit any detail which may throw light on the reactions of the shark, at a time when underwater fishing is on the increase in the tropics.

A short digression on the natural behaviour of the shark, when faced by an underwater fisher, may well be appropriate at this point. The 'gogglers' who work in tropical waters have noted that in spite of its reputation as a 'mobile digestive tract', the shark is a relatively timid fish in the presence of a swimmer who appears to be at home in the sea. I have always found this nervousness, on the coast of Annam, in the Annambas Archipelago, between Indochina and Singapore, and finally off the richly stocked coasts of Mauritius. There I have counted up to half a dozen sharks weaving gracefully below me but maintaining a respectful distance while I tried to approach more closely. I have seldom, in fact, come closer than ten feet to a shark for they seem to be really frightened of the peculiar fish which the 'goggler' represents for them; his lithe, natural, movements seem to the shark those of an animal perfectly adapted to the medium of water.

So far I have been concerned only with the 'quiet' shark, as normally found, that is, at the beginning of an underwater expedition. The picture can change completely as the hunt develops. Suppose, for example, a 10-15lb. tunny has been hit by the spear. This is a fish which fights back ferociously and bleeds freely. If one or more sharks are in the vicinity they will soon put in an appearance, attracted by the vibrations produced by the wounded fish. Nevertheless, the catch can generally be brought back to the boat without incident. After some minutes' fishing, if one has a good bag, the shark will become bolder and will often tear the speared fish from the weapon. He becomes increasingly more daring and soon there are no limits to his audacity. It is then that the shark may well become dangerous, if one challenges him over a quarry which he regards as his own. One Sunday, for example, when a number of us were fishing in a passage to the south of Mauritius, the sharks became so insistent on their rights that, in order not to lose the whole of our catch, we had to swim within arm's length of the pirogue, firing at a shoal of carp. The moment each fish was hit, we passed the gun to a companion in the pirogue; he pulled in the fish while the men in the water climbed hastily on board. For my own part, I preferred to swim quickly away from the pirogue while attempts were made to save the still hypothetical catch. I did this in order not to lose sight of the sharks, for a great deal can happen between beating a retreat and finding safety in the bottom of the boat.

However, a shark which had seen itself neatly cheated of a prey it almost had hold of, made a sharp swerve and came right at me. I only just had time to let out a shout and give the water a violent smack, or there might have been a nasty accident. We then decided to pack up, since this part of the coast offered no other suitable fishing ground.

It is worth recording the reactions of a school of thirty to forty sharks which we watched from the British warship *Loch Glendhu,* in which I travelled to Mauritius after my shipwreck. We were crossing the large Saya de Malha Bank, some hundreds of miles east of the northern tip of Madagascar, when the captain decided to take the opportunity of exercising the crew in dropping depth charges. Apart from the training value of the operation, he had the further objective of catching some fish, of which there is any amount in the banks in the Indian Ocean. The catch, in fact, was pretty poor, but the behaviour of the sharks attracted by the explosions was most interesting. It was not long before we had lines out in an attempt to hook one. It was a beautiful sight, thirty-odd sharks swimming lazily round the ship with wonderful grace.

Suddenly the picture changed: a shark had been hooked and we were afraid that he would free himself. Two rifle-shots rang out. Blood poured from the wounds and spread out over the water, lashed by the tail of the struggling fish. In spite of these precautions, the shark, which had not been properly hooked, got away, seen off at the last moment by a well-aimed bullet in the top of the head. The whole group were now excited by the blood, swimming more rapidly, with acrobatic twists and turns. A second shark was caught; this one, with four bullets in its body, did not get away. More blood stained the sea; three others took the hook, whereas it had taken a quarter of an hour for the first to make up its mind to accept the bait.

So much for that incident, from which I shall try to draw some practical conclusions, even though (since my experience is not based on a large number of observations) they cannot be regarded as final.

From what I have said, one fact emerges which I can safely assert: the shark behaves in two distinct ways: so long as there is no blood in the sea, it remains quiet, timid, cautious to the point of moving off if you try to approach it. But once there is blood in the water you must look out: the boldness of the quietest shark will rise to a crescendo, and the wise man will decide to fish somewhere else. It is always a good rule not to stay in a place where you have shot many fish, since the shark, attracted by the vibrations produced by the wounded fish might well suddenly find itself in an over-exciting environment, even if the blood is so diluted as not to be visible. I should add there is evidence to show that certain varieties of shark,

like the tiger-shark, attack on sight—but you try to tell a tiger-shark
from a lamb-shark!

There are a few points that should be emphasized before leaving
this subject. Captain Young, a professional shark fisher, writes in his
Sharks about an experiment he says he made, with a net dyed in
three colours, one section white, one blue and the third black.
Practically all the sharks were caught in the white section, with not
a single one in the black.

In his *Secrets of the Red Sea,* Henry de Monfreid says, I believe,
that the Somali pearl-fishers smear the palms of their hands and the
soles of their feet with a black substance, for they have noted that
it is the lightest parts of the body which arouse the shark's interest.

The same author tells how one of his crew, who was standing on a
rock, was afraid to swim to the boat because of the sharks which
could be seen. Monfreid threw him a line, telling him to roll himself
up into a ball, since sharks generally fasten their teeth in the tapering parts of the body—arms or legs. When the man was ready,
they all rapidly hauled in the line and brought him on board (in
view of the swell, a fifteen-ton sailing vessel could obviously not draw
alongside a rock).

Thus a well-bronzed 'goggler' would appear to be less liable to
attack. Further it is advisable, I think, to use rubber flippers in
shark-infested waters. Apart from the assistance they provide, they
have the advantage (being dark in colour) of not attracting sharks
too much. Moreover, should a shark bite a flipper, there is a chance
that he may be content with hanging on to the end of it, without
touching the foot (I was fishing without flippers, it will be remembered, on the day I was in trouble).

It should be noted that a shark will take a line much more
readily at night than during the day. It is at night too that he is
most apt to enter narrow channels and that he hangs about the
coast. The fishermen of Mauritius and of the Cargados-Carajos
Islands, where I later spent a year, often make no attempt to fish
at night, since it is then that the sharks are most troublesome,
attacking the fish caught on their lines.

The shark would appear to do most of his feeding at night.
Personally, I have *never* seen a shark attack a fish while I have
been diving. Neither I, nor any of my Mauritian friends, many of
whom are first-rate underwater fishermen, have ever done so. (I do
not mean a fish already wounded by a spear.) So, if the shark

does not feed during the day, he must do so at some other time ...
and you may be sure that you will not find me swimming for fun
in tropical waters at night.

A final note: in Mauritius, I was attacked at a depth of some
twenty feet. Some months later, when a group of us were fishing
together in the Cargados-Carajos Archipelago, I was on the point
of being attacked as I was retrieving a spear I had lost at a depth of
fifteen feet. A shark had suddenly emerged from behind a lump of
coral, and things developed so quickly that Christian Couacaud,
whom I had asked to keep a look-out, had no time to see it coming.
I missed a bad accident that day by a hair's breadth. And yet
that shark was no more than five feet long.

Now, Cousteau, in his *World of Silence,* relates how close to their
last hour he and his companions thought they were, when they were
trying to get back to their boat off the Cape Verde Islands, laden
with their diving equipment. As soon as the group of swimmers
approached the surface to signal to the boat, the circle of sharks
closed round them. Some feet deeper, Cousteau and his men felt they
were comparatively safe.

In the part of the Indian Ocean which I know, it is the other
way about. At the surface, I feel safe, but much less so on the
bottom. Thus the behaviour of sharks can vary from one sea to
another, and even from one place to another in the same sea, as is
clear from the numerous observations made by Bernard Gorski and
his companions.

Here are a number of rules which I find useful. Others may
have different ideas, and behave as they think best.

1. The shark is shy, and does not attack during daylight hours,
with the exception, perhaps, of some rare species. As a general rule,
he is afraid of man, and will seldom allow him to approach.

2. The most timid shark can become savage if there is blood in
the water. Speared fish nearly always bleed, and, what is more, the
vibrations produced by a fish struggling at the end of a spear will
almost unfailingly attract sharks. In such cases, it is prudent to fish
elsewhere.

3. The shark will let himself be bluffed by an aggressive attitude:
but you must be able to see him. Beware, therefore, of turbid water.
For my own part, I refuse to swim in such water in the tropics.

4. The shark feeds chiefly at night. It is at night, too, that he
comes closest to the beach and enters some of the narrow channels,

where he is not normally found during the day. Beware of bathing at night in shark-frequented waters, for not only will you not see him, but, to make matters worse it is his dinner-time.

5. The shark shows a marked preference for the lighter and tapering parts of the body: arms, legs, hands, feet. Numerous observations attest this fact.

6. Even if you are bitten, the game is not lost. You have to persist in your bluff. In any case, there is nothing else you can do. Had I not put on a show of attacking, when the furious shark was pulling me about, things might have taken a much more serious turn.

7. It is safest to accept, once and for all, that sharks do not necessarily behave in the same way in one place as in another. Off the coasts of Mauritius and in the Cargados-Carajos, for example, accidents are practically unknown. Off the coasts of Madagascar, some hundreds of miles away, sharks would appear to be much more dangerous. Again, in Mauritius and the Cargados-Carajos, I have noted that the shark tends to become rather more inquisitive near the sea-bed. Cousteau (off Dakar, if my memory serves me correctly) notes the contrary.

8. Endless stories are told about sharks. In this connection, people who have never even got their feet wet often have the most to say. On Ascension Island, where I put in later, swimming was forbidden because the sharks, it would seem, are so ferocious. I made some inquiries, but no accident appears to have been reported on the island. I stayed there a week, bathing every day in the water around my boat, without seeing a single shark.

*

That was the end of my underwater fishing, for the time being at least, for it was many weeks before my painfully swollen foot allowed me to use flippers. No more dancing, running or long walks, either. I shall limp, I thought, for the rest of my life, but better to limp than have an artificial foot.

And then—everything worked out almost miraculously. A month after the accident I was walking normally, I could run as I used to and I could wear flippers. My only legacy is a large scar, in the shape of a half-moon, on the underside of my foot. Gérard Dufourmentel had done a first-rate job.

And since miracles never arrive singly, I was engaged by 'Raphael-Fishing' to manage their fishing and guano business on St. Brandon.

27

The St. Brandon (or Cargados-Carajos) Group emerges from the sea 240 miles north-east of Mauritius. It consists of ten or a dozen coral islands and sandbanks scattered in the shape of a crescent, strung out some twenty miles south of the large Nazareth Bank. White sand, rugged coral, stunted bushes, turtles, countless sea-birds, casuarinas and coconut-palms that had managed to survive the cyclones—such was my background for nearly a year of the fascinating life I lived in the company of my men and my boats. We had a dozen 20- to 30-foot sailing boats for fishing the rich bank, and some thirty narrow pirogues, very fast, drawing practically no water, to skim along the coast in the lee of the archipelago.

The staff of St. Brandon consisted of twenty negro fishermen and thirty-odd landlubbers to extract the died guano. No women, no drink, no cinema. And I have never met a business managed with such perspicacity, nor such pleasant and understanding employers as Louis Couacaud and Wilfrid Larché: these two were the directors of Raphael-Fishing, with their headquarters in Mauritius.

There was no money, even, on St. Brandon: the men bought what they wanted at the Co-operative and their account was debited. Thus the problem of stealing was solved without any police. And the strict rule excluding women and alcohol from the islands prevented a great deal of useless trouble and tension. The contracted labour spent six or eight months on the island—one spell, no more, working and saving money. The system was simple and effective, and worked wonderfully. At the end of their contract, they went back in the Raphael-Fishing boat, which was bringing in the new intake.

My assignment had two aims: to increase the production of salt fish and to cut down the time spent each month in loading guano. I gave all my energy to jobs which really interested me: repairing the fishing fleet; marking the channels with light buoys, so that when the fishing was good the men could come back after sundown; installing lights visible from ten miles out to sea; and organizing the loading of guano in a methodical way, for it could be done much more rapidly with half the staff normally employed, thus releasing as many as possible for the fishing.

After ten months one could say that the target had been reached. On the other hand the selling of Raphael-Fishing salt fish was becoming difficult. The Chinese, who for years had been snapping up the landings, were being more difficult to please. Indian merchants in Mauritius were beginning to import salt fish from their home country, and the quarter million Indians on the island preferred this to fish from St. Brandon.

*

This period on St. Brandon put me on my feet financially. My old dreams, long relegated to the back of my mind, took shape again as my eyes turned to the dim line of the horizon. In spite of all the punishment I had taken in years gone by, I had not yet thrown off the virus of the sea.

'If you can stay, then stay: if you must go, then go'—and for me it was 'must'.

The timber for the keel, bows and stern-post was bought in fine mahogany, and then the planking; and Rousseti, the shipwright, and I began to shape and plane it, working under a baobab on the big south-eastern river, some miles from Port Louis. It was a peaceful, shady spot practically on the water's edge, and near enough to Port Louis for the numerous comings and goings that are inseparable from the building of a boat not to be troublesome. My friend Francis Lahausse de la Louvière offered to share with me his bachelor establishment in Curepipe. He dropped me each morning and brought me back in the evening after lending us a hand. Jean Galea, owner of the land on which I was building *Marie-Thérèse II*, and of the magnificent sloop *Liberty* moored close by, used also to look in every day to check the progress of my boat. He is a fine seaman, extremely intelligent, with a great gift for fixing up a job neatly; his help and advice were most valuable and his visits a most pleasant interlude.

At the very beginning we came up against a serious difficulty. Curved lengths of wood, for the shaped frames, were almost unobtainable on the spot. Mauritius, however, specializes in miracles, or rather, it is the people who are miraculously obliging. My contacts in the New Mauritius Dock found three fine pieces of jack-wood under a pile of rubbish. They approached the manager, who sold them to me at cost price—ten years old, in other words for nothing. To this Marcel de Nanclas added a magnificent log of black-wood on the same terms. So far as the frames were concerned, I was fixed up.

The building began by laying down the long keel, straight upon its parallel guides. The stem- and stern-posts were then fitted, bolted and held upright by posts driven into the ground and nailed to either end of the embryonic boat. We then had to build up the framing. We did this 'Eastern-style'. I drew out the central frame, life-size, and cut it out (sorry: it was Rousseti who cut it out). We then tried it in position. 'Open up a trifle, Rousseti . . . no, too much. Close up a little. No, not like that—I don't want a *Firecrest!* Ah, perfect! For Christ's sake don't move now—I'll be right with you!' —and I would dash round, jumping over the bushes, to nail the transverse beam which would ensure the correct distance until the construction was completed. The floor-frame was then cut out and riveted to this first frame, and the whole bolted to the keel. Two other frames, almost identical but closing in a little more, were then drawn out, cut, and riveted to their respective floor-frames, and then bolted to the keel, two feet forward and aft of the central frame.

The whole (three frames, keel, stem- and stern-posts) already gave a vague idea of the shape of the boat to be. It was then that the battens came to lend a hand: thin wooden rods were nailed by their middle, every eight inches, to the central frame, then led back to bows and stern, where they were held by small nails. The picture was now clearer.

I then spent the rest of the day moulding the final shape with lengths of string and pieces of wood: the lashing served to pull the shape inwards, while the pieces of wood were used to force the battens outwards, where more width was needed. Poor Rousseti was worn to a shred: no lunch at mid-day, no little siesta, not even the ritual cup of tea we normally brewed up in the tin over a fire of shavings and chips. I, however, was jubilant. My boat was taking shape. We finished in one burst, from eight in the morning until four in the afternoon. God of sky and sea, what a splendid craft you will one day have to nurse!

When Francis Lahausse and Jean Galea came for me at the end of the afternoon, I was sitting on a log with the amazed look of the young mother whose eyes caress her offspring, the eighth wonder of the World.

Marie-Thérèse II had just been born.

The rest of the frames were drawn using an iron rod, a quarter-inch in diameter, bent inside the hull at the points where each frame would lie. As soon as it was drawn, each of these frames was cut out, checked in position, riveted to the floor-frame and bolted to the keel. We thus moved on, frame by frame, from the midships to the after-part, and when that section had been framed, we worked forward. This gave us the possibility of correcting the little surprises which are inherent in so empiric a method, which progressed with much trial and error and a few fits of blind rage. Rousseti, fortunately, takes things pretty calmly.

Three months after laying down the keel the whole framing was in position and the eight stringers could be put in: four stout ones (4in. by 1½in.) on each side. Then came the laying down of the deck-beams, each made up of two planks fastened together and placed in position after being rounded-off to give the deck as pronounced a camber as possible. It may seem surprising to use planks instead of the traditional curved pieces of timber normally used for deck-beams. The reason was that curved timber is extremely expensive in Mauritius (as it is everywhere else) and, further, such choice pieces are difficult to find. My beams were stout enough to stand up to any strain, since only the upper portion was cambered, the lower part being left straight.

The framing was now complete and we moved on to the planking of the hull. Poor Rousseti, whose experience was confined to building pirogues and narrow, shallow-draught fishing boats, began to be out of his depth (and, what was worse, to lose weight); for *Marie-Thérèse II* with her ten foot beam to a length of twenty-eight feet was by no means easy to plank.

After two months' work we managed it, though with improvisations that would have made an expert weep.

Then came the positioning of the intermediate curved frames, made from guava wood. This is an extremely strong wood, very flexible, very hard, with a close grain which allows it to be bent cold; but no nail in the world can be driven into it without a hole first being prepared to receive it. This work took a fortnight and the less said about it the better.

Speed now became important, for my bank balance was growing lean even more quickly than Rousseti. Another fortnight saw to deck and coach-roof. Then came the huge rudder with its half-inch iron gudgeons, bolted to the hull; the chain-plates for shrouds and at the stem, the masts, etc. I was almost cleaned out and would never have been able to get as far as I did without the invaluable help of friends whose names are too numerous to mention.

Once again, a miracle happened: Louis Larcher, the owner of a sugar plantation and factory, asked me one day what was the weight of my keel.

'I shall only carry inside ballast. If it is suitably bolted to the keel, there will be no shifting in the event of a capsize.' (Several examples had confirmed me in my belief that no small sailing vessel can claim to be uncapsizeable. You either right yourself or you do not, and that is that.)

'And you think your boat will right herself on her own, without the help of outside ballast?'

'I'm almost certain, and in any case I have no choice in the matter.'

'Almost certain, but not quite certain, eh? Now listen to me like a good fellow and don't be an ass: first thing in the morning leave a full-scale drawing at my office, with all the measurements, of the cast keel you really dream of having. I'll give you a present of it, and if you don't accept it, I'll give you a kick in the pants.'

A week later the keel, weighing a quarter-ton, arrived on a truck ... and, as you will read later, by this royal gesture Louis Larcher probably saved my life.

Nine months after laying down, *Marie-Thérèse II* had her first baptism of water and was towed into the quiet basin of New Mauritius Dock in Port Louis. There, with the help of the excellent Caspierre, the dock-yard sail-maker, I put in her masts and rigged her, as a fore-and-aft ketch. The sail canvas and running rigging were supplied to me at cost price by my former employers in Raphael-Fishing, Wilfred Larché and Louis Couacaud.

How does one design the sail-plan of a boat? Most people think that that is a question for the designer, and in one sense they are quite right. Speaking for myself, this is how it was answered in the case of *Snark, Marie-Thérèse* and *Marie-Thérèse II*. You draw a diagram of the boat, on as large a scale as possible. You then draw in the sails, trying to make the mean centre of sail area (the centre of lateral effort) fall a little forward of the centre of the wetted surface. Then, when the sails have been cut out, sewn and roped, you can make a short trial run. You then find that the boat is a little too lively or a little too slow on the helm. It is like tossing a coin: heads or tails—seldom does it fall edge-on.

If the boat is too lively, all you have to do is to reef the mizzen until equilibrium under sail is arrived at. Back at your mooring, you can then correct the sail. Instead of reducing the mizzen you

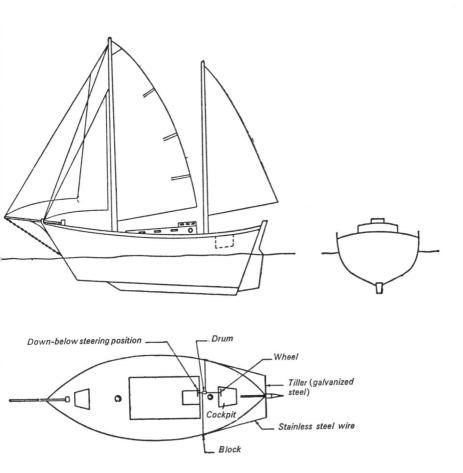

Fig. 1. Rough plan of *Marie-Thérèse II*.
Note the three stays forward,
two of them in the bows.

33

can also fit a bowsprit with an extra jib, or lengthen the existing bowsprit in order to carry the jib a little further forward.

If the boat proves too slow on the helm, then you have to increase the area of the mizzen or shorten the bowsprit, if there is one. Or again, you can quite happily reduce the area of the staysail.

This may sound like a great deal of work. In fact, it is not so very much. Moreover, it is great fun. (There is another point, too: if you want a naval architect to design your dream-boat, you will have to reckon on a fee of several hundred pounds.) *Marie-Thérèse II*, however, ready to put to sea, cost me 500,000 francs in all—though I must not forget my Mauritian friends.

Nevertheless, the money I had saved had now run out, and I was faced with two possibilities: either to find work in Mauritius or leave immediately to look for a job in South Africa. My equipment, however, was far too rudimentary for me to consider the second alternative. I had practically no provisions, no spares, and no stand-by anchors or chains, only a single set of sails, a sextant and a borrowed chronometer. I could no doubt have made Durban or Lourenço-Marques, but it was not simply a question of making a port. I had to be able to stay there without starving, in case finding work proved difficult.

As for a job in Mauritius, that was certainly possible, but would not have been a complete solution to my problem. In fact only a sugar-plantation owner could have taken me on, and in that case I should have had to live a long way from my boat, without being able to work on it regularly (for work on a boat is never done).

Mauritius, however, as I have said more than once before, is an island of miracles.

M. Calabrèze, the French consul who had succeeded Hector Paturau, was going home to France on leave, taking with him his daughter Marcelle, who worked as the secretary in the Consulate. This left her job vacant and the new consul, Fernand Saugon, took me on as assistant secretary as soon as he arrived. Thus I became 'Monsieur le Chancelier', a couple of steps away from my boat. I could live in her permanently (though not, I fear, in office hours).

I spent a year in this interesting job, working for an extremely agreeable man who was as much my friend as my boss; and this enabled me to complete *Marie-Thérèse II*'s trousseau. My friends, too, were wonderful. Without them the boat would never have been able to leave Mauritius in such excellent trim.

Numerous trips around the island and then a voyage to Réunion, accompanied by Francis Lahausse, enabled me to make some useful observations about the rig: the gaff mizzen was replaced by a more manageable Bermudan sail (all the more readily, in that *Marie-Thérèse II* was too lively, and I refused to entertain the idea of a bowsprit). Then, with the assistance of my dock-yard friends, I installed two wheels: one forward in the cockpit, and the other inside the cabin. This latter proved extremely useful both in thick weather and in clear.

Bardiaux arrived after a record passage from the Cocos Islands to Rodriguez, and from Rodriguez to Mauritius. As for me, I had respectfully given in my notice to the French consul, and was completing the purchase of my provisions, supplemented by presents from my friends.

I reserved my last three days, to spend them at Riambelle. And then it was goodbye to my dear adoptive family. My thoughts were often to return to them, remembering the treasured warmth and kindness which radiates from *Port d'attache*.

CHAPTER 3

Mauritius to Durban:
1,550 miles

It was with a heavy heart that on November 2nd, 1955, I hoisted my sails for this first stage: for there could not but be sadness in leaving this favoured island, on which I had lived for three years and could count so many good friends. However, such is the seaman's lot: the old saying is only too true—the sailor's friend hardly has the time to feel the warmth of his handclasp. Nevertheless, in the case of Mauritius, I can still feel the warmth of many a friendly hand.

The trade wind, however, had set in; and soon I was completely occupied in adjusting myself to the seaman's way of life. First, there was a certain amount of tidying up to be done on board. That was no great problem; all I had to do was to stuff everything into the big lockers which filled two sides of the cabin. A completely superficial tidiness, it is true, but I could see better how I stood.

Then came the tricky business of adjusting the helm for a following wind. This took a long time, and I was not completely satisfied, for I had not been able to treat myself to twin staysails. The mainsail was sheeted to port while the staysail, guyed out to starboard with a makeshift boom (too short—you never have time to do everything before you first start), more or less balanced the pressure on the mainsail. The mizzen is handed, of course, so that the wind's centre of effort lies as far forward as possible in the boat.

The result works out more or less correctly in a moderate wind (up to Force 4) because in those conditions the seas are slight. I had good weather, however, for ten days, as far as the southern extremity of Madagascar. I rounded this at a distance of a hundred miles, for in that area you often meet thick weather, and I like to have plenty of sea-room.

In the Mozambique Channel the weather immediately deteriorated,

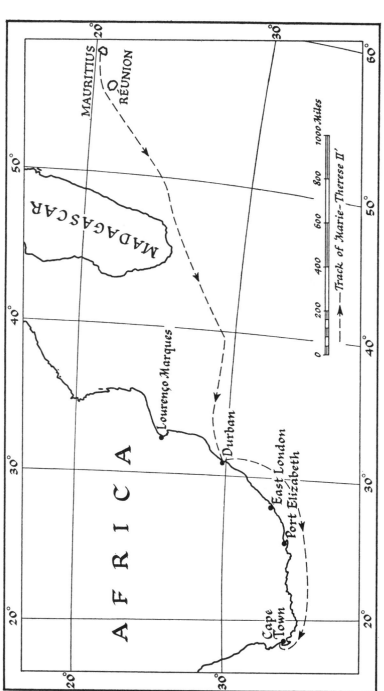

Mauritius to Cape Town

with a strong south-easterly and the seas often breaking. With the wind aft she no longer held her course. In this heavy sea with the wind from astern, the boat's trim called for constant alertness, and my watches were long and arduous. The current in the Mozambique Channel is responsible for this, for it sets almost directly against the wind, churning up the sea and causing the waves to break.

My hands had become soft from my long spell on dry land, and I suffered a good deal from small scratches incurred when handling the ropes; these were aggravated by the electrolytic action produced by contact with the brass of the wheel. (This brass wheel was later chromed; the electrolytic action stopped, and my hands no longer suffered.) I made excellent progress in the daytime, but I had to heave to at night, for there is a limit to my powers of endurance—and this is reflected in my averages. Nothing makes me more furious than being unable to take full advantage of a favourable wind. I decided that things would have to be different after I left Durban. Sailing, after all, is a delightful occupation, but you want to be able to use it as an opportunity to enjoy living—and at least have time to read, and dream, and cook, or even to do nothing at all—without keeping your eyes glued to the compass.

Even so *Marie-Thérèse II*, bless her, consented to hold her course for a few minutes on end; but this was not enough to allow me the complete relaxation I was to enjoy from Durban onwards, and in particular after leaving Cape Town. When I set out again from the latter I was really organized. To return, however, to the Mozambique Channel.

After three days of this somewhat damp sailing, the foul weather was replaced by a dead calm, which was to last for two days. At first the rolling was dreadful, and I was afraid to check it by hoisting the mainsail and sheeting it home because of the serious chafing of the crotch against the mast (there is no such difficulty with the Bermudan mizzen). I then tried a system which proved excellent. The sea-anchor was put out to port and stoutly lashed to the aftermost shroud of the mainmast, the bottle screw being tightened so that the downward pull could not cause wear in the ironwork. I then dropped a 45lb. iron pig into the sea-anchor, which settled down at a depth of five feet, the wide opening upwards. The effect was immediate. The rolling was cut by half, and I am certain that with a second sea-anchor put out on the other side it would have been almost entirely eliminated. Unfortunately my sea-anchor, which had been fudged-up from salvage material, let me down during the night. The rolling started again in earnest and meanwhile the current was carrying me inexorably south at an average of thirty miles a day.

Should the calm last too long, I was going to find myself taken south of the latitude of Durban into the Agulhas Current, which again makes fifty to a hundred miles a day, according to the time of year and its mood. The wind, however, returned, still from the south-east, bringing with it rain and a heavy sea. I maintained a north-westerly heading for some days, in order to stay well 'above' Durban. Sun-sights were difficult and at times impossible, and a dead-reckoning position had often to serve instead of an astronomical position. For the moment, however, I was not worried, for there was still plenty of sea-room.

Finally, on November 24th, after two days of clear weather which had enabled me to fix an exact position, I sighted land. My excellent Omega watch (for which I was indebted to José Poncini) had only a fifteen-second variation. Allowing for the current, I had selected Cape Santa Lucia, 120 miles north of Durban, for my landfall. Three days later I dropped anchor in the harbour of Durban.

My experiences in the meantime are worth relating in some detail. On the 24th, as I said, I sighted land. For the last two days there had been a fairly fresh wind from the north-east, with the barometer low, which was grounds for anticipating a stiff blow from the south-west with the next rise in pressure. I therefore kept well away from the coast, and at sundown my arrangements were made to heave to under the mizzen, with the helm a-lee, as I always did. At about 10 p.m. the barometer began to rise while the south-easterly wind set in; in a few minutes it had reached a considerable force, dropping after some hours to Force 7 or 8 on the Beaufort scale. This it kept up all night, gusting violently at times.

Marie-Thérèse II behaved admirably hove-to, swinging between forty-five degrees and zero degrees of the wind, in a sea that had built up formidably under the influence of the strong wind against the current. At daybreak the sea presented a thrilling sight. On all sides the seas were breaking, except on the boat herself, which was protected from the breaking seas by the dead-water produced by her drift.

For my own part, I was curled up in my blanket, prepared to sleep or read while waiting quietly for things to settle down. I must even confess that I rather welcomed this interlude, which allowed me to rest with an easy conscience. In fact it is difficult to realize how gentle and smooth the motion of a boat can be when hove-to, with a scrap of sail to give the wind sufficient purchase to make the boat drift, and heel over. It depends, of course, on the boat. A deep-draught vessel will not be so inclined to drift. As a result she will benefit less from the protection of the dead-water, and she will sometimes be struck by huge seas that will shake her from stem to stern. On the other hand, a shallow-draught boat, drifting more rapidly (which is sometimes a disadvantage on a lee shore—for nothing, unhappily, is perfect) will be better protected by her dead-water, for it extends further to windward. To my mind, the ideal from the point of view of comfort at sea, would be a boat of very moderate draught but with sufficient external ballast to right her once the keel has been exposed by a breaking wave.

Marie-Thérèse II was not, strictly speaking, a boat of moderate draught, for five foot, after all, is quite a considerable draught. On the other hand, she had little ballast and was lightly laden. (I had gone on board with ten shillings in my pocket, which gives you an idea of the comparative slimness of my provisioning and equipment.) As a result her drift produced a dead-water sufficient to protect her—until the time when the wind dropped to Force 5 (about fifteen knots) and complications developed. For, although the wind had dropped, there was still an ugly sea, covered with vicious breaking crests, caused by the Agulhas Current.

About noon on November 25th the wind, accordingly, had lightened considerably; there was no question, however, of getting under sail in this dangerous sea. I was in the cabin, when unusual thumps coming from the tiller roused me from my indolence; I went on deck to tighten the lashings, which had dried and so expanded. As I went up, I had omitted to close the sliding cabin hatch. I had hardly finished my work when I saw a huge sea coming. It was one of those isolated waves which come from a great distance, strike with extreme force, and when they had moved on leave behind an impression of comparative calm; they then roll ahead, striking out blindly at irregular intervals, to die out in an impressive mass of boiling foam on some far distant strand.

Marie-Thérèse II was lying head-on to this wave, and was completely covered by at least three feet of water. I can still see this picture of my boat, only the two masts emerging from the sea of foam. For my own part, I had had the time to wrap both arms round the mizzen mast, while my body went water-skiing on the surface of the flood. The impact, however, drove the boat back with great violence, so that she lay beam-on to the wave, which, still breaking, laid her right over, and then a bit further, and then a little bit further still. I found myself first lying in the mizzen sail and then swept overboard by the still foaming torrent. *Marie-Thérèse II* must have had her keel nearly forty-five degrees above the horizon. Fortunately she righted herself very rapidly, but with a list of some ten degrees to starboard. This was caused by the shifting of my stores, which I thought I had stowed most meticulously. It was fortunate, too, that my inside ballast, made up of lengths of rail and old chains, had been firmly bolted to the keelson. Otherwise the ending would have been a catastrophe.

I hastily clambered on board and immediately noticed that there was something not quite right—the cabin hatch had disappeared! It was floating twenty yards away—which meant diving in and recovering this essential fitting, an awkward operation in water lightened by the countless air-bubbles now incorporated in it. At that moment the boat lay in a protective screen of water which was almost solid white with air-bubble, and there she remained for some minutes completely shetered. No wave broke over her, the foaming layer acting like a film of oil.

Although the copper slats of the slides were bent, they were still held in position by some of the screws at the ends, which had not been pulled out, and I had no trouble in quickly putting them back, using a hammer to straighten the slats and a screwdriver to refix the screws that had been torn loose. I had no time to ram a match-end into the hold holes, to give my screws a better grip. That I left until better weather, or until I reached Durban. What concerned me most, in time and importance, was to replace the hatch, for I was dreading the coming of a second sea of similar dimensions, which could have finished us off.

All this was because I had made the mistake of not closing the hatch as I came out of the cabin. It was the pressure of the water on the underside of the hatch-cover which had forced it up and then torn it away from the guide-rails. With the hatch properly closed the pressure could only have been produced horizontally, on the forward surface, and that would have closed it even more firmly. The boat would have taken only a few buckets of water through the portholes, which were also open, on the lee side. Still, you have to breathe, do you not?

My second concern was the mizzen sail. Again it was fortunate that it had survived without splitting in two. The mizzen mast must have been extremely firm not to have snapped the standing rigging under the enormous pressure the sail sheeted home had to take. As it happened, the cleat of the mizzen sheet, or rather the metal eye, the width of your little finger in diameter, which held the block to the deck and which I had not thought it necessary to weld —this opened, allowing some slack to the sheet and thereby checking the effects of the deluge on the rest of the after-rigging. I patched it up temporarily with some wire, and then went forward to pay out all my chain, the warp and the anchor. The bows were thus held by this new-fangled but most effective sea-anchor, and remained stem-on to the seas. I then lashed the helm amidships so that the boat would have no tendency to swing beam-on should another breaking sea force her violently back. (The iron tiller-bar, one and a half inches thick, had been bent at an angle of twenty degrees by the pressure of the rudder at the impact.) With everything fixed on deck, I went to clear up below.

The cabin was in a state of indescribable chaos. Everything was swimming in water. The floorboards had piled themselves into the bunk, which in turn had flattened itself against the bulkhead. Tins of food were rolling to and fro; empty boxes, pots and pans, and an assortment of tools were lying in a ghastly muddle; mattress, blankets, all my clothing—the less said about them the better. They were soaking, and when I say soaking I do not mean they were just damp. In the forepeak the situation was less complex. Everything in it formed one solid mass plastered against the starboard side: spare sails (not many of them); ropes, chains, pots of paint, drums, flooring, had all flown off at random.

Before getting down to sorting things out—and re-stowing them— I decided to start by baling out the tons of water that were splashing around below. Since I could not risk leaving the hatch open, I could not use a bucket, which is quicker than the Chinese pump. This pump, which consists simply in a copper pipe which runs across the deck forward of the cockpit, is a marvel of simplicity. It can operate endlessly without jamming, spitting out water, tinned-food labels, oakum, and even a flying fish which I had picked up on the deck the evening before, and which had disappeared mysteriously while I was preparing my breakfast of porridge. So he was returned to his own element, and offered as a edible delicacy to his own kind. It took me several hours of monotonous work before I heard with relief the 'pfit, pfit' which meant that there was only air in the hold. 'Carry on if you like, chum,' this excellent pump seemed to say, indefatigable and always ready for work.

Meanwhile, the sea had subsided, and the wind had dropped considerably. The sky itself was not so overcast and in any case it was no longer raining. A few more hours' work and the stores would be back in the place in which they should have remained if that blasted sea had not thrown them about. Night was closing in by the time I had things ship-shape.

It was then that I began to feel cold, for in accordance with a habit acquired in the tropics, my sailing kit is ultra-light—you might even say non-existent. All my under-clothing was soaked. I looked out a warm pullover. The first contact with this wringing wet garment was most unpleasant but it soon became tolerable and I quickly warmed up. Cooking that evening was confined to opening tins, but a fine bowl of steaming coffee consoled me, after that cold dinner, for all the petty misfortunes of the day. Moreover, I was aglow with pride at the thought that my wonderful *Marie-Thérèse II* had stood up to and weathered a real sea. At the same time, this had made me realize the danger represented by inside ballast in a sailing vessel which has to take the weather as it comes and to meet all possible conditions. After all, supposing some slight play in the bolts holding it to the bilge had allowed the minute initial movement which, assisted by the inertia of this huge weight, had enabled the ballast to break loose: that would have been the end of *Marie-Thérèse II* and of me. I must therefore, I decided, find some completely safe solution. Moreover, the present disposition of this ballast (consisting of lengths of rail and old chains), and also the method of fixing it, raised a problem of accommodation to which I had not found the answer. I had, as it was, to be satisfied with an extremely rudimentary cabin, with no central passage-way. The bunk, in fact, occupied the whole of the cabin, stretching from one side to the other, with lockers on either hand for clothing, books, and light stores. This arrangement surprised my friends: and, I must confess, not without reason. All this, however, was something I could think about when I arrived in Durban.

After a night spent rolled up in my wet blanket, thinking of the joys of life on dry land, where, without disrespect to the forces of nature, one can count for certain on sleeping in some more or less dry spot, I climbed somewhat arthritically on deck. There I found a perfectly calm sea with practically no wind. This did not prevent the boat from rolling unpleasantly, held only by her mizzen, which was too small to check the motion effectively.

The calm lasted until midday. The staysail helped the mizzen in reducing the rolling, but I would have preferred a nice breeze from the north-east, as anticipated by the *Sailing Directions,* after the strong south-westerly.

At midday a sun-sight taken in perfect conditions placed me seventy miles south of the position I was in when I sighted the Cape. I was amazed at having travelled seventy miles against the wind in thirty-six hours, while my boat was drifting in the opposite direction. With such a current it was hardly surprising that the sea should have been in such a state during the last blow. I congratulated myself, accordingly, on having chosen a landfall so far north of Durban. It was as well not to have to beat back against that current.

Soon, however, the wind came: light at first and from the north-east, as it should, which for me was the right direction. From four o'clock in the afternoon it was to blow with great force, and the deck began to be wet. This is good for the wood: a boat will never rot so long as the sea and spray wash over her and impregnate her with salt. It is not so good, however, for the shrouds and ironwork, especially when it has not been possible to galvanise the latter.

On the other hand, it is over-lengthy lying in harbour which tends to introduce rot into the topsides of a boat: the Asiatics know what they are doing when twice a day they pour buckets of water over the deck and the deck-house, and splash the outside of the hull with a paddle or piece of planking. This long-term maintenance takes place first early in the morning, in order to wash away the dew from the wood and replace the fresh water which encourages rot with good sea-water; as the latter evaporates it desposits its salt in the numerous cracks and fissures, than which there is no better treatment for timber. The work is repeated in the evening at sundown, in order to counter so far as possible the harmful effects of the dew which will fall during the night. It is thus that, in spite of the arduous climatic conditions for boats in the Far East, they nevertheless survive to a great age. A good master is well served.

At last, on November 27th, at 11 a.m., we rounded the breakwater at Durban. Customs and Immigration picked me up in the channel, once I was inside the harbour. I had no trouble with the Customs, but shall have more to say about Immigration.

CHAPTER 4

A Year in Durban
shipwright and underwater caulking specialist

The secretary of the Point Yacht Club offered me the hospitality of his club, with an excellent mooring in the yacht basin. A charming, affable man, he was pacifying the Immigration officer, who was furious because I had only ten shillings to declare.

'How do you expect to stay here with that trifling sum?'

'By working on shore, of course.'

This innocent but unfortunate answer drove the official into a frenzy. He spoke volubly to his assistant in a language which I could not understand, Afrikaans, which is dervied from Dutch. But I could perfectly well guess what he was saying: South Africa is not an asylum for all the vagabonds in creation, and if this oaf of a sailor imagines he is going to be allowed to land and work on shore, and stay here for several months until he has saved enough to pay for the hundred and one modifications he wants to make to his boat, and then push off with a loaded wallet to go and infest some other place—then he's making a very big mistake. No knowledge of Afrikaans was needed to understand the meaning of this outburst.

For my part, I played the half-wit, put on my most cretinous grin, and in my halting English asked him if I had in some way contravened the port regulations. This produced a new explosion. I began to be a little worried—was he going to collapse in an apoplectic fit? After a while he calmed down and allowed me to explain the plan I had meanwhile concocted.

'Sir, you must excuse me, please: I have explained myself very badly, but, you know, English is not my native language, and so we have misunderstood one another. Money? Of course I have money: how could I sail without money?' (still behaving like the dimmest

46

idiot). 'I have to call at the Bank of Indo-China and find out from the manager whether the draft I arranged from the Paris office has come in.' Then I babbled on, to prevent him from asking me any more questions, which I probably could not have answered without lying outrageously and sooner or later being caught out.

It was past midday and the Immigration officer must have been getting hungry, because he showed signs of having had enough of this. The papers were signed, and he kept a copy of a declaration by which I undertook to observe the law relating to tourists, prohibiting them from undertaking any paid work during their stay on South African territory. At last he went away and I was left alone with the Yacht Club secretary. Not for long, however, for I heard an unmistakably French voice.

'Ahoy there!' It was Joseph Merlot, a great hunk of a man, with a fine, open, friendly face. He must be six foot tall and weigh fourteen stone, every bit of it muscle. Introductions were soon made and after five minutes were were old friends. (He had pulled across in his dinghy, home-made but as robust as the man himself.) Joseph and his family, consisting of his wife Madeleine and his little daughter Brigitte, were soon to become real friends: the sort of friends on whom one can land unannounced at any moment, without any fuss at all.

They had left France, the two of them, in their fine cutter (*Korrigan*, moored in the yacht basin) and had arrived as a trio in Durban. Brigitte had been born when they put in at Tobruk, which they had left as soon as she was old enough to go to sea. And that had not taken long: Red Sea, Mombasa, Comores, Madagascar, Lourenço-Marques, and Durban. They had been in Durban for six months, and Joseph had found a job in a French firm making concrete pipes. It was heavy work, well paid, and *Korrigan* was being improved every month: for however fine a boat may be, it is still never finished.

A few minutes later, Joseph took me on board *Korrigan*. Brigitte, who was a little angel, showed me Caroline, the ship's tortoise and *Korrigan's* mascot. Caroline was no trouble, even though she had grown five times the size she was when a Malagasy had given her to Brigitte during their long stay in Madagascar.

My new friends were delighted to find a Frenchman of their own sort, a marine creature, that is, with salt water in his veins. And I need hardly say how much I shared the same delight. Soon, however, my eyelids began to droop. Madeleine noticed this and was worried: was I all right, she asked. I should add that with my month-old beard and shaggy hair, I could hardly hope to pose for a picture of well-nourished tranquillity. The fact was, I was starving and had only just realized it. Madeleine and Joseph were quick to understand; 'Why didn't you say so sooner? And here we have been bombarding you with questions and talking ourselves silly. Anyway, we'll soon fix that.' The pan was put on the stove and soon I was sitting down to a huge omelette. The table had even been laid, which necessitated a certain amount of furniture-shifting, and some by no means flattering comments from Madeleine on Joseph, still full of jokes as he struggled to set up the table as quickly as possible, while the table refused to fit in between the chocks fitted on the floor of the cabin. This consoled me for my own table, 'Ah, Madeleine, if you could see my table, it would take your breath away!' I smiled at the thought, even though my thoughts were becoming very vague. Joseph reassured me: 'You know, Bernard, this is how it is here: Madeleine and I have these little squabbles quite often, but it never goes any further.'

My example roused Joseph's hunger; he joined me and we emptied a bottle of that excellent South African wine, which I found particularly delicious on that occasion. I felt a great deal better after that, and returned to my boat, feeling that the world was an excellent place, after a good meal, a bottle of good wine and the warm welcome of these French sailors. Before entering the cabin I looked with pleasure and a modicum of pride at the two French ensigns floating from the two mastheads of *Korrigan* and *Marie-Thérèse II*. There should in fact have been three, and I was surprised that Bardiaux had not yet arrived. A letter I had had from Mauritius told me that he had left Port Louis the week after my sailing. Knowing the capabilities of *Les Quatre-Vents*, this delay surprised and worried me, for nobody at sea can be completely free from the chance of an accident. One can so easily be slived in two at night by some vessel making its 15 or 20 knots. That great sailor Slocum certainly vanished in the Caribbean, before the start of the cyclone season: and how can one explain the disappearance of a seaman like him?

I was too tired to think any more. My mattress and blankets had been in the sun all day: in a real sun, which had dried them thoroughly and made me look forward to a refreshing sleep. I would shave that evening, and the next day, Monday, have my hair cut. I was as happy as a child, and not in the least worried about the remainder of my stay, and the many difficulties which were waiting for me at the Immigration office, nor about finding work (for my ten shillings were not going to allow me to go far afield). All that could wait until the morning.

Next morning I went across to *Korrigan* in my dinghy: for since the day before I had my own dinghy. Or rather, it was practically mine, thanks to the kindness of a yachtsman who had sold his yacht (poor fellow). For to hold on to garden, house, wife, and boat all together, is not always easy.

A big cup of coffee in *Korrigan's* cabin, followed by a second cup. In *Korrigan*, all hands are up at five in the morning, since Joseph has to catch the six o'clock train to work.

'Above all,' he told me, 'don't bother about Immigration's work-prohibition. When you've found something, send them a request for a permanent residence permit, with a letter from your employer certifying that he is ready to take you on. By the time the papers come back, whether they agree or not, you'll be over the horizon. It's six months now that I've been waiting, and there's not a sign from them—and, of course, I've been working for these six months.' If only, I thought, Joseph could know with how light a heart I left *Korrigan* that Monday morning, November 30th, to tramp the pavements of Durban looking for a job (which would not be my first, and by no means my last).

Transport is cheap in South Africa. No more than threepence to go almost anywhere you please by bus. The great thing is to set out with a good meal already under your belt, and not to have to go into a café for one. In this way, my ten shillings would hold out for several days, and it would be the devil's work if I could not find a job inside a week.

*

Some friends to whom I had spoken the day before advised me to try my luck out by the beach reserved for bathers, where, I was told, there is a shortage of life-guards. The life-guard is a man in swimming trunks who stands on a little wooden turret quietly waiting until some fellow (or it may be a woman) gets into difficulties through underestimating the strength of the rollers and overestimating his own.

When this happens (which is not often but by no means exceptional) the life-guard dives in, fishes out the rash bather, hauls him to the beach by the scruff of his neck, and if necessary, gives him artificial respiration. The perfect job, in short, for a former South Vietnam free-style champion, with experience, too, of under-water fishing.

Not so perfect, however, when you look closer: for in order to put in for the practical test in the Durban rollers you have to hold the bronze life-saving medal.

I contacted the 'right man', who sent me into the town to buy the little textbook you study for the bronze medal. 'You'll find it easy enough to learn. Come back when you think you know it properly, and we'll soon have you fixed up. We're short of people, and you look the right sort.'

So, it was in the bag. Wait a moment, though, and don't let's count our chickens before they're hatched. To begin with, I found that the booklet was not quite so simple after all: the method of artificial respiration was well explained, with clear diagrams; and I had a little practice on Joseph's back. The massage did him good, and he did not choke too much.

Next in order came twenty different holds for controlling a man on the point of drowning and bringing him back to shore. This seemed to me rather much. However, I was only too willing, since with £60 a month, when it cost me only £10 to live in my boat, I should save up a nice little sum in six months. I thought of the Immigration officer who had received me and I thought of the rage he would be in if he only knew.

Three days later, I presented myself to the same 'right man' at the swimming pool by the beach, a fine fifty-yard pool, with salt water, very clean, and sunny (when the wind was in the north-east, of course). 'Ah, there you are! First, let's see you do fifty yards.' I started with a crawl, not too fast, so as not to annoy him, in case his inner self-conceit was as strong as that which he affected externally: for if he wanted to overtake me racing, he would have to get up earlier in the morning (he was already swimming when I arrived). Another fifty-yards back-crawl, then fifty yards breast-stroke, ending with fifty on my back without using my arms.

'Fair enough,' he commented, 'now for the rest: show me hold No. 7.'

'Hold 7? Can you tell me in what circumstances you should use it?'

'All I want you to do is just to show me hold 7—come on, make up your mind. I've got a lot to do today.'

Between ourselves, I did once happen to fish out a friend who got into difficulties, but I would have had to be a mind-reader to know which hold this bastard wanted.

'Come back and see me when you know your holds properly by heart, with their numbers.'

I went back on board thoroughly put out.

*

A tap on the hull. It was a new friend, for anybody who travels in a dinghy loves the water and the sea, and therefore ranks as a friend.

Raymond Cruickshank: 'I think your boat is "very nice" (which is how an Englishman puts it), but I didn't like to come earlier for fear of disturbing you. I've a boat, too, *Vagabond*: tied up at the club jetty. Have you seen her?'

Had I seen her? An adorable little sloop, twenty-two feet at the waterline. Small, but really good; it would sail like a dream in any wind and reach!

We were friends from the start. Ray (as he was called) is no novice in sail. He began by fishing in the ill-famed waters of the Cape, and then became a shipwright, a most useful trade for a man who wants to build his own boat.

We drank some coffee—as we did constantly in *Marie-Thérèse II*, whether she was swinging to her anchor in harbour or under sail reaching out for the distant horizon. I told Ray about my problematical career as a life-guard. 'I know that bunch of so-and-so's,' he roared. 'I have been one myself and, believe me, I soon got their number. But there might be something much better. What would you say to being a shipwright?'

'Just the ticket—except that I'm not one!'

'It's not a question of being one or of not being one. You only have to say that you are, and there's no difficult about that, is there?'

His optimism won me over. Why not, after all, be a shipwright? It's not so grand as a bank manager but it's better than a chimney-sweep; and above all, nothing could be more useful for a sailor.

Our plans were completed there and then. The next morning, Ray was to pick me up at the jetty at 6.15 and drive me to the manager of Louw and Halvorsen's shipyard, to whom he would introduce me as a new recruit: a shipwright who had built his boat with his own two hands, with the assistance of his brain. References? They were lost in the wreck on the Chagos, but take him on trial and you'll soon see what he's like. My tools? They're on board, and I'll bring them tomorrow. Ray, in fact, had a fine set of tools, inherited from his father, who had also been a shipwright, and he would lend me all I needed, for *Marie-Thérèse II*'s tool-kit was extremely meagre. Even so, it did contain the tool which to my mind is irreplaceable, though frowned on in a workshop worthy of the name: a hatchet. You can use it for everything: to chop, of course, though that is not often needed on board, but also to drive a nail, as a screwdriver (which perhaps you had never thought of doing), to sharpen pencils, to extract nails, for caulking (and that is another use that had not occurred to you), and for scraping the hull free from barnacles. The Chinese even use it as a plane, but I am not such a star performer.

The most surprising thing was that it all happened as planned, when next day we met Mr. Nixon, manager of Louw and Halvorsen. He was a charming man, moreover, young and dynamic; and, by good fortune, he needed a large staff to start a branch in Durban of what was the largest repair and building yard for wooden vessels in South Africa, with their headquarters in Cape Town. He did not waste time, either his own or mine, but put me to work there and then.

Ray took me under his wing. Just then he needed someone to finish the repairs to a trawler in the roadstead. If Mr. Nixon 'does not mind' (another English phrase that amuses me), the help of a shipwright who is also a seaman could expedite the work. That was agreed, and I went off in the wake of my mentor, pondering on the shameless good luck that has never let me down. This time I was to learn one of the most useful of all manual trades while being paid £60 a month, plus £20 overtime—a fortune for a man who lived on £10 a month.

However, I had a rough time at first and that was to continue for a while. The first thing Ray did was to teach me the elementary principles without which I could not keep up the pretence for long: in the first place, the way to hold a tool. This is of the utmost importance and it is impossible to bluff the foreman on that point. You either know how to hold the tool or you do not. For a week our little gang worked together, and I made great progress, particularly, I must admit, when it was a matter of improvising.

When, therefore, I was put into the main gang, under Peter the foreman, I was not a complete dead loss. Moreover my workmates, who knew the story but did not mention it, were sympathetic and helpful. They helped me considerably as I steered my course among the reefs, neatly making good the work I had not carried out properly, and explaining to me what had to be done. On my side, I slaved away, doing my best to make progress along the arduous road of manual dexterity. At the end of a month, I was almost up to scratch, though that does not mean that it was all plain sailing as yet.

There was no lack of work for firms that specialized in the repair of fishing boats and the fitting of shifting-boards. South Africa exports its surplus maize crop, which the ships take on in Durban, the principal port for loading South African grain.

Shifting-boards are fittings constructed from strong beams, designed to hold the grain in position and prevent it from shifting to one side in rough weather. This shifting was probably the principal cause of the loss of the *Pamir* in the Atlantic: with the shifting-boards giving under the pressure of the cargo, the latter's movement to one side would have given the vessel a list that was all the more fatal in that the weather made it impossible to correct it.

Installing these boards was an exhausting day-and-night job for Louw and Halvorsen's gangs, for, unlike the yachts, the ships concerned had not come into harbour to lounge around in Durban's lovely sunshine: they were always in a desperate hurry.

The drill was almost the same for each ship that came in to load maize. Five teams of two or three European (i.e. white) shipwrights went down the ladder leading to the five holds (one team for each hold). Each white man had two coloured helpers to pass him tools, carry and hold the beams which the white man measured and sawed to the required length, and to keep them in position so that the white could fix them correctly with six-inch nails. Nowhere in the province of Natal is a coloured man allowed to use a tool. That is a privilege reserved to the whites and they are quick to defend it.

Work on the shifting-boards generally lasted a week, the last two days being extremely arduous, because of lack of sleep and the physical exhaustion we all suffered. Hasty meals of a sandwich or two, which our stomachs could not even digest in peace, produced towards the end of the week attacks of indigestion which in turn were a source of bad temper. There was considerable nervous strain, but we had so much to do that we had little time to brood on that; in any case the wages matched the work we put in, which was a consolation and made us forget after a couple of days the nightmare of the previous week. Then the ships would sail, and work on the new repairs would send us back to the same routine, until the next grain-ship, whose arrival, in the end, we awaited with impatience.

Money, money! The things you made me do in Durban! But there were many consolations. I was in excellent health and spirits and my bank balance was growing. Coming home exhausted in the evening, I used to look with pride at *Marie-Thérèse II* and run over in my mind all the improvements I planned. The most important was to find a foolproof solution for stowing the ballast, and I nursed grand schemes for making my cabin pleasant and elegant. The position of the ballast and its stowing had obliged me to be satisfied with a very rudimentary cabin, with no central passage-way. The only spot where one could stand upright was a space two feet square by the cabin hatch, where I had located the galley and the down-below steering position. The door opening aft could be made into a table by swinging it round on its hinges, with a length of fishing-line to hold it horizontal. This peculiar arrangement obliged guests to lift their feet in order to clear the table, before setting them down on the floor, hardly two foot square. I realized that it could be made infinitely more comfortable, but it would take a great deal of work.

I had heard nothing from Immigration, but to forestall any trouble I drew up my request for a residence permit in due form. I took my documents round to the 'right man', who was more polite on this occasion, and even distinctly favourable to my plan for permanent residence. He had no doubt but that my visa would be granted, even though my request had not been forwarded through the South African Consulate of my country of origin. Meanwhile, time was on my side. The wind was in the right quarter and life was good.

*

It was, indeed, a good life, with plenty of work and plenty of good friends. One of these was soon to become as close to me as a brother. This was Henry Wakelam, the son of an English father and a Russian mother, himself born in Shanghai. His parents had settled in South Africa at the time of the Sino-Japanese war. Henry had arrived there at the age of seven, and was to leave the country at the same time as I did, in his cutter *Wanda,* twenty-two feet on the waterline.

Raymond Cruickshank's *Vagabond* had also been built from the same plans; but although both boats originated from the same design, they were very different from one another. Ray had kept to the original plan, carefully following the specifications in order not to add weight. *Vagabond's* cabin was roomy for so small a boat.

Henry, on the other hand, had built everything more solidly and heavily, even massively, at the expense of lightness. The coach-roof was as small as possible, the deck was strengthened with huge stringers, and the framing was twice the weight allowed for by the designer. As far as strength was concerned, it would be difficult to imagine anything better in a wooden vessel. He had built it entirely by himself, under a tree, achieving miracles of ingenuity in getting round difficulties. Only when it came to riveting the planking to the frame had he been obliged from time to time to grab a friend by the arm, lead him to the boat, and push a heavy dolly into his hands with which to hold the heads of the copper nails. With countless oaths and threats, Henry would hammer away inside the boat, riveting until his companion was dropping with exhaustion. Apart from this work, which called for two men, everything else had been done by Henry on his own, with just his two hands and his brain.

For Henry had a real brain. I have never met a man so clever at doing any job that may crop up, with practically non-existent materials. He was the very personification of resourcefulness and practical intelligence. The friendship that was to unite us for a number of years was to be a real enrichment to me.

In addition to his uncommon gifts of practical intelligence, Henry possessed another that is equally rare: he had a heart of gold and an unselfishness that could make him forget everything else to help a friend or even a complete stranger in a difficulty. A few minutes' thought was enough for him to find the solution to a practical problem which would have taken a long time and much trial and error for a person of average endowment. Later I shall be describing the improvements, great and small, he introduced into *Wanda,* some of which were real masterpieces of simplicity and execution, and almost always made with means available on board. What a desperate worker he was, too, whether on his own boat or when giving a hand to a friend.

One morning, as I was pulling ashore to work, as usual, a new boat attracted my attention. I pulled harder and turned towards the newcomer. There was no mistaking that this boat had come a long way. The small indications one notes when looking at a sailing vessel often tell one at a glance whether it is an inshore pleasure boat or an ocean ranger. And there was no doubt that this boat was the latter.

It was a ketch, called *Atom*. So this was the fine sailing boat mentioned in Jean Merrien's books. I felt a little pang in my heart, however, when I saw that it was the American flag this single-hander flew—for all that, in spite of her American naturalization, she had remained very French, as I was later to find out.

I laid my hand gently on the rail, taking care not to let my dinghy chafe the hull, for fear of waking up the owner. He had in fact come in during the night and he could hardly be as fresh as a daisy this morning. I had been knocked up myself more than once; so I tapped gently on the hull—the well-known (sometimes too well-known) signal among sailors. I tapped too gently to wake him up if he was still asleep, but loud enough for him to hear if he was already about. No reaction on board: so I went ashore to work.

Back at the Yacht Club, there was no Jean Gau in *Atom*. His dinghy, which in the morning had been folded up against the coaming of the cabin, was gone, too, and I immediately looked across to *Korrigan*. It was as I thought, he was there. Soon a third dinghy was tied up astern of *Korrigan*, mine. And a minute later, there was a fourth: Henry, too, was back from work. Conversation, as always when a group of seamen are gathered, was soon in full flood. At sea there are few opportunities for lengthy discussion, but one makes up for it at times in harbour.

Jean Gau was over fifty. He had left France as a comparatively young man, to settle in the United States, which he left about fifteen years ago in his schooner *Onda*, heading for France. Losing his boat on a rock off the Portuguese coast put an end to his dreams of long single-handed voyages. He then returned to his ranges and ovens in America, where he was chef in a big hotel, and by dint of scraping the bottoms of his saucepans he managed to buy and fit out *Atom*, in which he was to complete a trouble-free circumnavigation. He is now back in New York, saucepan-scraping in the same hotel, in the hope of saving up enough to end his days peacefully in Tahiti, with which he had fallen in love.

However, Jean Gau is a wise man and takes no risks. He has learnt to draw the dividing line between adventure and the serious side of life: the future that you cannot just shrug off without the risk of finding yourself one day landing up in swimming trunks on a desert beach, with no boat, and no money. When you are young, you may extract yourself from such a situation without much difficulty; but later in life, it can be very tough. Jean Gau had given much thought to this and had laid plans for his future so that any accident that might occur would not be for him, in his fifties, a catastrophe.

Apart from his solid commonsense qualities, Jean Gau has an astonishing artistic talent; we were dumb with admiration when he showed us his paintings of the sea and boats. Everything in them was faithfully represented, and, in spite of this perfection in detail, from the whole unity of one of his pictures you gain an impression of strength and truth which to my mind, makes them rank as masterpieces. I hope that the public will be able to see them some time, for such expression of the beautiful should not remain hidden at the bottom of a cardboard box.

I had a long conversation with Jean Gau on this subject, trying to make him understand that he should not expose works such as these to the dangers that are inseparable from long passages. In fact, when Jean lost *Onda* fifteen years earlier, some magnificent pictures went down with her. *Atom* was very nearly lost on a reef in the Torres Strait, in which the strong swell would have made it impossible to save the boat. The most he could have hoped to do was to save his own skin. It will be a long time before I forget the expression of horror on his face, normally so relaxed, while he was telling me this nightmare story. It happened at the entrance to the Torres Strait. The wind suddenly dropped. The great Pacific swell was breaking on the coral heads that line the entrance; and the current was taking *Atom* into them. There was still, however, enough wind to manoeuvre and Jean retained his usual composure. Suddenly the wind dropped completely, not a breath. Where *Atom* lay, the current ran faster, carrying her straight towards the coral, and Jean suddenly realized that he was going to be wrecked at any moment, for the bottom was too deep for the anchor to hold. That was the end. It is sometimes in just that way that a boat is wrecked. In a flash, you realize that it is all over and a few seconds later, in fact, you are finished, and another page is turned. Jean remained petrified, his mind ceasing to function, and completely impotent. It is odd and terrifying how, in a moment, the intelligence can be paralysed, at the same time annihilating the will, which is frozen rigid, incapable of any reaction. It is, perhaps, a mixture of fear, astonishment and resignation to the inevitable.

When this sort of thing happens the seaman cannot think of anything. Jean did not even think of his engine; he had forgotten its existence, because he had greased the cylinders before leaving Christmas Island in the Pacific, and was not expecting to use it until he put into Durban. All he could feel was an iron hand, the hand of fate, crushing his bowels in its grip. He staggered down into the cabin to get a cigarette, which he took as though in a dream. His lighter would not work! The temperature was too high and the petrol had evaporated. Petrol!—he thought—petrol! engine! Saved at last, if only there is time! Time! He could feel the boat rising up on the swell, more pronounced at the edge of the reefs because of the sharp rise in the sea-bed.

He grabbed the starter: and, miraculously, the engine, which had given nothing but trouble, started without a cough at the first turn. Jean had had a very narrow shave.

And I, too, thank the god who watches over the seas, for in consequence Jean Gau's pictures will one day delight the public. And yet those paintings came very close to keeping company with the sea-urchins and starfish of the Torres Strait.

Two days after Jean Gau came into the harbour Bardiaux arrived in *Les Quatre-Vents;* and so there were now four French sailing vessels in the Durban yacht basin, three of the four with a single-handed crew. The Durban papers were delighted. Tired of their country's lack of stable government, were the French emigrating en masse? (This, remember, was December 1955.)

Bardiaux had made a sensational passage from Mauritius to Durban: twelve days, I believe, which, like most of his passages, moreover, has seldom been equalled. As for wind, he had had all, and more, than anyone could want. Off Réunion, he had even, he told me, been flung out of his bunk onto the deck while he was asleep. The bruise had gone since then, but not his memory of the incident. As usual, Bardiaux had no fixed plan about the length of his stay in port. 'It all depends on what happens,' he said, a statement with which we all agreed. Why move on if you feel inclined to stay a little longer, and why stay if you want to move?

His delayed arrival was caused by a damaged knee, which had put him in hospital some days after my departure from Mauritius, which he himself was planning to leave a week later. Had he started when he intended, he would have been in Durban to greet me on my arrival, for *Les Quatre-Vents* is a very fast boat. Moreover, Bardiaux does not like heaving to, which delays him. He said to me once, very truly, 'The longer you're at sea, the more chances you have of finding trouble: so don't hang about waiting for it if you can outsail it.' For my own part, I was beginning to dream of my next boat, very fast, sailing windward like a dream. Once my first enthusiasm had calmed down, however, I came round to the idea of a happy compromise between *Marie-Thérèse II*, pretty slow (and sailing close when the wind is in the right quarter), and *Les Quatre-Vents*, which seems to laugh at the wind direction and leaps from crest to crest without a thought of the crew's endless work and cold meals.

*

Supper that evening found the three French single-handers in *Korrigan's* cabin, sitting down to Madeleine's excellent soup. The four dinghies lay quietly tied-up astern, like four little dogs obediently awaiting their masters' good pleasure. Soon, however, we had to restore order among them, because they were starting to come to blows. The south-wester which had developed was responsible for this growling and snapping (the sea gets up with the wind, even in harbour sometimes). There followed a certain amount of pushing and pulling in *Korrigan's* cockpit, each trying to protect his own first-born (for of course, each one of our geese are swans). Soon they were settled down or at any rate mastered, carefully tied up stem to stern.

We went back to the cabin, where Madeleine gave us a towel which we shared in turn, for the south-wester, now blowing hard, had brought rain.

There was a storm raging in the cabin, too: not an ugly storm, but somewhat acrimonious all the same—on a subject that rouses every seaman in the world and about which they can never reach agreement.

There were two items on the agenda: heaving, or lying, to and sea-anchors. The storm broke while Jean Gau was making me tell them about my last passage. I had just reached the famous sea that broke over us, 'And how were you hove-to at the time?' asked Jean.

'My usual way, under the mizzen, with the helm hard down, and, unfortunately, no sea-anchor.'

'One of these days,' answered Jean, with a little less than his normal unruffled calm, 'you're going to get into trouble, my boy' (twenty-three years difference in age and his long experience of the sea entitled him to this paternal tone) 'because you must remember that heaving to means placing yourself beam-on, or practically beam-on, to the sea under reduced sail. Drifting on her side, the boat produces an area of smooth dead-water acting like a layer of oil and preventing the waves from breaking. No other method, with or without a sea-anchor, will produce sufficient dead-water to protect the boat. A boat under bare poles with the helm hard a-lee will remain beam-on to the sea and will not drift sufficiently to produce an extensive smooth. Too many sailing men are satisfied by taking off all sail. The result is that one day they will be rolled over by a breaking sea and risk losing their masts, not to speak of the damage done on deck by the impact of the seas on the cabin-hatch: or the damage to the rudder, whose stock may be sheared clean. As for the people in the cabin, they may take some nasty knocks or at least a few serious contusions.' (I thought to myself of *Adios's* adventure—the cabin stove-in, the rudder-stock sheared; and of *Marco Polo*, which, as one of her crew of three told me when I met them in Mauritius, was lying a-hull, beam-on to the seas, under bare poles. The bowsprit snapped, and it was a miracle she was not dismasted, for the mainmast was stayed forward only by the bowsprit stay, their rig including no forestay. And one of the crew of *Marco Polo* had to be taken to hospital with the injuries he received in the cabin.)

According to what Jean Gau told us, this is what seems to be the safest way of heaving to: under stay sail sheeted home and hard, as close as possible to the fore-and-aft line of the boat, with the helm hard a-lee. The boat then lies beam-on to the seas, making no headway, and drifts sufficiently to receive protection. If the wind decreases and the seas are still dangerous, Jean Gau, if necessary, sets the mizzen while leaving the helm a-lee. The boat then lies a little closer to the wind, swinging with the wind somewhere between the bow and the beam—and she is still sufficiently protected by the dead-water of her drift.

I then asked him a question which had been very much in my mind since my accident off Durban. If a huge breaking sea should cross this protective layer of dead-water and roll you over like a pancake, will you not lose your mainmast, with this terrible pressure of water on the staysail? (That was aimed particularly at Jean, whose mainmast is stayed forward only by the bowsprit stay, the jib occupying the whole of the area between the end of the bowsprit and the mainmast; and I had the feeling that if he took a real monster on this large jib, bowsprit and mainmast would go overboard together.) 'No sea has ever done that with *Onda* or *Atom* when hove-to,' answered Jean, a trifle put out by my remark about the forward staying of his mainmast, and by my stupidity in not understanding what seemed to him perfectly obvious.

'As for the sea-anchor,' he went on, 'I have not much use for it. The last time I used one was in *Onda*, and I thought my bones were going to lie in the mud at the bottom of the Atlantic. What happened was that this blasted sea-anchor, paid out forward, held the bows so firmly into the seas, that they put a tremendous strain on the forebitts, so that I expected the bows to be torn away at any moment: and you should have seen the waves breaking over the boat—*Onda* was facing directly into them and was completely unprotected. Finally, I took my knife and zip!—one good slash on the line and I was free of that accursed sea-anchor: a very dangerous device, I think.'

In my own mind, I thought over what Jean had just said about the sea-anchor which held *Onda*'s bows so well into the seas. In my last two boats I had observed a tendency which was exactly the opposite. With sea-anchor or with nothing at all, it was the same, so much so that I was pleased to note the effectiveness of an ordinary anchor lowered on twenty fathoms or so of warp. The anchor, as a result of its own weight on the one hand and the drift of the boat on the other, lies obliquely, thereby presenting a considerable braking area and acting most satisfactorily. To each boat its own method!

'After getting rid of that infernal sea-anchor,' Jean Gau went on, 'I set the staysail, sheeted it home with the helm hard a-lee: and that was the end of my traumas. No seas broke over *Onda*, which nevertheless was hove-to beam-on to the sea, but was then protected by her drift to leeward. Since that experience, I have never carried that useless encumbrance a sea-anchor. I heave to under the staysail or staysail and mizzen according to the strength of the wind.' It should in fact be remembered that the state of the sea does not always depend on the strength of the wind. A wind of extreme violence will sometimes have the fortunate effect of blowing off the dangerous crests in the form of spume. But when that wind drops, you must be ready for trouble. The seas will start to break—and how!—particularly when a contrary current joins in the fun.

After Jean Gau's exposition, Joseph Merlot was asked to tell us about this theory, based on his own experience. (*Korrigan* is a cutter, with staysail stayed at the stem and jib at the bowsprit.)

'I had to heave to three times,' said Joseph, 'once in the Mediterranean, then off the coast of Africa, not far from Mombasa, and finally off the Mozambique coast. On the last two occasions, the wind was against the Mozambique Current, which was running at about a knot.

'I have always hove to under the staysail, except once, when I was under a jib, set upside down as a trysail. I have had no trouble with these methods, but I prefer heaving to under the staysail because in that case I continue to fore reach. I have even covered forty miles on my correct heading in one night.'

'But how did you lash the helm?' I asked him. 'For a boat hove-to must drift either to one side or astern, and not sail to windward.'

'The helm? It wasn't lashed, for I don't like putting an extra strain on the rudder when there's a heavy sea. It was riding free without any lashing, except at times a piece of inner tube from a car-tyre—just not to let it have too much play. As for the staysail, I don't sheet it home, but leave it as though I were simply sailing to windward.'

'And have you never collected a nice big wave in your staysail while you were sailing to windward under reduced canvas in that sort of weather?'

'Never,' said Joseph. 'Not yet, anyway.'

Jean Gau shook his head slowly and murmured, 'Chancy, very chancy! You, too, Joseph, will catch it one of these days.'

For my part, I, too, think that Joseph will catch it if he really comes up against the real thing, and the wave decides to break just at the moment it reaches the boat. For, to be dangerous, a wave must satisfy two conditions: the first is that it must be of very great size, and the second, that it must break right on the boat or a few yards short of it. If it breaks a little astern, it does not matter. If it breaks too soon, the crew will escape with a slight emotional disturbance, some spray on deck, and at the worst a nasty smack but without unpleasant consequences.

Furthermore, for quite a long time now I have not believed it possible that a really large sea should break exactly on a small boat: the chances of such an accident happening seemed to me so slim as not to be worth considering. There is in fact so much room around the boat: so why should the wave break just on that one little dot dancing on the sea? A mathematician might well amuse himself by working out the probability of such an occurrence. It is not unlike the problem of collisions at sea. How can one imagine that two dots moving across the vast expanse of the ocean should one day coincide —particularly when one of the dots is a small sailing vessel whose course is at the mercy of the god who controls the winds, and the other a steamship, which knows no gods other than the schedule and the most direct route? Nevertheless many a sailing vessel has been run down by a steel ship: was not Le Toumelin run down at dawn, when his lights were clearly visible?

We all looked with anticipation towards Bardiaux. None of us had any doubt: Bardiaux was the master who would let in the daylight on the problem for his three pupils. Bardiaux, however, was not interested in heaving to or not heaving to: he had seldom hove to though that had not prevented him from being flipped over like a pancake. It all depended, he believed, on the boat herself. It was the boat that determined the final result, for, hove-to or not hove-to, it was all the same to Bardiaux. There was, nevertheless, this very important difference, that when hove-to you generally drift in the wrong direction, while if you press on without bothering over-much, you continue to make some progress, or at any rate not to lose ground. This bold theory was supported by an irresistible argument: that it worked. Further, it is as well to get through as quickly as possible, without hanging about in the middle of the ocean waiting for worse trouble. As for a sea-anchor, he had never found it satisfactory and no longer carried one on board. He found it in the way in a small boat, and preferred to use the ordinary anchor with a good length of warp paid out.

Before leaving this subject, which must interest seamen, whether they sail in deep water or inshore, I would like to describe my own ideas and experience. First, the question of the sea-anchor.

I have never been satisfied with the conventional device popularized by Captain Voss. This consists of a strong canvas cone or pyramid, whose mouth (about three feet across) is held open by a wooden or metal cross-piece or ring. All yachtsmen will have heard of it, or know it from carrying one on board. It is heavy, cumbersome, and once the weather has improved, it is awkward to haul inboard again.

Moreover, the effectiveness of this type of sea-anchor is very doubtful. Its braking action is slight, and generally not sufficient to hold the boat head-on to the seas, the centre of drift lying almost always pretty far aft. As a result, when the sea-anchor has been paid out ahead, the boat will nearly always lie beam-on. For such a device to be effective it should have a much wider opening, which would make it intolerable to carry inboard and extremely difficult to handle.

I have myself had three conventional sea-anchors in succession and I must confess, with shame, that I have lost them all, and for a very simple reason. I do not find them satisfactory, and it almost gives me pleasure to see them disappearing each time, although I am sorry to lose the warp (which I had, of course, forgotten to protect against chafe).

Nevertheless, a sea-anchor can be extremely useful if it is essential to drift as little as possible; as, for example, when you are on a lee shore. Paid out ahead, with the assistance of the very reduced canvas used to heave to, it will cut down the drift to some slight extent. Paid out astern, without sail, it will slow down the boat while holding the stern into the waves and avoid the crew's having to take turns at the helm (*although this still depends on the boat*).

There is, however, a very little-known type of sea-anchor, which works perfectly. It presents a large braking surface, without the disadvantages of weight, awkwardness, and difficulty in handling associated with the Voss-type sea-anchor. It is extremely simple, and the construction is as follows.

A rectangle of stout canvas, four feet by three (for a boat of about five tons), is strongly roped. Each of the longer sides is laced to a cylindrical support: the upper support, which is wooden, is some four inches in diameter, and will act as a float; the lower is made of galvanized tubing and will act as a weight, holding the canvas vertically in the water.

From each corner, four 5-yard lines fitted with shackles meet at a thimble, to which is attached the warp connecting the sea-anchor with the boat. The important thing is to ensure that the four lines are of exacly the same length.

This type of sea-anchor can be reasonably large, since it is not cumbersome (it rolls up like a curtain); it is easy to haul inboard when the foul weather has gone (all you have to do is to take hold of the upper support and you can pull it in with ease); and the sailor can be sure that his boat will head into the seas and drift very little. For my own part, there is now no question about it: it is, so far, the most satisfactory type I know.

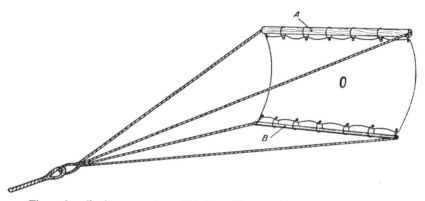

Fig. 2. An effective sea-anchor which is readily stowed inboard. It is important that the four lines should be of exactly the same length. A: wooden support, acting as a float. B: galvanized metal pipe acting as a weight.

Now for the second question: heaving to. In the first place, I think that I should emphasize that, no matter how you are hove-to, no sailing boat of small tonnage (I am speaking of yachts) is safe from capsizing if she is caught at the right moment by a freak wave breaking over her. I am speaking now of lying a-hull under bare poles or storm-canvas and without a sea-anchor. The instances of boats being turned turtle by a giant wave are too numerous to discuss. I need only mention Voss in *Sea Queen*, Bardiaux in *Les Quatre-Vents*, Vito Dumas in *Lehg II*, Tom Steele and Cruickshank in *Adios*, Bernicot in *Anahita*, and more recently Henry Wakelam in *Wanda*, my New Zealand friends in *Marco Polo*, and I myself in *Marie-Thérèse II*, and certainly many others. All these boats were lying a-hull when it happened: hove-to each in its own way, and probably in every imaginable way. But this did not prevent them from being rolled over.

There is no doubt that the protective dead-water produced by a boat drifting beam-on under storm-canvas will greatly reduce the risk of capsizing. But if a giant wave should ever cross this barrier,

c

the boat will then be caught from the side and violently capsized, with the risk of being dismasted and receiving other damage to her structure. So what should one do? My answer holds good only for myself, for I am far from claiming to be in the position to advise others, when much more experienced seamen than I disagree over the question of heaving to.

At the onset of the foul weather, I would do what I always did before my accident off Durban. That is, I would heave to under the mizzen, or under reefed mainsail in the case of a cutter or sloop, with the helm a-lee, of course. Hove-to in this way, the boat is very comfortable: with a slight leeward list, there is hardly any rolling. If the draught is shallow, the dead-water on the weather side will protect her perfectly, at any rate at the beginning. Life on board will be free from worry, without regret for the time wasted, since prudence insists on my heaving to until the sea is in a better temper.

If the foul weather continues, however, a further manoeuvre seems to me to be advisable. I go forward (completely stripped in order not to risk wetting the few dry clothes I still have) and pay out the sea-anchor: not the Voss anchor, but the one I have just described, *or even the ordinary anchor with the full length of warp*. If I am ketch- or yawl-rigged, I leave the mizzen (well sheeted home as it should be) but I put the helm amidships so that the impact of a wave breaking forward (thereby driving the boat violently astern) will not be in danger of breaking the helm as a result of the water's resistance to the rudder. One can readily appreciate, in fact, that were the boat to be driven suddenly astern with the helm lashed at 45 degrees, the resistance of the water to the rudder-blade would be enormous, and might well cause serious damage: breaking the blade, or the stock, or even—if the metal bracing holds firm—tearing away the whole stern-post (as would be by no means inconceivable)—not to mention the comparatively minor but highly disconcerting accident of breaking the tiller. Moreover— and this is important—a boat driven violently astern with the rudder at 45 degrees may well turn beam on and find herself rolled over again by the same wave, as happened to me off Cape Santa Lucia.

If boat and rigging are sound, there should be no trouble, the more so as the coach-roof is generally very low, forward (or at any rate that is how I generally build it). It is none the less true that with the sea-anchor forward, the rudder cannot but be put to a severe test. And if the skipper is fearful for his rudder, even with the helm lashed amidships, he still has the resource of running with the sea-anchor paid out astern. The rudder will then be under no strain, since, should a sea break over the stern, it will simply follow the boat as it normally does. It is the after part of the cabin that will have to take the impact; in some cases this can be extremely severe, the more so in that the cabin of a small boat is generally, in proportion to the boat, somewhat tall and exposed aft.

In such a case, one can also, instead of a sea-anchor aft, use a number of warps trailing astern. They will act as a brake (though not so much so as a sea-anchor) and will, even more, have a stabilizing effect on the course should a sea break aft. In connection with these warps paid out astern, I have noted (having sometimes used this method in my earlier boat, *Marie-Thérèse*) that a single warp with its two ends made fast at the stern, one at each side (so that the whole forms a sort of loop), has the effect of raking the surface of the sea astern and seems to produce for some distance in the wake of the boat a protective sheet of dead-water, unfortunately too narrow to be really effective.

But supposing the heavy weather sets in when one is fairly close to the shore and is being carried towards it by the wind?

Well, as a rule I like to give a very wide berth to the shore, fifty to a hundred miles is not too great a distance when the shore is exposed to frequent violent winds. For, generally speaking, a boat is far from being uncomfortable when she is hove-to, paradoxical though that may appear to some. However, if you allow yourself to be carried too close to the shore, then you do just what Bardiaux did—you stick your neck out, more or less. That is why, when talking of boats, I fully approve of the old French saw: 'better too strong than too weak'.

*

Atom and *Les Quatre-Vents* spent a month or so in Durban before setting sail for new shores. Jean Gau made a direct return passage to Cape Town in twenty-one days, for he met a good deal of bad weather. Bardiaux loitered along the coast, putting in at most places between Durban and Cape Town, where he was to remain for a long time, while Jean Gau was soon on his way to France to see his mother. He then sailed *Atom* back to New York single-handed, leaving New York once more to end his days in peace in the Pacific islands that had won his heart.

After the great exodus, Henry wanted to make a trial run to Beira, seven hundred miles north of Durban, returning to Durban to decide on his next stage.

Wanda's sailing north took place just before a south-westerly gale. In going up the African coast, you have no alternative: you must have a southerly wind, and such a wind is no joke off the Natal coast.

Henry's passage of some three hundred miles to Lourenço-Marques is one that he will remember for a long time; if he sailed at too great a distance from the coast, he would come up against the strong contrary current with heavy breaking seas; closer in, he would have to face the loss of sleep entailed by skirting the rocks, at the helm night and day, in the rain and spray. A week later I received a postcard from Beira.

Meanwhile, my work proceeded at Louw and Halvorsen's: but it proceeded at a pace that accelerated to the point where I had difficulty in keeping up. A change in manager was the reason for this. The consequences of the change may have been advantageous for the business, but they were less pleasant for me. In brief, the new boss had seen through me, to put it plainly, and this in spite of all Peter's efforts; for Peter (the foreman) had realized my position for a long time but had decided to take the single-handed French sailor under his wing.

On one occasion he had, in fact, made me come clean.

'It's no use trying to bluff me. What were you up to before you shoved your great clumsy feet into this joint? Don't give me any of your yarns—I soon realized that you didn't know much about handling tools before you came here: you can bluff the boss, if you like. It's all you can do, in any case. But not me. Come on, let's have it—I'm waiting!'

It was in fact useless to try to bluff Peter. This had always bothered me, but, after all, I had to live. So I then told him, and really meant it, that in life today I thought it was essential to be master of a trade, that the shipwright's trade seemed to me probably much more useful than the mechanic's, since I do not like engines, and that the best way of learning a trade is to plunge right in at the deep end, without messing about (here Peter began to smile)—particularly when you are in a sympathetic shop with even more sympathetic work-mates.

'All right, all right,' answered Peter, 'you needn't say any more:

but if you had told me this a bit earlier, I'd never have given you some of the jobs that had to be done quickly and really well. Do you know that I had hell's own job pacifying a customer yesterday? I had to go over the work in the evening; the only excuse I could make was that you never drink but this was the exception that proves the rule.'

Well, Peter, you were a good friend; and if St. Peter by some mistake sends you to the sailor's heaven, I hope the wind and sea will always be fair for you and that every new dawn will find your deck covered with flying fish!

Unfortunately, the new manager had his eye on me, for it is rash to imagine that all bosses are half-wits. Apart from caulking, which interested me greatly and at which I had become very proficient, and building the shifting-boards, which I could manage not too badly, at everything else I was still a passenger.

Caulking, however, and making shifting-boards were far from covering the whole of Louw and Halvorsen's activities. It was then that caulking came to my rescue, in the revolutionary form of underwater caulking. What a stroke of luck!

It happened as follows. One day, when things were looking really ominous for me, the skipper of a fishing boat brought his vessel into the yard. There was a bad leak. All Louw and Halvorsen's slips were busy and it would be three days before they were free. And my luck had arranged that those in their competitors' yards were also busy.

I had already mentioned to Peter my talent for stopping leaks in a way that would last, working outboard by diving under the hull. He did not believe me at the time, but remembered it then, for he came and took me off the shifting-board gang. 'Now, look, Bernard,' he said, 'if you're not as big a bluffer as I'm afraid you are, now is your chance to show us something.' He then explained the position to me. The manager, for his part, simply shrugged his shoulders: after all, it would be a good opportunity to get rid of me. 'We'll soon see just what his bluff is worth,' he must have been thinking.

The Indonesian seamen had shown me how to carry out under-water repairs, using a mixture of clay and cement, and I have used this technique successfully on my earlier boat, which, I must confess was by no means new. The clay and cement mixture had given me good results, but I had found a better way of stopping leaks between two planks.

As everyone knows, caulking consists in forcing a strand of oakum or cotton into all the parts of the hull at which two pieces of timber meet, in particular between the planks. This strand of oakum is applied, of course, from the outside. When the boat enters the water, the joint swells as it becomes wet, and all the interstices are solidly plugged.

It is important, it will be appreciated, that the packing should be even, and reasonably tight, and done with a really dry strand. And I was claiming to do this under water!

There was a solution, and a very simple one; but, as always, I was looking too far afield for it. The light dawned one day: not too blinding, since it left in darkness practically no detail of what was for me the realization of an old dream. Everything comes in time, but on this occasion it was certainly high time.

At this point I think I should describe in exact detail the way in which I carried out this operation. I repeated it successfully five times on Durban fishing boats.

The problem can be broken down as follows:

1. Find, inside the boat, the source of the leak.
2. Locate it on the outside, by diving under the hull.
3. Caulk it from outside with dry cotton.
4. The first operation is carried out by the conventional method. The only way of detecting a leak is to work by a process of elimination. I pump out the hold, dry the bilges with a sponge, and then pinpoint the little trickle of water: forepart, midships, or afterpart. One can generally have access without difficulty to the forepart and the midships part. In the afterpart the problem is more difficult: there is no flow of water to help you locate the source of the trouble. Moreover the contracted shape of the hull makes this part of the vessel difficult of access. Armed with a candle and a great deal of patience you have to be prepared for every sort of physical contortion.

Then comes the next series of eliminations: port or starboard—unless the water is coming from the keel rabbet, which is extremely trying.

Finally, working along the frame along which the water is flowing, it will generally be possible to locate pretty accurately the source of the leak. Listening has often saved me a lot of time, because I have been able to hear the trickle of water entering. Similarly, I have done it by feeling, in a Durban fishing boat. The water was in the afterpart, in the keel-rabbet. Running my hand gently along it, I felt the little eddy which revealed the position.

Once, after much patience, the leak has been found, then you mark the place inboard. You only hope that the leak is not in the keel-rabbet, the stem or the stern-frame. In this last case, particularly, it would be difficult to overcome because of the torsion forces produced by the rudder. Caulking the stern-post always calls for a great deal of care, and must be checked periodically.

It then remains to locate outboard the leak you have pinpointed inboard. I drill a hole in the planking about a foot from the leak, and into this hole I drive a copper nail thick enough to block the hole and long enough to project outboard. Before driving the nail, however, I make several notches in it near the point, with a pair of pliers. The reason for this will be apparent later.

This nail will mark outboard the area in which the leak will be found. I use a copper nail because it will have to remain in position until the next careening, and copper does not rust. To withdraw the nail immediately and replace it by a wooden plug would be to invite a ship-worm, for the plug would not be protected by anti-fouling: so better to leave the nail in position.

Everything is then ready for the operation of underwater caulking. I enter the water, wearing a mask, and carrying a white cloth and a pocket knife. The cloth will be hung on the nail, held in position by the notches, and will enable me to locate the working area without difficulty. On occasions I have spent a lot of time hunting for that infernal nail. The white cloth is readily visible and saves waste of time and breath. Similarly, a weighted belt will make it easier for the diver to maintain his position in the water.

The pocket knife (or a stainless steel kitchen knife) will enable me to detect suspect places in the caulking. A close look will save time, particularly inasmuch as the underwater image, seen through goggles, is magnified by one-third. In a well caulked place, the point of the knife will hardly enter, but as soon as you come to a defective spot it can be inserted with ease. You then mark the exact spot with another white rag, so that you can find it again immediately on your next dive.

If the area you suspect is very large, you have to look and look, and dive again and again. But here I was taught a dodge by the

Vietnamese fishermen. They do not really caulk under water, but can temporarily stop a leak with tallow mashed up with crude oil (small fish and prawns would eat the tallow, but they loathe the taste of crude oil). Their dodge consists in rubbing their head against the hull. The leak has a sucking effect and the diver feels his hair being flattened against the hull—only very slightly, it is true, but quite enough to notice. These Vietnamese fishermen then smear the defective area copiously, rubbing it in well with their hands: and you can be certain that some of the tallow will inevitably find its way into the hole. As so often, Asia, ancient as all past centuries, has the answer: and all this they do without diving goggles.

To return to ourselves: we have now located the leak, marked it with a rag, and now all we have to do is to caulk it with dry cotton, and under water.

Dry cotton, and under water? It is simple enough, in fact. To keep the cotton dry, all you have to do is to coat it with tallow. After a day, the water will penetrate the cotton, at least in places; it will then become wet, swell and set firm. Exactly the same principle is used in conventional caulking.

The practical application of this elementary principle is not easy, needless to say. You have to be a pretty good swimmer to be able to work under water for thirty seconds at each dive; and, above all, you have to *try* and not say from the outset that it is impossible.

In this connexion, however, I must note a little dodge in the caulker's trade. A beginner will be inclined to caulk only the defective part. The result may well be to stop the original leak, it is true, but also to open up two new apertures, one each side of the part that has been newly caulked. What happens is that when you pack the cotton between two planks, you force them apart a little. Water will no longer penetrate where you have just packed the cotton; but on either side the planks will no longer be in contact with the old caulking, which by that time has become almost as rigid as a wooden rod.

To avoid this snag, you have to do as the experts do, and start the caulking three or four inches before the condemned portion, ramming it in fairly gently at the beginning and working up to the maximum tightness of packing at the few inches of the leak itself; you then progressively ease off the packing, so that you finish very gently in a rat's tail five or six inches further along.

The tools used are a caulking iron and a four-pound hammer.

Lacking the former, a screwdriver will do, though it slows you down a little. There are certain places, however, where a screwdriver can be most useful—at a corner (where the keel joins the stern-post, for example); or for all the small leaks which make up much of the work of underwater caulking; and for caulking a leak through a rivet or nail. In old boats there are many such leaks and they are extremely difficult to locate. It is the same as with teeth: it is no use treating the one next door. Only a screwdriver allows you to force the cotton round the defective nail or rivet. As a result of a single rusted nail a boat can make an alarming quantity of water in twenty-four hours.

My employer now had in me a most useful workman. The fishing season was at its height, and the boats would not wait for the slip to be free to fix a troublesome leak which the 'Frenchman' could caulk in a morning, or in a couple of hours with luck; for meanwhile I had constructed a diving kit of extreme simplicity which allowed me to breathe normally under water for a minute. At the end of that time I had simply to return it to the surface, leave it there a moment and then go back for another minute's work.

I shall describe this rudimentary apparatus later (pp. 167-73), after it has been perfected by Henry Wakelam and myself during our time on St. Helena. Any yachtsman can make it in a few hours with the means available on board. It enabled us to breathe underwater for as long as we wished, using a system of recharging which was carried out on board in record time. For the moment, however, I must crave your patience, for we are still a long way from the roadstead of St. Helena.

There was plenty of work: so much, indeed, that I was doing nothing at all for my own boat. Weekends were devoted to recovering my energies for the next week's work. And the weekend might very well coincide with the arrival in harbour of a ship loading that infernal maize. No Sunday rest, in that case, but down into the hold with the rest of the gang until the work was finished.

However, this sort of life was not to last for ever. My bank balance was growing week by week, and there had never been any question of my settling in Durban.

It was *Wanda's* return that brought things to a head. One morning, as I reached the club jetty on my way to work, I found *Wanda* there.

The morning was spent peacefully in Henry's company. He, too, had any number of little things to arrange for the big day of his coming departure. Why, we asked ourselves, not sail together? Why not, indeed?

That same day I went and handed in my notice to Peter. 'If there's any caulking to be done,' I told him, 'you know where to find me. It won't be often that I leave the boat.'

'And if your savings run out before your work is finished,' he answered, 'you know where to find me, too.'

*

I had an impressive list of work to be done, for *Marie-Thérèse II* had left Mauritius only just in seaworthy condition. There is no need to bore the reader with a detailed account of all the work carried out, which kept me another three months in Durban. My first concern was for the ballast. The old ballast, of rails wrapped up in old chains, was not a good solution, even though in theory (and indeed in practice) it would have remained in position even if the boat had turned turtle and righted herself again. It took up too much useful space.

I replaced it with concrete ballast, reinforced with a ton of old bolts, and poured inside the boat along the whole length of the hold. Setting under the keelson and the first stringers in the bottom, it formed a completely immovable solid block. Whatever happened on board, therefore, it would be absolutely safe. This was the solution adopted by Slocum and suggested to me by Bardiaux. In addition to its complete safety, this method considerably increases the longitudinal rigidity of the hull, particularly if the concrete is reinforced with steel rods, as is done with concrete girders.

I cannot guarantee that the concrete will not cause the timber to rot, because I have no real experience in that matter. All I can say is that many fishing boats use concrete ballast. It is advisable, however, to see that the hold is perfectly clean before you pour the concrete.

Further, I thought it better not to pour my concrete until *Marie-Thérèse II* was once again in the water, after cleaning and painting the hull on the slip. I think, too, that I made a mistake in using paint on the bilges. A good coat of tar would have been better protection.

But why leave the concrete until the boat was back in the water, and not when she was high and dry on the slip? This was so that her ballast should be poured when she was in her natural element, and she would be spared the slight distortions which might have resulted if she had been out of the water on a slip. Another reason was that in this way it was much easier to find out how much concrete was needed to allow her to ride easily. When she is deep enough in the water, you stop pouring. Simple enough—but you must not, on the other hand, be too enthusiastic and pour in too much concrete. This is what I did in Durban, and I had to remove some of it in Cape Town with a great deal of trouble, giving myself some nasty cracks with the hammer on the hand that held the cold-chisel.

It is essential that a boat should carry such ballast that she can right herself on her keel if by chance she is capsized by a breaking sea. On the other hand she must not carry more ballast than safety necessitates. When a boat is too heavily in ballast, she will not drift sufficiently, when hove-to, to produce the protective area on the weather side; in this case she may well, if the sea is dangerous, have to stand up to quite a number of vicious waves.

Again, if a boat that is too heavy is struck by a sea as it breaks, she will resist with her own inertia; the force of the wave then becomes far more dangerous, and you must be prepared for damage. Had the boat been lighter, she would have given at the impact, thereby damping the effect. At sea, it is rather as in the fable of the oaktree and the reed. And that is why a sea that will destroy a ship of five hundred to a thousand tons, or cause her serious damage, will do no more than roll a small sailing boat without breaking anything that matters too much. If you tossed a watertight barrel into the sea in the middle of a cyclone, it would survive. On the other hand storms have been known to tear away sea-walls weighing hundreds of tons.

After the important job of the new concrete ballast, came that of all the metal tangs for the shrouds. I sent them into the town, and they came back three days later galvanized. I re-bolted them in the old position with bolts that had been similarly treated, after smearing the holes with a mixture of white lead and tallow (one part of white lead to three parts of tallow). I also smeared in the same way the inner surface of the metal where it was fastened to the hull.

You can make this precious mixture of white lead and tallow, cold, with your hands, although some prefer to do it warm in a double saucepan; and it is surprisingly effective in preventing rust. It sticks both to wood and metal, does not melt in the sun as would tallow alone (because of the white lead with which it is mixed); nor, because of the corrective action of the tallow, does it become completely hard, as white lead by itself does. And in addition to all these advantages the sea will not wash it away, even in the course of a long passage.

Next came the installing of the bowsprit. I have never liked a bowsprit. It is a source of annoyance in harbour; and this spar projecting beyond the stem is not really part of the boat. If you are manoeuvring in harbour it is like an over-long nose that tends to bang into everything. The boats, too, moving around you seem to have a predilection for this fragile appendage, which they some-times seem to be blind to until the last moment; and then, crunch, the shrouds are entangled, making you leap from the cabin with the feeling that your guts are being torn out. Our unfortunate *Snark* saw her bowsprit torn away—taking part of the bows with it. *Snark*, it is true, was riddled with rot, but even so, it was a horrible moment.

These considerations had made me swear that I would never have a bowsprit fitted to any boat of mine. With *Marie-Thérèse* this had been no problem. She had no need of one. With helm lashed, under all plain sail, on any point of sailing (including with the wind dead aft) she would sail like a dream. *Marie-Thérèse II*, however, had different views. No bowsprit, no care-free passages, she seemed to say.

For while the bowsprit can be troublesome in harbour, at sea it behaves quite differently. In the first place, by allowing an extra jib, it increases the sail area. Moreover, with the wind on the beam or quarter, it produces much better balance, by bringing the centre of effort further forward; and this, when the bowsprit is sufficiently long, makes control of the helm easier, because the boat carries less weather-helm.

Contrary to the generally accepted opinion, I have found that a boat that is artificially made to carry lee-helm by the addition of one or more sails forward, is not more dangerous than a boat which carries weather helm or is simply well balanced.

Better to explain my meaning, let me take an extreme example. Imagine a boat whose bowsprit was so long and carried so many jibs that her centre of lateral effort, lying much too far forward of the centre of the wetted surface, prevented her from sailing close to the wind. Such a boat would be slow in answering the helm, that is to say she would require a great deal of lee-helm and still she would hardly come up into the wind.

With the wind on the beam, this same boat would not sail so fast as a well-balanced boat, because the angle at which the rudder lay would make it act as a brake.

On a reach, she would sail much better: in the first place because of her large sail area, and secondly because in these favourable conditions, even though the helm is a-lee the angle is not so great, and the rudder does not have so pronounced a braking action against the water.

So far as reaching or running goes, such a boat would need no-one at the helm; after a certain amount of trial and error, the helm could remain lashed at an angle that varied with the wind direction. For if the boat tended to luff under the impact of a wave, she would be brought back to her original heading by the pressure on the sails at the bows.

In the contrary case, where she would have a tendency to pay off, that is to bring the wind further aft, the angle of the rudder would bring her back to the correct position, since the wind has less effect on the jibs when sailing with the wind aft. Thus there is no danger of gybing.

Accordingly, without going so far as this extreme case of a boat made to carry lee-helm by an exaggerated increase in the number (and hence the area) of sails forward, I had nevertheless decided to make *Marie-Thérèse II* carry some lee-helm by providing her with a bowsprit and jib. And I could not but congratulate myself later on my decision, during my second stage, from Durban to Cape Town. This passage turned out so much more satisfactorily than the first, from Mauritius to Durban, that on my arrival in Cape Town I slightly lengthened the bowsprit again. As a result *Marie-Thérèse II* was to sail like a queen; all that was needed was a few empirical adjustments for her to hold her course with the helm lashed in all winds, except dead aft. But there was better to come, and I shall be describing in detail Marin Marie's self-steering system (pp. 133 ff.), which enables any sailing vessel, no matter how imperfectly balanced, to sail for weeks on end without touching the helm (provided, of course, there is no change in the wind direction).

My bowsprit was accordingly fitted, stout, not too long (4ft.), and a spare staysail was hurriedly tried out as a jib—so hurriedly that later it was to prove pretty inefficient.

Henry, too, had had some trouble with sailing with the helm

lashed, during his preceding passage. He also was to be busy fitting a bowsprit in *Wanda*, even though his sloop had not been designed to take such an appendage. It is often so with boats designed by professional designers. In the literature they distribute, they boast of the capabilities of their brain-child, and offer it as an ocean cruiser; but they are careful not to point out that it will refuse to stay on course without a man at the helm. And it is not everyone who enjoys being glued to the helm of his boat for every minute of his ocean passage.

There are many yachtsmen who refuse to introduce some slight modification to this or that characteristic in a boat, on the ground that she has been designed by an expert. I am far from suggesting that the plans drawn up by an experienced designer are bad. There are many things I could learn from designers. But their plans can never be perfect, because they are generally designed for the benefit of a large number of amateurs who do not all use their boat for the same purpose.

The professional designer can design a waterline and a hull shape that are satisfactory, and even, for certain sorts of use, perfect. On the other hand, the owner of a boat can without hesitation carry out the slight modifications in detail which enable him to get the best results from the point of view of the use he wishes to make of his boat. This calls for experimenting, sometimes for trial solutions that lead nowhere, and is costly in time and money: but the final result is nearly always a boat that is better suited to the owner and the sort of sailing he is interested in.

I have seen so many people who have fallen in love with sail, building beautiful boats to be sailed in tropical waters, and meticulously following a plan drawn by a designer working in Europe. The plan included a keel that was weighted only in the middle, leaving aft a section of timber whose underside it would be practically impossible to paint when the boat was hauled up the slip or aground at low water for her normal bottom-scraping and anti-fouling. As a result the shipworms that infest warm waters would soon have driven their tunnels into the after part of the keel. A good sheeting of metal, an inch or so thick, covering the underside of the wooden keel, would have been sufficient to avoid this trouble: but there was no such indication on the plans.

Henry could not be classed with those who blindly follow the designer's instructions. He had the sense not to alter his boat's lines, for, being a novice, he thought the designer knew more about such matters than he did. On the other hand, he modified the line of the deck in order to increase the height under the beams, and changed the shape of the coach-roof to increase the solidity of the whole structure. Being a tireless worker and gifted with a fertile creative imagination, he then tried countless innovations in detail; he would scrap what he had just made, and start it afresh, with just that little extra addition which made all the difference between a passable and a perfect result.

The bowsprit he made was one of his real successes, both because of its strength at sea and its safety in harbour. It was made of galvanized piping, offering little resistance to the seas that might break on it (because of its slimness, about two inches in diameter): and it could be brought inboard in a matter of seconds.

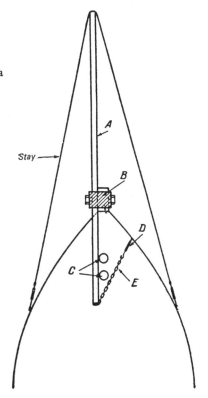

Fig. 3: Bowsprit used by Henry Wakelam in *Wanda*. It has many advantages. It can be brought in in a matter of seconds: you have only to release the hook D, and the boom slides in the collar B bolted to the stem. Its slimness (2 inches in diameter) offers little resistance to breaking seas.
A. Galvanized pipe.
B. Metal collar bolted to the stem.
C. Bitts.
D. Bottle-screw; tightening this prevents the boom from sliding inboard or shifting to port.
E. Chain.

A diagram will make it plainer than a lengthy explanation. I was only sorry that I had finished my conventional bowsprit before he had turned his mind to his own.

His experience of the life of a single-handed sailor during his last passage (which was also his first) made him interested in my down-below steering position. He had looked at Bardiaux' *Les Quatre-Vents,* too, and had made a similar wheel, very small and as cheaply as possible, from a bronze water-valve that was lying around a scrap-heap.

Next on my list of jobs to be done came the inside of the cabin. This was extremely simple. Everything in it, without exception, had to be changed.

The great clean-up took me a day, after all the equipment had been moved to the forward or after part of the boat, to get it out of the way. Then I got to work with a saw and hatchet (always the invaluable hatchet); and that evening the inside of the cabin looked like a room which has been cleaned out by an army of burglars disguised as furniture removers. There was then no alternative: I could only start again from scratch, forgetting what existed already and profiting from my earlier experience.

Three weeks later, my cabin had become a most elegant little room, with a double bunk, another on the opposite side, narrow but quite wide enough, which could be used to sit on; with a small table, hinged for convenient stowing; beautiful shelves for my hundred and fifty books; a locker at the entrance, for my shore-clothes, in harbour, or oilskins and pullovers at sea; a special place for the radio I had acquired; oil lamps hung on gimbals; little blue curtains with a pretty pattern of white sails; in short, it was a real room, small, indeed, but elegant, attractive, and comfortable.

After the cabin, I turned my attention to the forepeak. I made a quick job of this. Simple and strong, all in stout wooden battens, for free ventilation. And so my sails and rigging were at least stowed in two tiers, easy to get at and safe from damp. 'And about time, too,' the disapproving reader will say. True, but you must allow every man to go his own pace.

There is no need to dwell on the rest of the alterations. They included the hundred and one trifles that every sailor has to see to, and would have no particular interest for the reader.

The new Bermudan mainsail arrived at last from the sailmaker. In her new rig, which she seemed impatient to try out, *Marie-*

Thérèse II breathed an air of imminent departure. For my own part, although I often turned my eyes to the harbour entrance, I was no longer in a great hurry. Peter's prophecy had been correct: my bank account was as empty as my pockets. The Suez affair was diverting ships to Durban, and so I went back to work for some weeks with my former employers. It was only then that the boatman unit was really equipped. The boat with spares for twelve months, and the skipper with £40 saved up to flash around the next port of call.

I had no great weight of provisions, but with plenty of rice, dried peas, lentils, etc., and some tinned food, they would enable me to hold out until I could find work in Cape Town. For I should need work: holidays of this sort cost a great deal, and neither in the Caribbean nor in the Pacific could I hope to find a job that would enable me to build up a solid reserve. It would be as well to do so in South Africa where there is work for everyone: and comparatively well paid when you consider that I could live on £10 a month.

Henry and I had thought about this for a long time, and we had come to the conclusion that it would be best not to leave Cape Town until we were fully loaded with spares and food. The ideal would be to be in a position to live for two years without buying a single thing, from a length of line to a tin of bully. We would, of course, have to have a little money in reserve for the vegetables and fruit we would need when we put in, but so far as our basic rations were concerned we were determined to carry enough to last us a long time. And the odd thing is that we were to succeed in doing so, though not without a great deal of luck.

*

The Merlots now left Durban for Lourenço-Marques, but not in *Korrigan*. To their great sorrow, they had sold their boat in Durban, as no longer being suitable for three of them. Brigitte was growing and a thirty-foot boat is rather too short for a family to live in.

Sadly I witnessed the sailing of my three friends, Joseph, Madeleine and little Brigitte. A letter from Lourenço-Marques told me that they had bought a jeep, in which they crossed Africa looking for a spot to settle in. Their tour ended at Abidjan—until the next boat, larger than *Korrigan*, should be conceived and born.

Personally, I was now prepared for my next stage.

One last job remained to finish, which was to prove most impor-

tant for the peace and comfort of my future passages. This consisted in converting the after part of the cabin (that is, the inner
section, where it was possible for me to stand upright) into a steering
position.

To do this, I cut a wide rectangular opening in the sliding hatch,
and covered it with a sheet of perspex, $\frac{1}{3}$in. thick and 19in. by 26in.
in area, as used in aircraft. Thus in foul weather, whether hove-to
or not, I could close the hatch without producing the darkness that
is so bad for your spirits. For while it is often demoralizing at sea
to spend several days in thick weather, with the rain and spray
obliging you to close the cabin-hatch, my own morale has a distressing tendency to sink even further when I have to remain shut
up in a dark cabin.

Further, I could now keep an eye on the mainsail and mizzen
through this solid transparent sheet without having to open the
hatch and expose myself to the weather.

This transparent hatch would therefore make life more pleasant
for me both at sea and in harbour; for it can rain in harbour,
too, and this makes you close everything and live in semi-darkness.
It can become very dreary when the rain continues for several days
and you do not feel inclined to go ashore.

However, it was not enough that I would now be able to see
the sails. I wanted to be able to steer as easily down below as on
deck, and for this I needed to be able to see all around the boat.
To effect this, I cut a series of small slits, four inches high, through
the hatch-coaming; and all along its edge another series $2\frac{1}{4}$in. high
by $4\frac{1}{2}$in. in length; I covered these with plexiglass screwed to the
coaming and made watertight at the edges with my invaluable
tallow and white lead mixture. Only the two scuttles in the after
part of the cabin were larger, giving improved lighting in thick
weather.

These small watertight windows were at eye-level, so that I
could see what was happening in the sea without having to stoop,
as you have to do when you look through a porthole, which is
always placed too low.

Thus, standing upright in the after part of my cabin, with my
hand on the wheel, which was placed against the after bulkhead, I
could continue to sail in dirty weather: completely dry, in a natural
position, without getting stiff, and watching the seas. I could also

be cooking at the same time if I wished, for the primus, swung in gimbals, was ready to my hand.

Everything was now ready on board: halyards rove, blocks and sheaves oiled, sails roped, impatient to go. I even brought in my anchor, dropping it again immediately in the same place, in order to avoid one of those last-minute surprises which oblige you to strip in the cabin and dive into the water to release an anchor that finds the mud of the harbour bottom too comfortable to leave.

Wanda was ready, but not poor Henry: he was to be detained in Durban for another fortnight by an operation to remove his tonsils. A great disappointment, for I should have been delighted if we could have sailed in company on our next stages to Cape Town.

However, the end of the dry season was at hand, and we were soon to be having wilder weather. Nor was I too happy now in Durban because if you spend too long in harbour your boat is inclined to develop rot—and the crew, too.

It was time, then, to move on, towards the wind and the spray that would soon impregnate *Marie-Thérèse II's* sturdy hull with salt, and wash the stains from her captain's soul. I have always had the feeling that these long voyages act upon my system as a thorough cleansing of all the nastiness that accumulates during a period on shore. Once out of sight of the coast, a man is all alone in the presence of his Creator, and he cannot remain a stranger to the forces of nature that surround him. Soon he will be part of these himself, regaining his simplicity and refining himself in contact with the brute forces that embrace him and swallow him up.

And it is, I believe, this need not simply for novelty, but for physical and spiritual cleanliness which drives the lone sailor towards other shores; there, his body and mind are freed from their terrestrial ties and bondage, and can regain their essence and integrity in the natural elements which the ancients deified.

Wind, Sun and Sea: the seaman's triune god!

CHAPTER 5

Durban to Cape Town
seventeen days at sea,
thirteen days foul weather

At the beginning of February, *Marie-Thérèse II* spread her sails to a north-easter, blowing that day with great force. My friend Rex King in *Jeanne-Mathilde*, too, put to sea on the same day, three hours after I had cast off.

There was an ugly tide-rip in the neck which lies between the harbour mouth and the open sea. We had to short-tack out of the narrow channel which very nearly kept *Marie-Thérèse II* on its sharp rocks, for on the last leg she refused to come about on the opposite tack.

There was not enough sea-room ahead to attempt another tack. We therefore had to gybe, and an electric light, hanging too close to the wheel down below, chose just that moment to jam the latter. Fortunately the current was taking us out to sea, and the hull only just grazed one of the large rocks at the edge of the break-water.

Fortunately, too, my friend Peter Gibson had come to lend a hand, and his courage saved *Marie-Thérèse II* from more serious damage. In spite of the risk of being badly hurt, he jumped onto the rock, up to his waist in water, and helped me fend her off. The off-shore current did the rest and we were soon safe at sea.

Seamen will know from their own experience, or will have no difficulty in imagining, how I felt during the few seconds we were in contact with the rock. Every jolt went straight to my guts, and I felt as though my heart was gripped in a vice. This first day at sea was spoilt by the sort of nasty taste that stays in your mouth, and with which I was already too familiar.

In the open, the sea, without being vicious, was nevertheless a little difficult, even though current and wind were in the same direction, both setting towards the Cape. From every point of view, this suited me, in the first place for speed, and secondly because of the state of the sea—which could have been easier.

When I was well away from the shore, I handed the sails and then, wearing underwater goggles, I went overboard to check the damage. They amounted only to scratches which did not affect *Marie-Thérèse II*'s rightness and solidity.

Not knowing, however, when I would be able to scrape the bottom again (particularly since the anti-fouling had been applied a week before), it was important to see that the few square inches of hull stripped to paint by the rock should not be attacked by worms. I was proposing to spend a long time in Cape Town, and although the water there is cold there was always the threat of these pests which can be found to some degree in almost any waters.

I returned on board, accordingly, and made up the clay and cement mixture (half clay—half cement, as taught me by the Indonesians); I applied this carefully to all the exposed surfaces, after I had driven half-way into the timber a good many small half-inch copper nails; the heads of these and the part that projected from the hull would hold the protective mixture in position. Once it had hardened, shell-fish would be able to attach themselves to it, but at least the borers which are attracted by bare timber would crack their teeth if they tried to penetrate it. However, the mixture I had carefully prepared and applied proved to be too slow in hardening; after some days at sea there was none of it left, as I found out when I took advantage of a morning of dead calm to dive in and check it. The friction of the water produced by the boat's speed had washed it away before it had had time to set. It needs, in fact, twelve hours to become sufficiently resistant.

This did not matter at sea, since the speed prevented the larvae and barnacles from attaching themselves. It was when we were in harbour, with the boat at rest in still water, that the danger would come: and in such circumstances, the mixture of clay and cement has time to harden without being washed off. Further, thanks to Henry Wakelam's advice, I was able in Cape Town to perfect a mixture which sets in ten minutes, and with which one can make a solid and durable job at sea, and under water; this will even cope with a serious leak, such as might be produced, for example, by collision with a floating tree-trunk or a rock.

Here is the recipe for this magic substance:

One part of ordinary cement, as used in normal building work.

One part plaster of Paris (which can be had at a chemist's).

A touch of clay.

And it is prepared as follows: first mix together the two equal parts of cement and plaster, without water. This mixture constitutes the basis of the final product: cement, because it becomes extremely hard as it sets, whether underwater or exposed to the air; and plaster, because it hardens very quickly (in five or six minutes). However, if this powder were stirred up with water alone, it would be impossible to spread the paste so produced without its crumbling away almost immediately.

To prevent this, the water must have a binding medium. Clay is perfect for this purpose. All you have to do is to thin down a little clay in half a glass of water (two dessertspoons to each cup of powder). Next, pour the clayey liquid into the container which holds your powder, stirring quickly and thoroughly, and watching the consistency of the paste: the ideal consistency is that of modelling clay.

Once you have made this paste, you have to be quick, because it will harden in a very short time. So take a handful of it, and keep it in the hollow of your hand so that it will not crumble away while you are making your way under water to the part that has to be repaired.

Apply it without rubbing (which would make it crumble), pressing it pretty firmly, with your palm slightly hollowed, so that when the paste is applied it looks like a miniature, slightly flattened, tortoise-shell. Then carefully smooth off the edges without applying pressure: the fore-finger should just stroke the paste.

If you are using this procedure to stop a leak, then no preparatory work need be done. The paste will make its way into the hole or joint, working itself in and making an efficient plug. If, however, you have to protect a part of the hull where the paint has been damaged, leaving the wood exposed, it will be as well first to insert a number of copper pegs (or galvanized steel if you have no copper) which will serve as an armature and prevent the protective shell from falling away.

*

For two days, the weather was hard on my poor stomach. My

morale, already low as a result of the ridiculous accident of which I was so ashamed, had no chance to recover. Moreover, the day had been so busy, that I had neglected to have a good meal before leaving Durban: and I like to go to sea with plenty (but not too much) ballast inside me. It is much the same as with a boat. Sick and pale, I soon returned my breakfast—through the cabin hatch. Too depressed to wash down the deck, and with my stomach empty, I continued to vomit intermittently. Anyone who has been sea-sick with nothing inside him will know how unpleasant that is.

As night came on, I began to be worried. I had never had such a prolonged bout of seasickness. It lasted for practically two days, during which nothing I ate would consent to stay where I had put it.

The odd thing was that there was no loss of my physical strength. At the end it began to be almost entertaining and I even tried to keep count of my abdominal spasms. Twenty-one, twenty-two . . . let's see if we make it to thirty.

Marie-Thérèse II, on the other hand, was happy, very happy. Even though over-ballasted she was going flat out in a quartering wind which was strengthening. Its strength was even approaching the safety limit, in spite of the rather too moderate sail area she was carrying; but it was so delightful to be making such progress and to feel a boat living up to her full capabilities. On the wind, the violent gusts made the boat groan, hard-driven as she was; but with the wind round on the quarter or aft (provided there were no sudden squalls), my boat, with her short masts, stoutly stayed, seemed to known the joy of living and to be calling for even more wind.

Heading towards the open sea, so as to get outside the shipping route, I then ran parallel to the coast at a distance off of about thirty miles. I would benefit less from the current, which was a pity, but at least I could sleep in peace, or at any rate not worry about shipping.

Ships making for the Atlantic sail as a rule ten miles off the coast, or even closer, following the hundred-fathom line, where the current reaches its maximum speed. The others (moving up the coast of Africa) keep as close inshore as possible, where there is little or no current. Some coasters familiar with local conditions even make use of the eddies very close in: so close, sometimes, that when the ship goes into dock for its annual bottom-clean, the shipyard workers are surprised to find dents in the bottom.

By standing well out to sea I wanted to be able to heave to

without being haunted by fear of the proximity of land, should one of those south-easterly gales, pretty frequent at the latitude of Port Elizabeth, catch me without warning.

However, the sky was clear and the north-easter was blowing strongly. The motion of the sea was more regular, and *Marie-Thérèse II* was sailing with the helm (or rather the wheel) lashed, under mainsail and mizzen on one side, staysail set on a boom on the other, at her maximum speed of six knots.

On the third day of this wonderful sailing, my stomach at last consented to settle down. I very wisely saw to its ballast, as a matter of duty, for I was not really hungry and I felt perfectly fit—in spite of the Adamite costume I am in the habit of wearing at sea, which might have encouraged calorie-loss.

At noon on this third day at sea a position fixed in good conditions placed me forty miles south-east of Port Elizabeth. Only three days to cover half the distance! I had to admit, of course, that the favouring current was partly responsible. It might be half-way in miles, but not so in time. That would be altogether too easy. Nevertheless the barometer reading was promising. So were the wind and sea—even a little too much so, for the sails were on the point of flapping idly and I had to tauten the staysail foreguy. I replaced the staysail with the largest jib in my sail-locker, my Genoa. With its huge area, this holds a light wind admirably, and *Marie-Thérèse II* was now gliding at two knots as though on a sea of oil.

If only that could have lasted—but, no, we must not anger the gods of the Cape of Good Hope by asking them for the impossible. The gods of the Natal coast had already smiled kindly enough on *Marie-Thérèse II's* white sails, and soon it would be the great lord of the west wind on whose goodwill I should depend: for it is he who holds dominion over all the coast of South Africa, a tyrant of uncertain temper, wearing an almost constant frown; and his outbursts are feared by all who sail in his domain.

Nevertheless, the domain of that mighty west wind is, at times, invaded by the troops of another lord: the east wind, or rather the south-east, who from time to time likes to move in for a week-end, particularly in the summer months. The south-easter is much more formidable than the westerly, for it often blows with gale force, and drives one on to a coast without shelter. Woe to the boat that is driven onto that coast after being surprised too close in by the black-south-easter, for that wind has no mercy on the rash.

On the other hand, when the lord of the west rages, the sailing vessel can find refuge in a number of inlets on the coast, spaced out some fifty or sixty miles apart. Even there, it can happen that a huge swell from the south-east follows her into her shelter, forcing her to run and heave to in the turbulent kingdom of the western monarch.

Marie-Thérèse II was gently making way in the calmness of the night, unhurried and unbuffeted. It was as though sailing in a dreamland, completely at peace, with no care for ships nor coast, the latter too distant to be present in one's mind. The temperature, too, enhanced the charm of this night at sea, the sky studded with stars—their brilliance slightly dimmed by a thin film of mist which had spread over the sea, but nevertheless very noticeable. The moon, in its last quarter, rose some hours before dawn, and seemed to bring a blessing to *Marie-Thérèse II* and to be preparing her for the rude ordeal that awaited her. For that was the last of the fine weather for the rest of the passage.

In the morning the wind was back, variable in strength, from the south-east. A tack inshore enabled me, before sunset, to distinguish the mountains of Port Elizabeth. The barometer had fallen, and I made my preparations to meet a possible gale from the south-west or west. The night passed, however, without incident, even though I had to be constantly alert; for in this area the weather can change with disconcerting rapidity, with squalls from every quarter forcing one to heave to under bare poles or very much reduced sail.

The sky was still clear in the morning, and after a few severe gusts, one of which laid me over almost on my beam ends, the west wind reasserted its authority. It blew Force 6 to 7, for five days of arduous sailing close-hauled; the seas had risen greatly, but were, fortunately, still fairly regular, for the wind was constantly from the west, without any variation.

By keeping well out, I would meet heavier seas, for outside the great Agulhas Bank, the current sets west (against the wind, therefore) at its full strength, reaching four knots at the steep southern edge of the bank.

On the bank itself (with a depth of less than a hundred fathoms) the *Sailing Directions* state that the sea is much less difficult with the wind in the west, and so easier to ride. On the other hand there was the danger of shipping. Whether their destination is east or west, ships hug this coast in order not to lengthen their passage unnecessarily. The safest thing to do, accordingly, would be to close the coast during the daylight hours and draw away at night. In so doing I would be cutting across the shipping lane twice in every twenty-four hours: once in daylight, and again at nightfall. I would have to be alert, therefore; but rounding the Cape is no holiday, and I could not neglect any precaution.

I spent nearly all the hours of daylight at the wheel inside the cabin, in order to make good as great a distance as possible; for even if a sailing vessel almost always sails well on the wind with the helm lashed, it will do better still with a man at the wheel; he can take advantage of the slightest variations in the wind, and play hide and seek with the seas, avoiding any sudden checks and maintaining the boat's best speed.

After five days of this sailing close-hauled, in seas that were too heavy for *Marie-Thérèse II*, with her bluff lines, to ride gracefully, I was still only a hundred miles west of Port Elizabeth: an average, in fact, of twenty miles a day.

I congratulated myself nevertheless, on having adopted the Bermudan rig, which is much closer-winded than the gaff rig. With my former rig I would certainly still have been even closer to Port Elizabeth. I might even have been still in harbour there, waiting for the westerly to drop (which can mean a long wait on this part of the coast) in order to round Cape Agulhas. Later, in spite of the equally bad storms which attack the Cape of Good Hope, the wind pattern would be more favourable; and the north-westerly direction of the coast-line would not oblige me to tack in a westerly.

As things stood, however, I had not yet rounded Cape Agulhas; I still had a long way to go, and I had to continue tacking, hoping that the crew would hold out as well as the boat. I was completely exhausted and beginning to suffer from lack of sleep. My eyes, heavy lidded, were red from the wind and the strain of keeping awake, and I could hardly keep them open during the long hours at the helm which I spent below. When I was tired of standing up, I would steer for a few minutes sitting on the edge of the cockpit, but the deck was continually swept by seas and spray, and I did not stand it for long.

I would then go below into the cabin, close the sliding hatch, jam the wheel for a few minutes while I made a cup of hot coffee (it took only a moment to jam the wheel or free it again); then back to steering again, down below, keeping an eye on the seas through the slits I had made round the coaming of the cabin, dry and (with the galley just beside me) warm. For no matter what the weather, it was always possible, and indeed easy, to cook. In some boats that are fast close-winded, cooking can become impossible; but it is quite remarkable how in all the sailing boats that have made long passages, a spell in the galley, even in the most severe weather, raised no serious problems.

During these long watches it is as though the organism reacts by adapting itself to new conditions, rather than by calling on the will. After several hours at the helm, the brain becomes stupefied: and then the senses come into action on their own.

Hearing, I believe, is the most valuable of the seaman's senses: so valuable that very often, when holding the wheel, with the upper half of my body clear of the cabin in order to see better through the spray, I had pulled back the hood of my oilskins so that I might not be hampered by the deceptive noise of the wind in the hollow of the hood. It was too bad, of course, about the cold water that runs down your neck and soaks shoulders and chest; but you must above all be able to hear, particularly on a dark night, when your eyes are of little or no use. It is then that your ears take over. They note every noise the water produces against the hull, the murmurs, the creaking of the frames, the whistle of the wind in the sails and rigging, the rattle of the halyards against the masts. All these noises, which are part of the boat, are noted and recorded, and translated into sense-impressions. Meanwhile the body is at rest, and the brain too. Suddenly the brain is wakened. The ears have detected an abnormal sound, not included in the range which the intelligence had drawn their attention to before it drowsed off.

Even before rousing the brain, and interrupting its master's rest, the hearing has been able to communicate a direct order to the sleeping seaman, telling him to switch on the electric light which illuminates the compass in the deck-head above him. Lying in his direct line of vision, it has already told him that there is a difference of several degrees in the heading. Meanwhile, the sense of touch has noted a change in the motion or speed of the boat.

The brain, awake now and refreshed, rested, thanks to the vigilance of sight, touch and hearing, will then be able to guide the seaman to his next task; to tack, in order to take advantage of a variation in the wind, to reduce sails, to adjust the tiller and the sheets, or simply to close the port against the wind.

And when the hearing is tired, and dozes off, then the touch takes the watch: the touch of the wind, spray and rain on the cheek or nape of the neck which will warn the seaman of the slightest variations in heading. Although touch is not so accurate as sight and hearing, it is a complementary sense, often most valuable and always useful.

It is only then that the mariner is completely at peace, for the work is done automatically in a fraction of a second. It is the reflex period which will allow the exhausted organism to hold out beyond the normal limits of conscious movement.

Thus I was on watch all day at the helm, and on watch without holding the helm all night: for then I jammed the wheel and the boat held her course close-hauled.

Even so, it was more a half-watch than a watch, spent for the most part on the bunk (damp, for everything below was now wet, clammy and sticky). Eyes closed, brain dulled, but ears alert. I do indeed believe that at sea, a seaman's ears are never asleep, particularly if he is single-handed.

During the night, I was free from the wheel after nine o'clock. It was then time, first for cooking a meal, followed by coffee (great mugs of it) and a cigarette—not the first in the day, nor the last. For on this occasion I had had enough of the stupid plan of going to sea without tobacco, as I had done several times before. No spirits, of course. It has never had any attraction for me and I have enough vices already without adding that one. Coffee takes the place of alcohol for me. It does you less harm, is cheaper, and you can drink as much as you like without rolling under the bunk.

As for tobacco, it will probably always be an indispensable part of my ship's stores, now and in the future, and I am always grateful to it for what it has sometimes enabled me to put up with. At the same time, I have put a slight check on it so that it will not get too much out of hand. I carry it in the form of plain tobacco. There are no manufactured cigarettes in my boat. It would be too easy to shove my hand into a tin and take out a cigarette. No, it is important to roll them yourself. It is cheaper, and you smoke less, for rolling a cigarette with wet fingers is quite a business. There are, it is true, little machines you can get for rolling cigarettes, and

I had taken one with me. It was quite a distraction during my hours on watch or when I had some leisure.

I had a pipe with me, too. It was a souvenir from Jean Gau, one of two he had given me from his collection.

'But why give me two, Jean?' I asked him. 'One is all I want.'

'Take the word of a man of much experience, my boy,' he told me. 'You'll soon find out that at sea the mouthpiece wears away.'

And in fact I found to my surprise that the mouthpiece gradually got shorter and shorter.

The pipe was kept for the night watch, when there was one, because it kept my hands warm—and my nose. A little furnace under the tip of your nose can be most comforting! Besides, a good pipe lasts a long time, and helps to while the hours away, without being put out by the spray, and disintegrating in wet fingers, as a cigarette does.

*

Until that day the weather forecasts I heard at night on my radio had been good, although they spoke of strong westerlies between Cape Agulhas and Port Elizabeth. On the other hand, south-westerlies were expected between Cape Agulhas and Cape Town.

That night, however, there was a gale warning, the announcer slowly giving out the co-ordinates of the area in which it was expected. My heart sank, for it was in that area that I was sailing.

In spite of all my confidence in my boat, I could not help being somewhat anxious—because that confidence was qualified. She was solid, indeed, and had proved herself such. She was even too solid, if one can say such a thing. She reminded me of the English phrase, 'solid as a rock', meaning a boat that heels very little. This was the case with *Marie-Thérèse II* since I had poured the mixture of concrete and old bolts into her bilge. She did not heel sufficiently, and had become much too heavy. When hove-to she did not drift sufficiently and would take on board some frightening seas, if they decided to become really vicious. The radio led me to anticipate this, for it had twice repeated, slowly, the words 'strong gale', and that meant a violent westerly.

Supposing I hove to with too heavy a boat? There might well be damage on board; and I had already seen what the sea can do to a more resilient boat, as *Marie-Thérèse II* had been before we made Durban.

93

There was no point, however, in going searching for trouble. The light marking the entrance to Krom Bay, thirty miles further east, is visible from a great distance; and I had large-scale charts of the whole coast (I had consented to provide myself, at Durban, with charts for the passage round the Cape, and I was congratulating myself on my forethought).

To my surprise, the barometer had not fallen as the gale warning had led me to expect. Perhaps they had made a mistake: but then I told myself that weather-maps are built up from information provided by ships' radio. There is any amount of shipping in the vicinity of the Cape, and one can hardly doubt that the South African meteorological service is well supplied with information and can therefore draw its maps accurately.

Accordingly, I listened to the voice of prudence (with which my tiredness agreed) and headed for Krom Bay. We practically flew to this shelter, and two hours later I could see the sweep of the lighthouse beam. The barometer was still steady; my doubts returned and I was beginning to regret my decision. It seemed absurd to retrace with the wind after a course I had so much trouble to make good in the other direction. And then there were the *Sailing Directions*, which spoke of a violent westerly which, a few years ago, had lasted without a break for seventy-two days.

Further, the wind, naturally, dropped in the early hours of the morning; I was then two miles from the lighthouse which had been in view for a long time.

A twenty-ton fishing boat came out of the bay under her engine, in my direction, followed by another one; and then I became convinced that the gale was as much a myth as the sea-serpent. After all, these fishermen know the area and can interpret the signs that herald the coming of the western tyrant.

The first boat, interested in *Marie-Thérèse II*, passed close by and reduced speed. As befitted the occasion, I had pulled on a pair of shorts, but I was still shirtless in the fine sunshine and the wind, which was now very light and only just sufficient to keep her under way.

To satisfy my conscience, I passed on to the crew the gale warning I had heard on the radio. Not understanding me properly, they came round in a circle and came closer in (rather too close, indeed, for I am not too fond of such proximity) and asked me to repeat what I had said. This time they heard, looked at one another, shrugged their shoulders, thanked me, and continued on their westerly course.

For my own part, I quietly anchored in the place marked on the chart, a little closer inshore even, in four fathoms. I put out my little 25lb. C.Q.R. anchor, with the ¼-inch chain I normally use for temporary mooring in a safe place. I like its lightness and convenience, for I have no windlass and keep my heavy chain for more serious conditions.

As for the gale warning, I had completely forgotten it, and had already forgiven the Meteorological Office, thanks to which I was now relaxing in the sun, safely anchored, and able to spend three days, say, getting everything dried out and catching up on my sleep. What a pity it was, however, that I had not had time to build myself a dinghy before leaving Durban. The shore had such an inviting look.

'Not had time to build your dinghy?' asked my conscience quizzically. 'How long were you in Durban? Over a year, weren't you? And how long were you working in the shipyard? Ten months? Right? Then your reckoning must be badly out, mustn't it? You had a good three months to get your boat ready and make your improvements in her. In that time you could have made a proper job of re-making that dish-cloth you have the nerve to call a jib: and with a proper jib we might today be a bit nearer Cape Agulhas. And what about this dinghy you didn't have time to make? It took Henry just a week to make his. Call it ten or twelve days for you to make yours, particularly with Henry ready to give you a hand. No time to make it? You must be kidding!'

I could only hang my head in shame.

Nevertheless, I was to give myself the pleasure of a victory over this intransigent conscience of mine. For if I had had the collapsible dinghy I had been thinking of making after seeing Henry's and Bardiaux's, I would most certainly have pulled ashore to the lovely strand which glittered in the sunshine a quarter of a mile away. And the dinghy would certainly have been lost, for it would have been a desperate business getting back on board in the 70 to 80 knot gale that got up in two minutes. It blew with hurricane strength, under a completely clear sky, while the spray flew, cloaking the edge of the strand. After ten minutes, this peaceful haven had become an inferno, with short, irregular seas that made me fear for my light chain and C.Q.R. anchor. It was a beautiful anchor, which had withstood, unassisted, the worst south-westerly gusts in Durban harbour. Burying itself deeper in the mud as the pull increased, it had never dragged, except for the few feet that allowed it to bite deeper into the bottom it had no intention of leaving.

Today again it obstinately refused to drag in spite of the wind and the seas it churned up and the violent pull transmitted by the chain. Although I had paid out the full length of warp, I soon began to feel that the chain would not hold much longer.

Two other anchors of the fisherman type were hastily attached to the same chain—a huge chain, this one. This system has never failed me; I find it much better than putting out two anchors separately, for in the end they drag one after the other as the boat yaws. The pull comes on each chain in turn, dragging first one anchor and then the other.

I had the job done just in time, for the light chain broke close to the warp. Had I had more warp on board, this wonderful anchor and my excellent chain, so useful in moderate weather, might have been saved by paying out a sufficient length to allow the other anchor to hold.

It was then that I remembered Henry's method. The shackle he uses to connect anchor and chain is always slightly narrower in section than the chain. Thus, should it prove impossible to bring the anchor in (because of fouling a rock, for example), he can be certain of saving at least the full length of chain; for if something must give, it will be the shackle, which is weaker than the chain.

Losing an anchor is no joke. But to save the chain is some consolation. With a little ingenuity and work, you can make an anchor, if you can find a forge on shore or if you have a friend who does arc-welding: but to make a chain is quite another matter.

I thought of the windlass I would have liked to install on deck. It would have allowed me to bring in my small chain in time to anchor the other big chain. However, you cannot carry everything on board; not, at any rate, at first, unless you stay such a long time ashore that you can make the most meticulous preparations—and in that case you may find that you never get to sea.

'Over a year in Durban, and no windlass? And yet Henry had shown you a very simple way of making one, seeing you had friends who were experts in arc-welding. . . .'

'Pipe down, conscience! I've no time to argue right now.'

It was not, indeed, the right moment for an argument. There was work to be done on deck, where the warp had worn through its anti-chafe gear and was on the point of snapping. The strength of the wind, now colossal, made it impossible to take in the few feet between the worn portion of the warp and the mast, to which I had made it fast.

One strand was almost completely worn through, for things sometimes happen with alarming speed, and I could already see myself putting to sea, leaving behind all my anchors, my chains and a new warp.

Two minutes later, using the tackle from the mainsheet (quickly unshipped and secured to the anchor warp) I succeeded in taking in the few feet required. This time, the serving was strongly made up from the reinforced rubber tubing which provided an extension to my bilge-pump. I had to cut it lengthwise in order to protect the part of the warp which chafed against the stem. And I thought longingly of the nylon warps which Bardiaux used: but nylon is so expensive.

The night passed more peacefully, for the wind dropped: squalls became less frequent and shorter in duration. The sea, protected by the shore, had become almost calm.

In the morning, the barometer had risen again, and at noon the wind was manageable. It was still a little soon, however, to hoist sail. I decided to wait until the seas offshore had subsided a little, particularly since I was busy drying everything in the cabin. I had collected my bedding and wet clothing and it was airing on deck (the westerly gales have at least the advantage of blowing through a clear sky leaving the air very dry).

While this useful work was being completed, the saucepans were simmering on the stove, and I was anticipating a first-rate meal in the evening: rice, lentils and corned-beef curry, the quality as satisfactory as the quantity. A nice bottle of South African wine to round it off, and then to bed!

*

Was it my hearing that, about midnight, whispered to my brain that it would be as well to take a turn on deck? The noise of the sea breaking on the shore had become unmistakably clear; it was the swell from the south-east, heralding a south-easter.

The barometer was up to its tricks again, and I thought prudence was the better part. The wind was now very light, and still from the west. No matter: it would be better to leave this spot, quiet though it was for the moment, because if the south-easter I feared should suddenly appear it might well turn into an inferno.

It was heavy work taking in the chain, with two anchors in succession. I had to make several attempts, with intervals to get my breath. At about one in the morning, *Marie-Thérèse II* left her shelter, where she would have been happy to sleep at peace until dawn, and glided lazily and almost regretfully towards the open sea, just free to windward, in the light ruffle from the west which was left over from the last blow.

The barometer continued to behave oddly, but the shipping forecast for the coasts of South Africa had not mentioned anything out of the ordinary the evening before: it spoke of the winds as 'light and variable between Cape Agulhas and Port Elizabeth'. That was true enough. On the other hand there had been this unusual swell from the west during the night.

About noon, there was a light breeze from the east. With the mainsail against the rigging and the large staysail boomed out on the other side, *Marie-Thérèse II* left behind her just the suggestion of a wake.

Towards the end of the afternoon, the black south-easter was blowing with full force, under an inky sky; *Marie-Thérèse II,* with a bone in her teeth, was forging through the sea in a great flurry of foam and spray. The sea was rising and already breaking in an unusual way, considering that the current, slight though it was, was setting with the wind: this should have tended to keep the seas down; maybe it was, a little.

As soon as the seas began to break, I brought in the boom which stays the jib outboard with a following wind, and got the staysail flat, sheeted to the foot of the mainmast. This checked our speed (though not for long, for the wind continued to strengthen), but at any rate it would save the boom from possible damage.

I now had to remain constantly at the wheel. In the shelter of the cabin this was no hardship, even should a wave break over the stern and sweep the deck.

My down-below steering position, with an all-round view of the sea, now proved extremely useful. It could rain, freeze and blow outside, without inconveniencing me at the wheel. Moreover, with both hands on the wheel as I faced aft, I was of course in an ideal position to handle the boat with a following wind; for I had a clear view of the seas aft through the glazed windows. It was comfortable below with the cabin hatch closed, sheltered from wind and rain, the stove close by me, hissing under the coffee-pot, and everything on deck stowed so that there would be no need for me to emerge.

Although it is my rule to sail clear of the shipping lanes, caution suggested that I keep my navigation light burning. I had bought in Durban an excellent pressure lamp, with Pyrex glass, which resists rain and spray in spite of the high temperature of the vaporized paraffin it burns. I hung this as high as possible in the main rigging, on the opposite side to the mainsail. This powerful light (250 candle-power, I think), was an insurance against possible collision, should shipping be blown seaward of its normal route.

The mainsail and jib were now brilliantly illuminated and would be seen from the side which masked the lamp. The other side was lit up, including the sea and particularly the slope of the waves towards my side, which I could see clearly through my little windows aft, in the reflection of the light on the spume.

After some minutes, I managed to estimate their height, present the stern of the boat dead-on to them, and then return to my slightly south-easterly heading. This was to keep me well clear of Cape Agulhas, which I prefer to round at a distance of twenty miles or so.

I had always realized that this lamp could serve as running lights; and reading Monfreid had taught me that once I was in the trade-wind zone it could be used to attract flying-fish on deck as well. I would also perhaps be able to use it for fishing for swordfish at night, on the reefs of an island in the Pacific, as I had done on Diego-Garcia. I had not yet used it to work at night on deck when I put in, as Henry sometimes did; but that remained quite a possibility, even for me. But it had never occurred to me that I would be using this 250 candle-power lamp to steer with the wind aft, in heavy weather, almost as well as in full daylight.

The wind meanwhile had reached its maximum strength, and *Marie-Thérèse II* was holding her course without faltering, deviating from it only to allow the passage of a breaking sea, and immediately recovering. My eyes were smarting a little, for it was now nearly past midnight. Without this perfect steering position, I am sure that I would already have hove to under mizzen and sea-anchor, or rather with the normal anchor and with the full length of chain and warp paid out in order to keep her head into the seas.

But in the warmth and, even more, the safety of the cabin I did not yet think it necessary, even though I had once already been pooped by a breaking sea a little before midnight. In spite of the thunder of the impact, *Marie-Thérèse II* had not fallen off.

This incident enabled me to confirm something I had already noticed in the Mozambique Channel: with a heavy sea astern it is better, with this boat at least, to release the helm at the moment a heavy sea is about to break on the stern. And for this reason: when a heavy sea overtakes the boat, it propels her forward with great force. If the boat's stern is at right angles to the seas there is no danger (except perhaps in the case of an exceptionally large breaking sea). But if the boat makes even a small angle with the direction of the wave, she will tend to turn beam-on under the influence of two forces: first, the sideways thrust of the sea on the stern, and secondly the resistance of the bows to this force; and this produces an accentuation of the movement that has already started. If the sea is not too heavy, and particularly if it does not decide to break just at that moment, nothing too serious will probably result; at the worst there may be danger of a near-gybe. As the wave continues its course, it will pass under the bows and tend to bring the boat back in the right direction. All one then has to do is quickly to bring the boat stern-on to the next sea.

What I had not realized, however, was that if the boat had not returned to the correct position, on a line with the direction of the seas, the best solution was simply to release the helm. If, in fact, you hold the helm firmly to the side on which it should logically act on the rudder, the wave, which is travelling faster than the boat, will exert pressure on the rudder blade and exaggerate the yaw you are trying to check, thereby increasing the risk of being driven beam-on and gybing.

It was in the Mozambique Channel, I said, that I noticed this. As I held the wheel, I had felt how strongly it resisted. I then amused myself by repeating the experiment in an easier sea. Every time, I felt pressure on the rudder when the sea caught up with it from astern, forcing the stern round in the opposite direction. On the other hand, if I released the wheel just at the moment when I felt the pressure, I found that the deviation did not increase: the rudder, being free, yielded to the sea instead of resisting it, and moved easily from side to side until it returned of its own accord to the right position.

Making six knots towards Cape Agulhas, with the seas, now heavy and breaking, coming from astern, I was able to gauge *Marie-Thérèse II*'s capabilities: for she seemed to have been designed for forging ahead in just such a sea. I even found myself falling asleep at the helm—though just in cat-naps.

The stern was never driven to one side by the heavy breaking crests that fell on her intermittently. They came sometimes in twos, threes, or fours, sometimes only one at a time, obeying, it would seem, one of those laws of nature that are unintelligible to man, and even to the animals one would imagine to be best equipped to read the secrets of the sea.

On countless occasions I have amused myself watching crabs feverishly hunting out a morsel of food exposed in the sand by the passage of a wave, and then even more hurriedly scurrying back before the arrival of the next bountiful breaker. They then wait above the normal water-line until the wave falls back. Quite often, however, their calculations are faulty and to their disgust and shame they find themselves struggling in the foam of a particularly strong wave. This was more than they had bargained for.

Inshore, however, man has been able to codify certain rules. Crossing the bar, the crew of a pirogue counts one, two, three: and then away, the paddles working at full speed; but sometimes a fourth wave, stronger than the others, appears just when the pirogue is half across the bar. Their reckoning was out, and so they count one, two, and then wait for the third. But the third hangs back and when it does arrive much later, it brings with it three or four friends of the same massive size.

Marie-Thérèse II, however, seemed to know something of the secret of the waves, for she behaved magnificently, never deviating more than a few degrees.

I was now able to apply in practice the little theory I had developed in the Mozambique Channel. When a vicious white crest broke immediately astern of the rudder, I released the wheel, allowing it to swing from side to side for two or three seconds, before taking hold of it again. Even when the boat was exactly stern-on to the seas, the rudder still had this to and fro movement, and I left it alone, because at that moment *Marie-Thérèse II* seemed to know much better than I did what she should or should not do.

The crest would then divide as it broke, on each side of the canoe stern (which offered very little resistance) and continue forward. The boat, meanwhile, was travelling for a fraction of a second as fast as the sea that was driving her along, holding and guiding her by the beam.

For a second time during the night, a sea broke viciously on the stern, sweeping the deck from end to end, and for a moment I considered heaving to.

After all, since *Marie-Thérèse II* sails to windward only moderately well (to put it politely), she probably makes up for it by her unusual qualities running. Moreover, Cape Agulhas was quite close, and if the weather did not moderate too soon, I should double it before dawn. Once past the cape, I did not care from which quarter the wind blew; it would no longer matter much to me, for my course would then be west-north-west, and False Bay, just before the Cape of Good Hope, would provide me with shelter necessary in difficult conditions.

I decided, therefore, to hold on, since so far nothing had given. With Bermudan rig and without the dangerous yard I had always had in my various boats, foul weather presented no difficulty: I had only a single halyard to manage, no yard swaying as she rolled, less danger of gybing, and less nervous strain.

Looking back, I am surprised that I kept to the gaff rig for so long. It took me four boats before I came to the Bermudan rig, and now I shall certainly never abandon it.

By this time my eyes were giving me trouble. This was due to tiredness and the continual strain of running, and keeping stern-on to every sea. It was fortunate, at any rate, that the shelter of the down-below steering position saved me from the effects of the wind and the cold. The latter, it is true, was not extreme, though it was damp and penetrating; but I had to find some way of improving the arrangements for handling the gear from below. Hitherto it had been necessary to stay on deck exposed to the elements if I wanted to handle the sheets, the cleats being round the cockpit, as in the majority of sailing boats. This caused further fatigue. You will be thinking that I am very lazy, but nevertheless it is just that wretched laziness which is the basis of all progress, is it not? If there had never been a lazy man, we would still all be walking on foot, and would never have thought of bicycles or cars, and boats would still be propelled by paddles. So, with all due respect to the hardier brethren, I like to keep exertions to the minimum when I sail, be it single-handed or with a crew. To go out on deck other than for my pleasure represents, to my view at least, a useless exercise, a way to lose calories and run superfluous risks. So I must work out some system for the sheets—next time we're in port!

The beam of the Agulhas light had been gradually left behind to starboard. An hour later it bore some degrees further aft. I had rounded the Cape, and was congratulating myself.

But two minutes later came disillusionment. The wind had dropped very considerably, which was no good omen; for in this area, when the wind is no longer from the east, it is almost inevitably from the west, right on your nose.

Was the merry-go-round going to start all over again, I wondered: would Neptune and Aeolus never tire of their infuriating practical jokes? Was this their idea of fun, to watch a lone sailor struggling in the black night, with no guide but the flickering beam of a light-house almost out of sight? A glance at the barometer had shown me what to expect: a westerly gale. It looked as though I should have to retrace, hove-to, the course I had made good so far, and watch the brief flash of the light in the east slowly glide by again, powerless to help me.

Half an hour later, we were hardly making way. The barometer still looked grim, but the sky was somewhat clearer, allowing a few reassuring stars to appear, while the sea had become calmer and was no longer breaking. The log registered 135 miles since noon the day before, a good average for my boat. But that was all over now.

It was almost day when the wind veered, in an icy blast. I only just had time to lower everything, before there came a second blast, of terrifying strength, which made the hull shudder and gave it a thirty-degree list, under bare poles.

Rain, heavy and freezing cold, stinging my bare skin painfully, drove horizontally, while I fought with the mainsail, trying to furl it before the real trouble started. I then paid out the anchor with all the chain and warp, lengthening the latter with a second warp in order to produce a more pronounced braking effect on the bows and force them to remain head-on to the seas. There was no question of setting the mizzen, for it would have been torn to shreds, at all events at this early stage. I would have to wait until the south Atlantic had got over its first outburst.

With nothing more to do on deck, where everything was fixed, I went back to the warm (if damp) shelter of the cabin; I could not help feeling extremely worried, because if such a wind should persist the seas would fling themselves on my poor boat, and, with her excessive weight, she would be violently buffetted. For the moment, however, she was head-on to the wind, even without the mizzen, and that was half the battle. The rudder, lashed midships, would thereby suffer less, but I was not really happy about it. And I was thankful that I had reduced its area before leaving Durban.

The gale was at its maximum strength for only ten minutes or so; during that time the whole boat was shaken in the squalls that followed one another between short intervals of almost complete calm. For forty-eight hours the wind then continued at a strength that made it impossible to consider setting sail again, the more so in that the sea was breaking wildly, while *Marie-Thérèse II* was huddling in the hollow of the waves.

All I was doing myself was to listen, not unduly perturbed, to the symphony of wind and sea, waiting for it to die away. I was glad that the big battery for my radio was holding out. It was to be exhausted two days later, these batteries being very much affected by damp. Next time, I decided, I would wrap it up in a plastic bag, with another one round it, and even a third, and a little packet of silica gel.

At last it became possible to hoist the sails again. Not full sail— just the mizzen and staysail, at first, followed, after some hours passed without incident, by mainsail and jib.

The wind was still strong, but the sea was much easier. And, as I had foreseen, I had again passed Cape Agulhas, travelling in the opposite direction under bare poles. As the barometer was steady, I came up with the Cape close-hauled before heading out to sea, taking advantage of even the smallest variations to come up a few degrees into the wind.

At about ten o'clock in the evening, the light was visible on my beam, and in the early hours of the morning Cape Agulhas was on the starboard quarter. The wind was veering to the south-west, a more favourable quarter for me, which allowed me to sail much faster, under full sail, while we pressed on towards the Cape of Good Hope and the fine harbour the other side of it. We made Cape Town two days later. Ouf!

But what a crazy notion this is—to insist on sailing, when there is no snugger mooring for a boat, and for her skipper, than such a sheltered harbour as, for example, the Royal Cape Yacht Club basin.

CHAPTER 6

Nine Months in Cape Town

During the summer months, Cape Town is one of the most beautiful places I know. The sky is then almost invariably blue, with not a cloud to be seen; the air is wonderful, dry and with the fragrance of greenery, for, compared with Durban, Cape Town is rich in green growth: lawns, parks, trees, all contribute their shades.

The outskirts of the city are old, the centre modern with, here and there, older buildings and monuments which take you straight to the heart of the first settlers. That was my first impression as I strolled about the city, hands in pockets, nose in the air. Cape Town seemed to be born from the heart, or rather from the multitude of hearts, of those first Dutch settlers; and in this it is a contrast to Durban. Durban has modern geometrical buildings, spaced out along wide straight roads, drawn with a set-square and measuring tape. Concentrated around itself, Durban is a town created by the practical intelligence, for well-defined needs. Cape Town straggles along one of the most beautiful coast-lines in the world, a real Côte d'Azur, on a grander scale, of the South Atlantic.

First came a visit to the French consul, whose office was on the seventh floor of an elegant building. M. Cansou is a charming man, young, and, what is more, a sailor. We got on well from the outset and discussed boats and voyages and the countries we had been to. He knew South America from having lived there on a number of occasions and gave me his impressions of that part of the world, to which I have always been attracted.

We then turned to my own immediate problems. 'So you're looking for work? Well, it just happens that there's a French firm on the next floor of this building which might interest you. They deal in china and earthenware.'

I made a note of it and decided to investigate—but not immediately. My holiday was not yet finished, I thought, and I could treat myself to another week or two: enough to spend the £40

I had in my pocket, although *Marie-Thérèse II* had the first claim on it.

Late in the afternoon, I went back to the club. It was full, for in these English-speaking countries people understand that work is good for the health, but there is no sense in keeping at it until after sundown. In Cape Town they leave the office about four o'clock, or sometimes 4.30, and then everyone busies himself with his own personal way of passing the time.

All the talk and thinking and activity of the club centred on sailing. One of my new friends told me about Rex King's accident. He had been dismasted off East London, and he was still there at the moment, completing his repairs. His crew had left him, one of them seasick, and the other not liking to leave his companion, to whom, it seemed, he was acting as guardian.

He told me, too that he had news of Henry Wakelam through a friend in Port Elizabeth. *Wanda*, it appeared, had been capsized by a breaking sea in a south-westerly gale, after leaving East London, where she had put in. No damage had been done, apparently, and *Wanda* had left Port Elizabeth only a short time ago, bound for Cape Town. I was eager to hear Henry's own account of this.

We had a few drinks (whisky is cheap in South Africa) and life began to take on a rosy tinge—why not, after all?

Another pal—for they were all pals in that friendly club—gave me an address where I could get a first-rate C.Q.R. anchor. 'Clinch it first thing in the morning,' he told me, 'you'll get it for a song, if it's still there.'

I left when I had had enough, in spite of all the invitations to have 'one last one'; I was already too familiar with the dangers of 'one for the road'.

I was lent a dinghy by a man who told me that I could have it for a month, as he was going on holiday. 'By that time,' he added, 'you'll have made your own. In any case, there are any number of them lying about the boat-house. Have a word with the secretary, and he'll certainly lend you one that you can patch up for the time being.'

I went back on board my boat, happy as Larry and thinking what a delightful crowd they were, so kind and helpful to their transient fellow-devotee. And I must add that that kindness never varied, and never wore off, in spite of the long months I spent there after that first friendly meeting. So far as Cape Town is concerned, you may say that there is a real brotherhood between the shore-based sailors and the birds of passage. The only difference between the two sorts is that one has ties on shore and the other has not.

I slept that night at last without any rolling or motion, and without the least noise. It was the peace of a quiet harbour where boat and skipper can sleep with a quiet conscience, and wake up when they please.

I had, however, set my alarm, because I had business on hand in the morning. I needed that anchor, and *Marie-Thérèse II* would never forgive me if I got up too late to buy her such a beauty. And then I could go back to my bunk and take it easy for four-and-twenty hours if I liked. If boats could speak, I am sure that she would have added that it was not the first time she had known me do so, and would probably not be the last. In the morning, then, I went to have a look at the anchor. It was waiting for me; I came to terms with the owner and it was soon mine for the modest sum of five pounds. For an equally trifling sum I bought also twenty fathoms of fine $\frac{3}{8}$-inch galvanized chain of first rate quality. Mooring-wise, I was now fixed up.

As it happened, I no longer felt sleepy and decided to clear up the red-tape. This meant a visit to the Harbour-master's office, Customs, and Immigration. Here I met nothing but smiles and friendly inquiries; there were very few forms to fill up and I was soon through without any hanging about. 'My papers are all in order, and so are yours: so, we part as friends!'

I took advantage of the next few days to clean, wash and air everything in the cabin. The sails were dried out and stowed in the forepeak, and then the harbour maintenance routine started: buckets of sea-water on deck and coach-roof, every morning, and on the topsides of the hull, as a precation against the rot that is always a danger if you spend a long time in harbour.

I took things very quietly while I was waiting for Henry to arrive. In spite of myself, I was beginning to be anxious about him—and he told me, later, that he had been extremely worried about me during my passage round the Cape.

*

I spent that weekend a long way from Cape Town and from my boat, with my new French friends, Etienne Droulez and his wife. They lived at Worcester, some sixty miles from Cape Town. It is a small town built close to a large lake, and for the first time I was to understand the passion so many yachtsmen have for small boats.

Until that weekend the centre-board dinghies you see gracefully manoeuvring in sheltered bays and harbours did not seem to me to deserve their owners' excessive enthusiasm. I found it difficult not to regard such sportsmen as trophy-hunters. But that was until I found myself, muscles and nerves straining, in a *Flying Dutchman* making ten to twelve knots on the surface of Worcester Lake. If I say 'surface', it is rather by habit, because there was in fact as much water over the boat as under it.

God knows Etienne Droulez' friend who offered to let me crew for him—on condition that I did what I was told and kept awake—was no trophy-hunter. For in these small sailing boats, fast and lively as they are, you need to have all you wits about you if you are going to win, particularly if the wind decides to be the least bit vicious. Reef? Not on your life! Although some small racing-craft aces, dispute it, it's carrying all the sail you can that makes them worth steering.

And as for the crew, they are not just passengers. They represent the mobile (and extremely mobile) ballast, not to mention the speed and judgement they have to show in order to manoeuvre more quickly than the crew in the rival boat.

I had sometimes witnessed, though somewhat distantly, the noisy gatherings that follow a regatta, listening with amusement and a slightly contemptuous smile to the passionate discussions about the course sailed, the buoy that was just rounded without that fatal extra tack, the jib-sheet on which winning depended and which the clumsy crew-man had let go and ruined everything.

You silly pot-hunters, I used to think, when will you stop treating your bum-freezers as boats, and speaking of the sea when you never go outside your well-sheltered bays?

I was out that day only for an hour, but now I understood. I realized in the first place that these are no bum-freezers, but wonderful little thoroughbreds of real pedigree stock, highly strung, fast, answering to a touch of your finger but throwing you into the drink in a split second if you make the least mistake. A sailing boat of several tons will forgive you again and again, but these little craft, never!

A peaceful evening with my new frinds the Droulez, including their adorable four-year-old Nicole, was enough to turn me back again into a landsman, quite at home on *terra firma* and far from all thoughts of long cruising. And next day Etienne and I, after a lazy morning, were taking one another on at table-tennis; I was interested to find that although I had not touched a table-tennis bat for years, my play was just the same as it used to be, neither better nor worse.

We went for a drive in the afternoon, and back to Cape Town the next day. Stony mountains with vineyards in the valleys: there is a certain charm about these rocky masses but for my own part I prefer the green country round Cape Town and its shoreline, which rivals the French Côte d'Azur, though wilder and less crowded.

*

Marie-Thérèse II was lying at rest just as I had left her. If I had covered her with a tarpaulin she would have looked just like a baby sleeping under its blankets. The club boats are not so protected but are often covered with nets, to prevent sea-birds from taking up permanent residence on deck. Nearly all the masts have a pointed metal extension: not anti-lightning but anti-cormorant.

One morning while I was having breakfast at the galley table, which stands just under the cabin hatch, a small white something— no, a big white something—went splash on the table an inch from my plate of porridge: a big black cormorant was busy preening its feathers, perched on top of the mizzen mast.

A smart crack with a stone from my catapult knocked him off, but he escaped the pressure-cooker that day at least. These creatures are so strong that a mere stone does not worry them much. I should have used a half-inch nut, but all my half-inch nuts were of brass, and I really could not use brass on cormorants; I would try to find some old half-inch steel nuts, or ball bearings, for cormorants are quite tasty, especially after a spell in the pressure-cooker—in the pressure-cooker even a thick bone could become soft!

Henry came in ten days after my own arrival. He had indeed been well and truly capsized by a breaking sea, while hove-to, but nothing had been broken on board except the staysail boom. The truth is that to break anything in *Wanda* you would have to make an early start and hit uncommonly hard—particularly since she is quick to heel over and tends to give to the seas rather than resist them, meeting their strength by her own flexibility.

After leaving Port Elizabeth, Henry had wanted to stand out to sea, out of sight of the coast, in order to avoid the risk of being caught on a lee shore by a strong blow; he then found that his compass was giving him wildly contradictory readings, with variations of over ninety degrees. He could not understand why this should be so, and it worried him greatly during his last stage.

It was only much later, just before leaving Cape Town, that he found out the explanation. A large steel bolt had fetched up in the compass when he capsized. It was when he unshipped the compass to measure the box which housed it that he found the culprit: he was taking the measurement with a view to buying a new compass.

Henry, just as I, had to find work before he could hope to continue his voyage and see what was going on on the other side of the Atlantic. We were now a well-established team, and after dinner we got down to discussing our plans for the future. Henry's idea was to spend two years in Cape Town, save up a good lump of money and then be off. 'Two years,' I exclaimed, 'two years in the same dump! You'll rot, Henry, and your boat, too. Anyway, two years is a mighty long time. There's time for a war to break out; they'll grab us, and give us a nice uniform and before we know what's happening, we'll find ourselves aboard a cruiser or an escort vessel—it might be a submarine, even—in the middle of the north Atlantic. If we've got to be in the Navy, let's make it the Pacific, where at least we'll be a bit warmer. Right?'

'True enough, but what about the money? Not much fun, you know, in the Tuamotus when you're broke.'

'Yes, but we could work in Cape Town for six or eight months, say; buy all the stores we need for two years; carry our anti-fouling paint and spares for a good long time; and then leave, even if we have only a very little money. It's a hundred to one that we'll find a job in Venezuela or in one of the Central American countries; and then we can stock up again and make for the Pacific, and see if we can find our ideal corner of the world.

'Besides, it won't even be necessary to go as far as the Pacific to find it: take a chart of the Atlantic and have a look. You've got the West Indies, where we might find our corner. Venezuela is quite close, or North America, where we could go and work when the money gets low. And then a little further, there's England for you and France for me, both of which are possible meeting points, with the westerlies for the northern route out and the north-east trade, nearer the equator, for the passage back to the West Indies.'

All in all, that would seem to be the solution.

We went on talking about it until late into the night, and then we discussed another possibility for the future: a camera would enable us to take some interesting films which we could show to gatherings of sailors when we put in, and so be able to earn ourselves what would be a modest living, no doubt, but in an interesting and enjoyable way. It was, I think, a pity that we did not consider a little more seriously this idea that cropped up, because I now realize, looking back, that it was there that a solution probably lay rather than in our almost impossible dream of the West Indies.

Henry meanwhile had come round to the first idea: to stock up completely with provisions and spares in Cape Town and, in six or eight months time, to make for the West Indies.

It may seem over-optimistic to propose to carry food for two years in a small boat; but we were not thinking of bread and onions, of course, but of basic foods—such as rice, tinned meat, fish and vegetables, tinned milk, coffee, oatmeal, everything that can be kept, with care, for a long time.

There was no difficulty about tinned foods, but rice, in particular, presented quite a problem for keeping in good condition. It is very much affected by damp, and weevils (and woozles) are very partial to it.

During my earlier voyages, I had always kept it in the way the Chinese do, with a big lump of charcoal to absorb the damp, and successive layers of wood ash, to keep out the weevils; but the ash is a nuisance, as the rice needs so much washing before you can cook it.

Bardiaux had spoken to me in Mauritius of a chemical he used to keep his rice free from weevils. He poured this liquid into a glass tube or small open bottle, which he then left for five or six minutes standing inside the closed containers in which he kept the rice. The liquid is extremely volatile, and gives off gases which destroy the weevils and any eggs there may be. You then take out the bottle and close the container securely.

Henry had used the same stuff (I forget the name, but a chemist—or a baker—would probably know); but he used to pour a teaspoonful of it into his lentil and rice containers. 'You needn't be afraid of it,' he told me, 'I've been eating the stuff for six months now, and I'm none the worse.'

So, with this chemical to deal with the weevils and a good lump of charcoal for the damp, the problem of keeping the rice would be solved. Personally, I had, after two years, eaten rice that had been eight months in *Snark* and then six months in *Marie-Thérèse*, kept in the Chinese way. It was still exactly the same—perhaps a slight after-taste of wood ash—and had been stored in four-gallon cans, tightly closed but not soldered.

Cooking oil, canned food, tins of oatmeal, sweetened condensed milk and powdered milk, sugar—these and other basic stores will keep practically for ever if you take the precaution of wiping over the circular ends of the tins with a greasy rag, or better still dipping them in melted candle-grease.

I had myself used tins of sardines in oil and of vegetables which were eighteen months old and had been twice completely immersed in sea-water, without any protective layer of grease or wax.

*

The time had come, however, to look for work. My cash had quickly melted away. Henry's had no occasion to melt, for it had gone while he was in Port Elizabeth.

Henry was soon fixed up. The day after his arrival, the hooting of a car horn called me out of my cabin. It was a man on the jetty, gesturing that he wanted to speak to me. He had read the article in the paper about *Marie-Thérèse II*'s last passage, and it had mentioned my working as a shipwright in Durban.

'I own a small furniture factory,' he told me, 'and I have just had an interesting order: a customer wants me to build him a powered boat in ply-wood, which is something I know nothing about. As you're a shipwright' (I smiled to myself as I thought what Peter's reactions would have been if he had heard this), 'would you be interested in taking it on? I hear you're looking for work, or so the paper said.'

So I was still a shipwright, was I? I thought of Peter's advice when I said goodbye to him on leaving Durban: 'You're reckoning to stop and work in Cape Town, Bernard? Just let me put you wise about one thing. Here in Durban there are practically no fully-fledged shipwrights. We have had to take on all sorts and try to make them into craftsmen. But Cape Town is full of shipwrights: there's no question of your chancing your luck in a shipyard—you wouldn't last two days. You'll have to try something else.'

Peter was quite right. The few visits I had made in the harbour had opened my eyes. The Cape Town shipwrights know how to work well, quickly and accurately; and there is a world of difference between the handyman who can build his own boat, if he has the time, and the expert shipwright whose speed and accuracy keeps the price down and so enables the yard to meet competition.

On the other hand, I had no inclination to go back to the same sort of job. I knew how to caulk; fairly slowly, it is true, but well. And I had also learnt a number of useful things about the construction and repair of wooden boats. That was enough for me, for it is part of my character always to have avoided specializing; I prefer to enjoy a reasonable competence at a number of different trades.

The prospect, therefore, of buckling down to the same type of work did not appeal to me at all; I would much rather look for something else, even at the risk of falling between two stools.

Henry, however, would certainly be interested. A few pebbles tossed onto his deck brought out his bearded head.

'A job for you! Come and meet your new boss.'

It was soon fixed up, and Henry was to start work the next morning. The yard was a quarter of an hour by train from the town.

It was time for me, too, to get down to work, and so I went to see M. Pierre Cholet, the manager of Brackenware Ltd., of whom the French consul had spoken to me.

A graduate of an engineering school and an enthusiastic sailor who had owned several boats, he received me most cordially. I told him frankly that I proposed to stay in Cape Town for six to eight months, so that I could fit myself out properly for my next voyage.

'Work?' he said, 'yes, there could quite possibly be something. How would maintenance engineer suit you? You would have to be something of a carpenter as well, in order to fill as big a gap as possible; in my business, all the staff engaged in factory maintenance work really hard, with their hands, whether it's the production manager or the newest coloured help.'

If he was inclined to take me on, I would have to be able to do my share, like everyone else.

However, his offer was too frank and full of understanding kindness for me to think of bluffing. I confessed that I had never been a mechanic and never fiddled about with an engine, and that I had never been attracted by this mass of animated steel, with its precise, planned movements, all worked out to the minutest detail.

'It's not that sort of thing at all,' he told me. 'All our motors are electric, and only one person in the whole factory is allowed to touch them. The rest consists of heavy machinery, simple to understand and repair. Even the coloured workers, straight from the bush, become useful and efficient assistants. In a very short time, you'll understand the working of the plant and will be able to help the head of the maintenance department. Like most of the senior staff, he's a Frenchman.'

And without further ado, that was settled. For, besides all the extremely useful things I should learn, I was thinking of this workshop, with its machine-tools and its full equipment, and the possibilities of my doing a little personal tinkering during meal-breaks or at weekends. This I would quite probably be allowed to do if I showed that I was a keen worker. Once again I had hit the jackpot.

That evening Henry and I were together in *Wanda*'s cabin. He was delighted at the good news. From his point of view, the new job was interesting and would not last more than three months at the most. The boat would be easy to build, whole-keeled, with angular frames, and a ply-wood skin, quick and simple to make.

'Any furniture-maker you like,' Henry said to me, 'could have carried out the design, and I can't imagine why they asked me. At the most it'll be a three-month job, and perhaps even only two. I'll have to find something else before then. As for you,' he went on, 'try not to get the sack, because jobs aren't to be had for the asking in Cape Town, from what I heard in the workshop today.'

There was no question of that happening, as it turned out, because I was immediately fascinated by my new job, which I started the next day. Moreover, I was quick to adapt myself, thanks to my early introduction in Indo-China to mechanical fitting: when I was sixteen my father had put me in a technical school, with this wise comment: 'Since you refuse to work with your head' (I had just been turned out of one more school), 'you can try a bit of manual work. It may make you think perhaps, and will probably help you to take things more seriously next time.'

It had, in fact, made me think; and it had also been extremely useful to me later, for although I had never been particularly attracted by mechanical craftsmanship, I had a certain amount of training in exact work.

My foreman, Dubois, was very soon a friend and partner in work. He was interested in what I was doing—and trying to do. I was particularly attracted by welding, and in a few weeks I became sufficiently competent for him to trust me with increasingly important work.

Apart from oxy-acetylene and arc-welding, which really took some learning, my work as assistant maintenance engineer was comparatively simple. It was, at any rate, quite within the capabilities of any reasonably handy person who took the trouble to think before acting. Dubois, moreover, kept an eye on everything. He knew every piece of equipment in the factory like the back of his hand; he had run the place ever since it had been built, with the rest of the executive staff. They were a hand-picked team, all sent out from the mother factory in France, and all first-class workmates, only too ready to help me to pick up as soon as possible all the basic principles of my new trade.

During the next month, Dubois went on four months home leave, and the chief electrician took over his work as head of the maintenance team. Barlé was much the oldest of us. He was a Yugoslav and had left his country after the war. After some years in France, he had settled in South Africa. Noting my partiality for welding, Barlé took me seriously in hand, as some teachers know how to do. With my interest in welding and his excellent knowledge of it, he had decided to teach it to me thoroughly. It is largely to this friend that I owe my familiarity with the thousand and one little dodges of the metal-worker's trade, which are so valuable to the man who must be able to shift for himself, without too much expense, when he is making something he needs or carrying out his own repairs.

In a word, I had found the ideal job. There was one trouble, however: the distance of the factory from Cape Town. I had to wake early, hurry up with my breakfast, jump into my dinghy and catch the train which took me to work in forty minutes. I got back pretty late and there was no question of doing any work on board during the week. My boat maintenance had to wait until the weekends, and it was by the kindness of my employers that I was able to get the work done quickly, for they allowed me access to the factory on Saturdays and Sundays.

My first job was to make myself a collapsible dinghy. It took me just two days, working without plans, on the same system as I used for building *Marie-Thérèse II*.

A piece of timber two inches square by seven feet long was. laid on the floor of the empty workshop. Two other pieces, the same in section, were fastened at each end with wooden corner braces and small brass bolts. These were the stem and sternpost. The angle they made with the keel was determined by eye: about forty-five degrees for the stem, thirty-five for the stern-post.

The midships frame was then marked out, sawn, assembled and bolted to the keel. Stem- and stern-post were then joined by four thin battens on each side; with the keel, frame, stem- and stern-post, these were to make up the framework of the hull. Two other frames were then marked out, sawn and fitted, using as a basis the lines of the hull as indicated by the battens screwed to the midship frame and the two extremities of the tender (as in hard-bilge construction).

The whole was then dismantled and packed up in not too cumbersome a bundle which I took back to the club by train that evening. In twelve hours' work I had finished the framework and had only to cover it with canvas. I used the old gaff mizzen for this, and the whole job was finished on Sunday evening. Henry shook his head: 'You don't feel you've rushed it a little?'

'Just a little, maybe: but it floats, and that's the great thing.'

'It floats right enough—but it floats lopsided when there's no-one in it—it's all glue and guesswork.'

He was quite right. I had cut the midships frame in too pronounced a V, and the dinghy was so light (twenty pounds—I could hold it with one hand, like a bicycle) that it did in fact float lopsided unless there was some weight to hold it down. On the other hand, it was so stable that once in it, I could paddle standing upright, and it would carry two people easily in a ripple of sea and three in harbour in dead calm water. It took me half an hour to strip down or re-assemble, which is rather long, but its extreme lightness then made it very easy to carry. On the other hand it had to be secured carefully on shore or on deck because even a moderate breeze was enough to shift it and a stiff blow would have carried it away.

There was another disadvantage: it was too lightly constructed to use without some risk, should I ever need to put out an anchor close to my boat. In that case, I would be able to load the anchor and chain into the dinghy, made fast to the boat by a long line, and then tip it over at the required distance; but I would have to be quick about this if I did not want to see the dinghy go down to the bottom with the chain inside it.

Henry roared with laughter at this idea: 'All in all, it's taken you only two days to make this contraption: and if you lose it, it will be no great loss, you bloody Frenchman!'

A week later, Henry began to make his own dinghy, to replace the one he had had since the launching of *Wanda*. It had become too old, particularly after drifting against the jetty, where it had spent the whole night bobbing up and down on rocks covered with sharp-pointed barnacles. Half the canvas bottom had been left on the rocks.

It was to be a folding dinghy, like his old one, built on a foundation of canvas nailed to the keel, with two sides of very thin ply-wood to stretch it into the required shape when assembled, and to fold flat on the deck or to be stowed in any convenient place below when at sea.

It was wide and stable and could be made ready for use in thirty seconds. It could carry three in a calm sea, and, most important of all, it was most effective if, when anchoring, you had to take the anchor out to some distance. The wide ply-wood stern enabled you to pay out an anchor chain without risk of overturning: and with a sliding lee-board, placed to one side in the Dutch way, it would sail to windward fairly well for so small a craft.

*

Meanwhile I was myself engaged in making my galvanized iron water-tanks in the factory workshop; and this made me realize the fact that any one can contrive to make things that he used to believe should be left to experts.

I am still amazed when I think of how I enquired from an expert what the cost would be of two water-tanks, and one for paraffin, the latter with a tap.

The man with the know-how asked me to look in again the next day, as he needed some time to work out the cost of the metal, the man-hours, the quantity of tin he would need for the soldering, and so on—the standard procedure of the magician who has conjured up a fat pigeon to pluck.

The next day, he told me his price: £50 for the three tanks, including the tap; and in his generosity he would not charge for fixing iron fastenings in the places I needed so that I could screw the tanks to the frames.

Fifty pounds and in Durban I had been quoted £65. I was on

the point of giving the order, but thought I would do well to consult a friend—Henry, of course—to check the specifications of the tanks.

It was a brief but stormy conference. As soon as Henry heard that I was thinking of having the tanks made by an expert, 'An expert?' he bellowed, 'but for jobs as simple as that we're all experts! If you can make a cardboard box with scissors and glue, there's nothing to prevent you from making the tanks yourself. It's just like a cardboard box: all you have to do is to cut it out, bend it, and solder it where it's needed.

'Come on: we'll do it right away. Look! There's nothing to it: you take your measurements, you mark them out on the metal with a scriber, or better still with an ordinary pencil, you cut off what you don't need, you fold it (you'll need a vice for this, of course), and then you hold the whole bloody thing together with three or four rivets.' And so the box began to take shape.

'Now all you have to do is to mark out and cut the top and bottom: to do this, you stand your box on the metal you have left over, and draw it by putting your hand through the opening (the smaller side of the rectangular box). Simple, isn't it? You do the same with the other end, and then cut out the two rectangles, allowing $\frac{3}{4}$ inch outside your pencil lines, for the fold. A few rivets to hold it all together, then a blow-lamp and a few sticks of tin and you've got your tank.'

And so our cardboard box was complete, and, as Henry had said, it was simplicity itself. 'And remember, too,' he added, 'that this work you do yourself will be far stronger than what your expert would make for you: he would skimp the solder, because it's expensive, and use the absolute minimum, without taking into account the motion of the boat or realizing that the water gets flung against the sides of the tank and sooner or later will open up the seams.

'Haven't you done any soldering in your works? Well, I'd better give you a hand with the first tank to start with. You'll see how easy it is with a blow-lamp, a bottle of acid to scale the metal and some sticks of solder; there's no need for a soldering-iron—I hate those little contraptions. They're no good except for small jobs, and too many professionals use soldering-irons because this allows them to economize in tin. The bastards don't care if they make a botched-up job so long as they go easy on the tin.'

Two days later, I received the material which had been ordered by M. Cholet, at fifty shillings for two big sheets. The first tank was made on a Saturday, but not soldered. On the next Sunday, I made the other two, working alone in Brackenware's workshop. I brought them back by train to Cape Town and from there to the club, where I stood them beside the one I had made the day before. So far, they had cost me under £3. All that was then left to do was the soldering, which has the advantage over oxy-acetylene welding that it does not remove the protective zinc coating from the galvanized iron; tin, moreover, will not rust.

The next Saturday saw the work finished. Henry took the blow-lamp and a stick of soldering tin and showed me how to set about it. The secret is the use of the neutralized acid, at which he was an expert.

I carried on after his start, and before it was dark everything was complete, checked, and touched up where necessary. Again with Henry's help, checking for leaks was quickly done. To be certain that the seams of a tank are watertight, all you have to do is to fill it and then look for leaks, isn't it?

But Henry showed me a much better way: smear all the joints with soapy water, and then get someone to blow through the hole used for filling the tank. Any faults in the welding (and there are nearly always some) will be betrayed by the soap bubbles that escape through any cracks. The advantage of this method is that you can patch up without having to empty the whole tank; and a couple of such checks are generally all that is needed.

I did not fit taps to my water-tanks. I preferred to pump out a week's supply from the opening in the top. This was transferred to a small four-gallon tank with a tap, from which I drew it each day as I needed it. The total cost of my three tanks, including the tap for the ten-gallon paraffin tank, came to £6. The two water-tanks, each containing twenty gallons, with the four four-gallon jerrycans I used on my Durban to Cape Town passage, brought my total water supply to fifty-six gallons.

At half a gallon a day, and then some, this gave me water for a hundred days at sea; and this I regarded as ample, because you can nearly always, if necessary, collect rain-water on a long voyage. In *Marie-Thérèse*, I have collected thirty gallons in one rainstorm, using a big saucepan.

Rex King had developed a better system in *Jeanne-Mathilde*: he screwed a one-inch wooden moulding to each side of the cabin roof, which channelled the water straight into a bucket placed on the deck; he emptied the full bucket into his tank and then put it back to catch the flow of rain water again. As a result Rex King had never once, since he left Singapore, had to shift his boat in harbour in order to fill his tanks.

Every sailor who has experienced this irritating fatigue of watering will appreciate the advantage of Rex King's method: no heavy boat to shift at the last moment, no jerrycans to shuttle backward and forward in the dinghy, which is a slow business and sometimes hard work—particularly when the boat is anchored a quarter of a mile offshore and the nearest spring is half a mile inland.

Henry and I accordingly decided to follow Rex King's example. Rain-water would be caught on the cabin roof in guttering based on his system; but it would then flow into pipes and be fed straight into the tanks without my having to carry buckets.

After a week of working in our free time, we had completed the installation in *Wanda* and *Marie-Thérèse II*: so that was another improvement made. It was impossible, however, to benefit from it in Cape Town because of the deposit of soot which came from the generating station in the town and the whalers tied up in the harbour. It is quite incredible how much smoke a whaler can produce when they are overhauling the engines; and if a dozen of them are at this game to windward of your mooring, you despair of ever having your boat clean again. And if you get a little drizzle of rain at the same time the whole boat is dripping with black, sticky slime. Unless you scrub it off immediately it becomes ingrained in the paint on the deck; swilling it off with a few buckets of water flung over deck and cabin is no use at all.

*

Henry had now finished the work on the ply-wood boat for which he had been needed and was out of a job: not for long, however, even though there had been a time when the outlook did not look too hopeful. He spent a fortnight working on the club boats for owners who were too busy to do so themselves on weekdays: putting in some new frames in one, replacing rivets in another, making a boom and later a bowsprit for another. He charged them only what you would charge a friend, and he was a sound and conscientious workman.

He then found more permanent work, though rather poorly paid, as a clerk in an office, and there he stayed until we left. The time to sail was coming closer, but slowly. We did not want to leave until we were completely ready, and it is terrifying what that means in time and all sorts of minor expenses: these accumulate and make short work of swallowing a bank account that stubbornly refuses to grow fat.

All our requirements were discussed in minute detail before we bought anything, so that the two of us together could find the cheapest solution. Apart from our stores of food, our heaviest expense would be the running rigging that was beginning to need replacement. Even though you can juggle a certain amount with halyards and sheets, sooner or later you have to buy new ones if you are not going to be in serious trouble.

Once again we were lucky: Henry had discovered in a dustbin by the club, some lengths of line that had an odd appearance; they looked dirty, even filthy. And yet we could not help noticing a small detail: there was a shiny appearance about the ends—they were nylon!

There was a whole little bundle of these, and Henry salvaged them; his fertile imagination had already converted this pile of disgusting bits and pieces into lovely little lengths of line the thickness of a pencil—which we could use for lacing our sails to the boom and on the countless occasions at sea when you need short pieces of line; for such things wear out with disconcerting rapidity.

Back at the club that evening, I found a note from Henry on the table where the mail was put. 'Come for some grub on board. I've got something new.' I thought the something new would be a penguin, invited also to be present at the meal. Henry had had his eye on him for some days, on the slipway used for hauling up the club boats. It was there that the worthy bird was accustomed to sleep—with one eye open, it is true, otherwise he would already have been incorporated in a curry.

All that issued, however, from *Wanda*'s cabin was the customary savoury odour of rice and lentils; and Henry was busy below with a hand-drill twisting together strands of shiny nylon.

'What's the idea?' I asked him. 'Haven't you caught that penguin yet?'

'Let him have a bit more sleep. He was on the slipway when the sun went down, and we'll have a try later with a pincer movement. Now, have a look at this.'

He passed me a thin nylon line, about a yard and a half long, as smooth and perfect as new. He went on working, counting the turns, twenty-five, twenty-six, twenty-seven, twenty-eight, twenty-nine, thirty.

He then detached the twisted strand from the drill, keeping it stretched tight between two nails, and began the operation again with another strand, counting the turns. When he had done this with three strands, he fastened them together to the end of the drill and twisted them in the opposite direction. The result was a line the thickness of a pencil.

'Nylon,' he said. 'You see the importance of this find? All the odds and ends of line that wear out so quickly and cost such a lot in the end? Nylon is infinitely more lasting and doesn't rot like manilla or cotton. I'd like to know where this little collection in the dustbin came from: if we can find the mamma who produced it, a little courting would seem to be indicated.

'Each of these strands (which seems to come from some pretty stout rigging) is made up of an outer envelope of nylon; it's dirty and badly damaged, and looks almost as though it had been scorched in places by friction, but it encloses other strands; and these are sound, smooth and shiny, perfectly preserved inside their protective sheath.'

It was these that Henry had sorted out and made into serviceable lengths of line. The possibilities excited us so much that we took no notice of the fact that dinner was gradually getting cold.

'Look, Henry,' I said, 'just let me try something.'

I took the three lengths Henry had made, hung them on a nail and twisted them in turn, using the drill but with a nail bent into a hook fitted to it instead of a bit. The three strands were then twisted in the opposite direction and made a length of halyard or, if you liked, of sheet, about four feet in length.

In our excitement we forgot both penguin and dinner. However, there would still be people in the bar at the club, and we decided to go across and try to find out where the nylon came from.

I stopped first at my own boat to pick up the catapult for the penguin. In the club, the last customers at the bar had already gone home. The two barmen were still there—namesakes of ours, oddly enough—Henry and Bernard. They were good fellows, who had always done what they could to pass on to us interesting tips.

We asked them to have one with us, which they accepted, and

for a while we talked of this and that. 'By the way,' I asked, 'do you know anything about this?'

They passed one another the piece of dirty line we showed them. 'No: what is it?'

'We picked it up in a corner of the boat-house' (we hardly liked to admit that we had lifted up the lid of the dustbin). 'It looks like nylon—have a look at it.' And Henry (the sailor Henry) untwisted the strand to show the inside, smooth and shiny.

'Ah, yes!' said Henry (the barman), 'I remember now. It's a piece from a nylon warp the whalers use. They get through an incredible amount every voyage. These warps are as thick as your wrist.'

Bernard (the other barman) saw our very evident excitement and understood immediately. 'Look, you two,' he went on, 'why don't you make the round of the whalers before they start on their next season? You might easily "buy" ("acquire" his tone of voice suggested) some old ropes from them. One of my mates who used to go on their expeditions down south told me that he had made a net from perfectly sound strands in this old nylon rigging. I don't know how he managed to extract the usable strands from the pile of worn out, scorched, lengths, but I don't doubt you'll find out how to do it.'

We finished our drinks and left. The whalers were tied up, stern-on to the quay, and the next day we would inspect these treasure-ships. These old nylon warps, thick as your wrist, were no use to them and probably simply an encumbrance, but for us they represented untold wealth. We could only hope that the crews of the whalers did not have net-making as a hobby. The penguin was forgotten. He could spend his last night peacefully asleep, for tomorrow he would be for the pot.

In the morning I had to go to the factory as usual; but I asked Barlé if I might have the next day off because I wanted to be free to visit the whalers. Henry was to make the same arrangement with his office. The pair of us would probably be more persuasive than either of us alone.

Barlé was in a bad temper that day. One breakdown after another. Just my luck, on the day when I wanted to catch him in a good mood. I tried to make myself as useful as possible, and not get in his way (which was the one thing that exasperated him) and everything turned out unexpectedly well. The factory was running at full production, the clay was coming out of the mixers at the right consistency, and everything was fixed up before the evening. This was not very much due to me, but Barlé had recovered his good temper and this was reflected on me. I should explain that I had carried my good will so far as to abandon my little experiments with the mixture of clay, cement, and plaster, on which I had been working for three days in an attempt to find the ideal proportions.

On the first day, Barlé had been most interested to hear that it was possible to make this concoction adhere to the hull. On the second day, his interest was waning; and on the third day my surreptitious disappearances for a few moments were beginning to get on his nerves.

However, I had hold of the right end of the stick and I was getting close to the right formula. With a couple more tests in the course of the next week, I would have established the perfect proportion (the tank I used, I should explain, was in the factory yard).

So, I was given the next day off: I should lose a day's pay, of course, but I had every hope that it would be more than made up for by the cheapness of the nylon.

Operation Nylon began the next morning, continued all day and was not concluded until the evening, which found us in the cabin of *Marie-Thérèse II,* with the pressure-cooker on the stove, while with gleaming eyes we shared out the treasures we owed to the generosity of our new friends the whalers. Those excellent fellows thought they were simply doing us a slight favour, but we would have liked to be able to tell them how overflowing with gratitude we were in fact.

We were both a little ashamed, Henry and I, at the whole drill we had worked out the night before. In the first place, we had to attack each whaler together; because, we argued, if an old length of nylon was lying about the deck it must be because the bo'sun had not yet tossed all the rejects overboard, and he would surely be able to find another piece for the second sailor.

And if he had to look around a bit to find something for one of us, then he must be a good sort; and in that case he would hunt a little more and perhaps find another length for the other fellow.

This cool calculation proved to be excellent psychology, and almost doubled the success of the operation. It was, for me, a victory over Henry, whose plan had been to work separately and share the winnings afterwards.

Henry, however, had won a point against me, in insisting that I should keep my big mouth shut, and leave it to him to talk in an offhand way of the use we might find for a few lengths of nylon to replace our own warps, which might well let us down during one of the gales that often raged in the harbour. Gusts of seventy knots and over had often been recorded, and boats that had broken away from their moorings had recently been severely damaged against the jetties in the yacht basin.

'Get this into your head, bloody Frenchman: in the minds of our potential benefactors, these ropes are solely to be used in their present form, as mooring warps and nothing else. If we let on about making new rigging from them, they will want to do the same perhaps, considering the cost of nylon halyards. Suppose the crew got wind of what we're thinking of using them for—what do you think they'll do? They'll all make them themselves and sell them to us. And another thing, not a word about it in the club, until we're leaving Cape Town. We'll just mention it a couple of days before weighing anchor, in case we haven't quite scraped the barrel.'

Henry knew what he was about, for the barrel was never quite empty. The whalers used to come in, in teams of from two to four, to spend a few days in harbour, preferably at the weekend, before another week or fortnight at sea. We soon found that we had to keep a note of their movements so that we could remember the numbers of the ships that had had the honour of being visited by us; for, good though the going was, we did not want to over-do it.

For some weeks our evenings were taken up until a late hour in unravelling our spoil and then carefully saving the strands that were intact, each one representing one third of a complete length of line.

Henry used to stop work sooner than I. He would then do the cooking and we used to eat together in *Wanda*'s cabin. Then our two dinghies would set out for *Marie-Thérèse II*, and it was back to work in my cabin. The sound strands from the middle were made up into balls, while the outer strands were sorted; many of these, though worn in places, were still on the whole serviceable. We then cut off the rejected parts and knotted the two ends. The rest was thrown overboard, to join the hidden treasure and rubbish in the mud of the harbour.

Then came the real work of making the cordage. The chief tool was a hand-drill with the drill replaced by a nail bent into the shape of a fish-hook. Supplementary tools were a hammer, large galvanized nails, and short lengths (4in.) of unused nylon.

And this was the procedure: we went round at night to the club's boat-house, and each of us drove a large nail into the wooden door at one end of the building (the walls were of concrete, so we had to use the door).

We hammered these in as far as possible from one another (both on the same door), and then with pliers and hammer bent them into the shape of a hook. Nine strands of nylon were then firmly secured to each nail and stretched out along the full length of the floor. Any ends that projected beyond the others were cut so that all nine strands should be of the same length.

A loop was then made at each of the nine ends. Henry, meanwhile, had been doing the same, and we were then ready for the work properly so called—no, not yet, because there was a slight precaution to be taken, unless we had a friend to help us. (We preferred to work at night, incognito, when the club was deserted.)

This precaution consisted in driving several nails in a line into a heavy table which happened to be in the building: we even had to make it heavier still by piling on it a collection of all sorts of weighty objects, having first stood it in the middle, three-quarters of the way down the length of the strands.

Everything was then ready, and each of us could set about making a halyard from the nine strands of the same length, firmly secured to the nails at the end of the building. The reason why we worked together was first that it was more pleasant and secondly we could lend one another a hand if we got into difficulties.

One of the nine strands was hooked onto the end of the drill; we pulled on the strand to stretch it (but being careful not to overdo this) and then turned the brace, counting the turns. The first strand was twisted as thoroughly as possible, that is until the first kink appeared. A few strong pulls from time to time made it possible to give more turns of the brace.

The next step was carefully to unhook the twisted strand, keeping it stretched as tight as possible, and hook it again, by its loop, onto one of the nails driven into the table. The process of twisting had by then reduced the length of the strand by one fifth.

For the first strand, it was almost always essential to have a friend working with you, so that he could push the heavy table and ensure that the nail to which the loop was to be attached was in the right place and kept the strand well stretched.

Two other strands were then twisted in the same way, with the same number of turns and in the same direction. The three twisted strands we now had represented the first strand in the final length of rope. (There are generally three or four such strands, never two.) This strand was made by taking the three we had already twisted and hooking all three together onto the brace; they were then twisted together in the opposite direction and this gave us a length of three-stranded line the thickness of a pencil.

The initial process was then repeated with the six remaining strands, twisting each of them in turn in the same direction and with the same number of turns as the first three; two more lines were then made by twisting together each pair of three in the opposite direction. All three would be made into the final rope after they had first been twisted again, one at a time, in the same direction, and then hooked all three together onto the brace and re-twisted in the opposite direction. However, before starting the final twisting which was to produce the finished article, it was important to hold the three strands together by light whippings every sixteen inches along its length. This made sure that during the final twisting one of the strands would not ride over the other and so spoil both the appearance and strength of the finished work.

When the length of rope was complete all we had to do was to apply a lighted match to each end to fuse it together, and then rub it briskly between the palms of our hands so that there would be no danger of its unravelling later. This is a trick that is familiar to users of nylon lines: it makes it unnecessary to whip the ends, as you have to do with lines made from vegetable fibre.

These ropes cost us nothing at all, apart from a good deal of hard work. We had decided to work only at night, and that meant a night without sleep, from ten in the evening until five in the morning, in the boat-house: it was left open at night, thanks to the good offices of Bernard the barman.

*

Meanwhile the various improvements, big and small, were being carried out in the two boats. As Henry had no machine-tools available in his government office, I used the workshop in the factory to do jobs for him at the same time as for myself, working at meal-times or when the place was empty in the evening.

There was any amount to do: small welding jobs, holes to bore, parts to be forged. Thus, for example, I made two collars for the mast, on which the booms of the twin staysails could set; the metal tangs for the staysails, made from an iron ring cut out by hack-saw from a length of galvanized piping of the same diameter as the booms, and with four links of galvanized chain welded on top, to which the blocks and sheets would be shackled. The fitting at the mast-end consisted simply of a bolt, with a slot cut in it by hack-saw; another bolt, with a tenon cut into it, fitted into this, with a rivet to act as a hinge, and the whole was welded to an iron collar cut from a big pipe.

Then came the small ventilators we wanted to install on deck at each end of the boat; these were to prevent, in the tropics, the rot that was produced in the permanently enclosed parts of the boat by the damp and stagnant air. For these I bought several curved joints of galvanized pipe and welded each to a plate of galvanized iron in which I had cut a large hole in the middle to admit air, and four smaller holes at each corner for screwing it to the deck. These miniature ventilators (the hole was 1½in. in diameter) could be turned to face in any direction, and were extremely strong.

The main boom band was then replaced by a new one, to which I had welded eight stops; these were made of small iron rods whose ends had been slightly curved and rounded-off with emery-wheel and file.

We found a sea-water-tap for the cabin in a pile of rubbish in a corner of the factory yard. The handle was broken, but a little brazing put that right, and I had a better tap than I could have bought in the town; for the handle was now the exact length not to get in the way of anything inside the cabin where it would be fitted. A small copper plate was brazed above to provide the base, and a length of copper piping was then brazed to a small square copper plate with a hole cut in it. This was the inlet for the water, to be placed against the hull, below the waterline. A strong rubber tube connected this to the tap, so I would be able to use sea-water for my washing up, and also save my fresh water by not having to go on deck with a bucket to fetch sea-water for my rice. (It is an intelligent economy to add a little sea-water to fresh water when you are cooking rice, instead of using fresh water and adding salt.)

I used the same system for the automatic baling of the cockpit: two small copper pipes soldered to a round plate of the same metal, which would take sea-water or rain-water outboard through two rubber pipes emptying one on each side of the hull, above the waterline.

All these small jobs, not to mention others, cost us practically nothing, whereas the same equipment, bought at the ship-chandler's, would have left us broke.

We had not yet begun on the twin running staysails and their booms; but we soon got on with these, too. We needed strong spars, fourteen feet long, for them. After a north-westerly gale there was always timber floating in the harbour. We used to go out and salvage it in our dinghies, picking out planks and beams that might be useful to us some day, and carefully stacking them in the club's workshop, with our boat's name chalked on them.

The idea behind the twin staysails was taken directly from the system used by the Van der Wieles in their fine ketch *Omoo*. I had noticed how well *Marie-Thérèse II* maintained her heading with the wind aft, or very nearly aft, with the mainsail guyed to one side and balanced on the other by the single small staysail, boomed out. The boom pivoted on the mast and when not in use was made fast forward, providing a useful handrail between mast and stem, without fouling the working-jib or its sheet, which cleared it above.

The new, and longer, booms of the twin staysails were jointed on the mast, and when not in use, rested on the end of the bowsprit, in two metal hoops, so that they did not interfere with handling the forward sails.

There was the problem, however, of reducing the area of these staysails when, for example, the wind freshened. In *Omoo*, reefing the staysails involved a lot of work.

Henry Wakelam developed an idea which solved this problem and enabled each of us to cross the 5,500 miles of the Atlantic from Cape Town to the West Indies at a daily average of over 100 miles: and in perfect safety, too, using four sails instead of the two staysails normally used with the wind aft in the trades.

Henry's system, which worked extremely well in practice, was as follows: two staysails of moderate area, not requiring reefing in a strong wind, are hoisted to the head of the mast, each held by its boom. The tack of each is made fast by a line three or four feet long to an eye-bolt in the deck, about three feet forward of the mast.

Each staysail has its own fitting, and there are therefore two eye-bolts, about eighteen inches apart and about three feet forward of the mast.

The foot of each staysail is set therefore about three feet above the deck; this leaves room for two other quadrilateral sails, each made fast by four points: at the two ends of the boom, at the deck and at the clew. The system may seem complicated to describe but is in fact quite simple; it should be remembered too, that it is used only in a light or moderate wind (see Figure 4). If

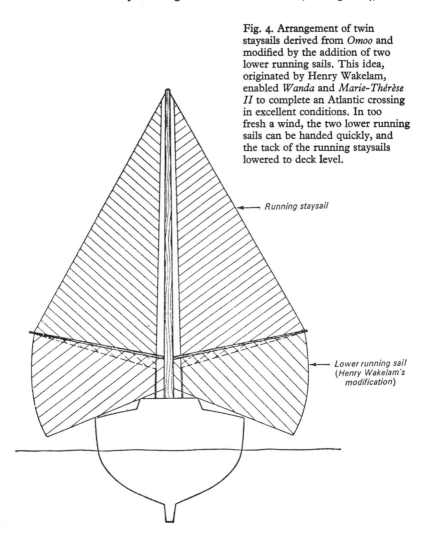

Fig. 4. Arrangement of twin staysails derived from *Omoo* and modified by the addition of two lower running sails. This idea, originated by Henry Wakelam, enabled *Wanda* and *Marie-Thérèse II* to complete an Atlantic crossing in excellent conditions. In too fresh a wind, the two lower running sails can be handed quickly, and the tack of the running staysails lowered to deck level.

Running staysail

Lower running sail (Henry Wakelam's modification)

the wind strengthens, you have only to hand the two lower sails —no trouble at all.

If the sea is such as to make it necessary, one can then lower the staysails to a height that is governed by the length of line attaching them to the deck, and make them fast directly to the latter.

A fine piece of timber, free from knots, was selected to replace my bowsprit, which I found too short. A Saturday's work with adze and plane and it was ready. The next day it was fitted in place of the old one, with a new bobstay, and stays on each side of galvanized chain. Henry had come to lend me a hand so that we could finish it as soon as possible, and we then started on the twin staysail booms: after a meal of rice (needless to say) and a cormorant brought down by catapult on the neighbouring boat. This time, however, the ammunition was heavy steel ball-bearings taken from an old ball-race. I had collected a little bag of these, and we were eating more meat than we used to. The day before yesterday, it was curried penguin and today it was cormorant (curry again, of course). The great thing is not to get caught by a policeman, because sea-birds are protected in this country, to whose wealth in gold and diamonds they add the further wealth of fresh guano.

In harbour, however the catapult is an ideal weapon: silent, almost invisible and much more powerful and deadly than an airgun —much more accurate, too, in my experience, when it has to be fired from a tossing dinghy.

Quite a few cormorants which Henry had shot from the deck of *Wanda* with an airgun, had simply shaken their feathers (which are most effective armour) before flying away: but once they stopped the full force of one of these heavy ball-bearings propelled by my catapult, their career generally ended in the pressure-cooker.

At weekends there was no cooking for Henry or me, for our friends Joyce and Mary took over. At first, Joyce found the dark cormorant meat rather revolting, but she soon grew accustomed to it and asked for more, so long as I undertook to pluck and draw this economical and, indeed, extremely palatable form of game. (It needed plenty of spice and curry powder.) With our new cooks the menu was, necessarily, no more varied but I must admit that as a rule it tasted very much better, with Joyce cooking in *Marie-Thérèse II* and Mary in *Wanda*.

They used generally to get together at weekends in the cabin of *Marie-Thérèse II*, gossiping, knitting and cooking while Henry and

I busied ourselves with our various little jobs. We worked together, helping one another, either on deck or in the club workshop, where there was a most useful vice.

At lunch-time Joyce would give a few blasts on the foghorn and we pulled across in our dinghies. The two girls were so charming and kind that our boats became a meeting place for our friends from the club: anyone who happened to be on board used to stay for lunch or dinner, for the pressure-cookers always held plenty of steaming rice or cormorant curry; and there would be lentils, too, if I had not forgotten to put them in to soak the day before.

When there was no cormorant in the pot Joyce saw to filling the gap; she would keep an eye open and 'Hi, Bernard!' she would call, 'look here, a cormorant has just settled on one of the club boats. See him? The fourth boat to starboard.' A quick glance around—no copper in sight. I tossed the catapult and bag of ball-bearings into the dinghy, and set off. With a very casual air, like someone just looking around, I quietly paddled in such a way as to pass twenty yards or so away from my target. My dinghy, meanwhile, was drifting slowly towards the bird, who had completed his toilet for the moment and was watching me. I pretended to be dozing and sat motionless, my eyes half closed. If he showed that he was uneasy by raising his tail and depositing a small white offering, I would have to fire quickly, for he would be off in a split second. But no: he went back to preening his feathers, and wham! —I put paid to that. There were occasions, of course, when I missed, but I was successful often enough to keep the pressure-cooker full most of the time, to the great satisfaction of our little community (now augmented by Rex King, who had come in recently after a voyage that had been not without incident).

Evenings at weekends were a time for relaxation with our friends on board: Mary, Henry, Jack, Rex, and a little devil called Wilf, a fifteen-year-old who practically lived in the water when he was not at school (or in detention). The little demi-john of 'Mardi Gras' (the cheap but delicious South African white wine) was uncorked and the glasses were filled and re-filled while the washing-up from the meal of curried cormorant and rice lay about the deck.

Then, when it was time to get our heads down, I would send off my guests with a few tunes on the squeeze-box: by that time I had started the second one, they had generally disappeared and the dinghies set off into the darkness, to the club or the sailing boats swinging at their moorings.

*

Our work on board was now practically finished, except for one last big improvement: the reduction of my inside ballast by one third.

The mere thought of the work involved was making me constantly postpone this important job until later. Moreover, it would take me at least a week, working eight to ten hours a day, to finish. A brief experiment, just to see how it went, had made this quite clear.

Further, it was work that could not be done in my free time, as my earlier small improvements had been. Once begun, I should have to work really hard at it and get it finished as quickly as possible, for it would make my cabin impossible to live in, with all the mess of concrete and iron flying in all directions, and the dust.

Meanwhile, M. Cholet, the boss, brought me one day a copy of an English nautical periodical. 'Have you seen this?' he asked, and showed me an article which described the use in an English boat of the self-steering gear invented, constructed and used by Marin Marie during his transatlantic voyage in *Arielle*.

Using this ingenious system, Marin Marie had sailed from New York to Le Havre practically without touching the helm. This is sometimes possible with a well-balanced sailing vessel, but quite out of the question in a powered craft without installing a gyro-compass, which would be much too costly for a small boat: and *Arielle* was a motor-pinnace.

Arielle's main rudder was clamped at an angle to correspond with that for the approximate required heading. An additional, and quite small, rudder or trim-tab was used to correct the heading by means of a wind-vane which swung on a vertical axis.

I do not know how long it took Marin Marie to work out this extremely ingenious device, and it is a great pity that the book describing his passages in *Arielle* and in his sailing boat *Winibelle* has not been published in French.

There have been any number of long passages with small crews or single-handed, and the crew had sometimes to be at the helm for eight, ten, or even eighteen hours a day. And how many such passages were bound to be excessively arduous if they were not to be too slow, or too slow if they were not to be excessively arduous —occasionally they were both!

Nevertheless the solution was ready to hand all the time: Marin Marie's self-steering gear.

There are, of course, tricks of the trade to cope with a boat that refuses to maintain her heading with the helm lashed, such, for example as installing a system by which the staysail sheet operates an alarm that brings you quickly back to the helm. The boat then maintains the correct general heading but sails a somewhat zig-zag course and loses ground. Moreover, the setting of the sail that is connected to the helm prevents it from holding the wind as well as it should and the result is a further loss of speed.

With this system of using a trim-tab operated by a vane, all the sails are used entirely to propel the boat and are therefore working to the best advantage. The boat will sail faster, and with no-one at the helm. The crew, whether single-handed or not, can read, listen to the radio, cook and sleep soundly until the wind shifts, which is not a thing that happens very often in the trades.

My earlier *Marie-Thérèse,* lost on the Chagos, was one of that fortunate class of sailing vessels which were well-balanced under sail, whatever the angle of heel, and sail well under any arrangement of sails. Such boats are seldom to be seen; they are generally large, rather broad in the beam and stiff.

In *Marie-Thérèse II,* the extra staysail on the bowsprit had proved very satisfactory since Durban and my boat held her heading satisfactorily in all conditions, even, with the wind aft, the main fully paid out and the large jib, boomed out, balancing it; but it was still not perfect because with the wind on the beam or quarter, the mizzen had to be slackened a little too much in order to reduce the pressure on the after part of the boat; this produced a loss of speed and a zig-zag course, the mainsail, jib and staysail being at times blanketted by the mizzen and therefore not doing their full work. This happened mostly in a quartering wind.

The article and diagrams M. Cholet lent were discussed in great detail that same evening in *Wanda,* for in all practical matters Henry was the acknowledged master. He could take in a complicated diagram with incredible speed, digest the whole thing, and then produce from his own head a method that was twice as simple to carry out and infinitely cheaper, using materials to hand.

In the first place the small correcting rudder shown on the diagram was modified. Henry wanted to add an extension or tab to the blade, projecting forward of the stock, at the lower end; this would 'balance' the correcting-rudder and allow the vane to be made smaller and less cumbersome. This idea turned out excellently in practice and our self-steering gears were so well balanced that the least motion of the vane was sufficient to turn them.

The stock and axle of the vane could be made from old galvanized tubing. We found a suitable piece on a rubbish heap in a corner of the club yard. The braces for the rudder could be made from lengths of ungalvanized iron we already had and could weld in the factory workshop, each of them being clamped round a short section of the galvanized piping. Bolts driven into these lengths of piping, on the same side as the blade, would serve as the male members of these braces.

The movable and adjustable joint connecting the vane to its axle could also be made from short welded lengths of galvanized piping. The wing-nuts for tightening could be replaced by ordinary bolts with a small metal lug welded on the head that would allow them to be tightened or slackened without using a shifting spanner.

The movable part between the stock of the vane and that of the tab would also be easy to make, again with lengths of piping. And that left the vane itself. This could be made from a broom-handle sawn lengthwise for half its length and a sheet of ply-wood from one of the numerous empty packing cases lying about the club.

All we then had to do was to get on with the construction, and we lost no time about that. We dived in to measure under water the braces which were to be fitted to the after end of our main rudder; they were made that evening in the workshop and bolted under water the next afternoon.

The spaces between the braces were then very accurately measured, and the next day I came back by train with two lengths of piping, to which I had welded the other tenoned braces. I went back to the club by the last train, but both our rudder stocks were finished. Henry would make the blades in the club workshop the next morning. We had the timber we needed in the store of planks and beams we had salvaged.

Meanwhile, I would still be working in the evening, using the factory workshop, on the two revolving stems for the vanes. This was more intricate work than the rest, but Dubois gave me valuable help, and two days later both Henry and I had our mountings. Dubois had been greatly taken by this idea for a self-steering gear, and he had found me four old ball-races to reduce the friction;

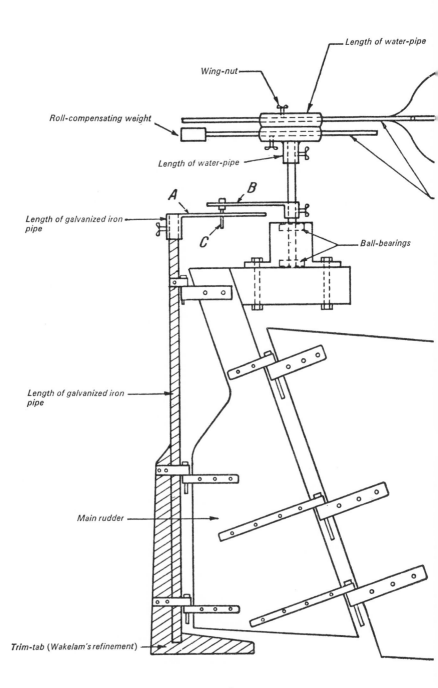

Length of water-pipe

Wing-nut

Roll-compensating weight

Length of water-pipe

A

B

Length of galvanized iron pipe

C

Ball-bearings

Length of galvanized iron pipe

Main rudder

Trim-tab (Wakelam's refinement)

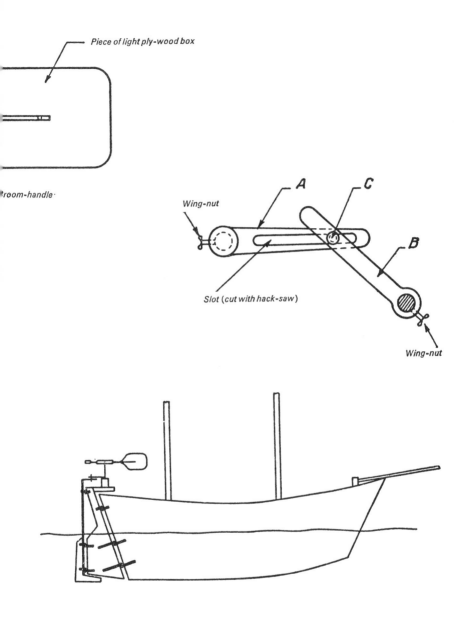

Piece of light ply-wood box

room-handle·

Wing-nut

A

C

B

Slot (*cut with hack-saw*)

Wing-nut

Fig. 5. Marin-Marie self-steering gear. Above: general view Left: details of assembly, and materials used for construction with means available on board.

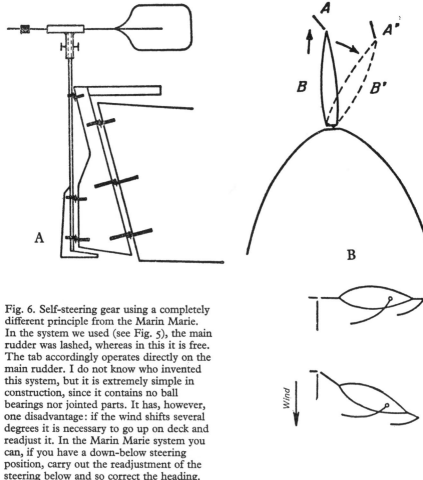

Fig. 6. Self-steering gear using a completely different principle from the Marin Marie. In the system we used (see Fig. 5), the main rudder was lashed, whereas in this it is free. The tab accordingly operates directly on the main rudder. I do not know who invented this system, but it is extremely simple in construction, since it contains no ball bearings nor jointed parts. It has, however, one disadvantage: if the wind shifts several degrees it is necessary to go up on deck and readjust it. In the Marin Marie system you can, if you have a down-below steering position, carry out the readjustment of the steering below and so correct the heading.
A. General View.
B. Operating principle: if the tab A is no longer in the same plane as the main rudder B, the pressure of the water flowing past A forces back the blade of the main rudder B and corrects the heading.
C. (Reading from the top). The boat is sailing with the wind on the beam. The tab has maintained its position in relation to the wind; the yaw is corrected by the action of the tab on the main rudder, and the correct heading is restored.

each of the mountings was welded to a plate with a hole bored in each corner to bolt it to the tiller of the main rudder (see Figure 5).

The whole of the installation was carried out one Saturday morning. It was magnificent weather so that the constant diving required for fitting the bolts into the braces was not too unpleasant, especially with Joyce to provide hot coffee in between.

After putting in the final touches, we both set out the next day on a trial trip in *Wanda*. The system worked perfectly and we were delighted, Henry in particular. The sails continued to fill, and the vane worked as it should, correcting the least variation in the heading. There was a great exchange of congratulations—no more long spells at the helm! In *Wanda*, the system worked on all points of sailing, and must therefore be applicable to any sort of sailing vessel. Marin Marie and Pierre Cholet had indeed earned our gratitude.

*

Our sailing date was coming closer. Apart from a few details, we were practically ready. I still had to sew a new jib for my new bowsprit. This took a week, working for an hour every evening in *Marie-Thérèse II*'s cabin after getting back from the factory, and the next weekend it was proudly stayed on the bowsprit.

It was now time to give up my job and get busy with hammer and chisel removing my excess of inside ballast. Ten days' hard work and that was done. My poor hands had a very rough time, and I now understand something about the strength and solidity of the metacarpal bones!

Marie-Thérèse II had been considerably lightened, and Henry made no more of his usual jokes about the 'cormorant ship'—because cormorants swim with their backs (their deck, perhaps, I should say) at water-level.

Good, so we were ready—well, almost ready. Our provisions had not yet been loaded, or even bought, apart from the rice. This was in five-pound bags, each of which we had put into another plastic bag, sealing it by twisting the open end and fastening it with rubber bands. This would completely exclude the damp, and an 'anti-weevil' chemical injected with a small syringe would keep it free from pests. Taking everything into account, we preferred this system of storing our rice in separate bags that would be thrown away as we used them. If we kept it in sealed canisters, they would be in the way when emptied, unless we had had special canisters made to fit the shape of the hull. This would have been the best solution but you cannot have everything when time is limited, and on the whole we had nothing to complain about.

The rest of our provisions were still in the shops: or rather, at the makers. For I had had an idea which was beginning to penetrate Henry's thick head. (Henry could sometimes be pretty slow in the uptake.) We would buy from the maker, because, provided he agreed to sell us cans of food at wholesale prices, it would be cheaper. But there was something even more important. It stood to reason that in manufacturing and subsequent handling, a great many cans of food must suffer apparent damage without the contents in fact being any the worse for it. Some batches, for example, could have been over-cooked without the food being made unfit for human consumption from the medical point of view. Cases, in transit from the factory to the wholesaler, could be knocked about, and the damaged cans could not then be sold at the normal price.

Bearing this in mind, common sense argued that cans of food, sub-standard on the outside, would not be dumped as rubbish for so trifling a defect—not with the millions of under-nourished people in the world!

Continuing this line of reasoning, it was clear that these defective cans would undoubtedly end up in restaurants at knock-down prices. 'What do you think, Henry?' I asked him; 'if the restaurants can get canned food at knock-down prices, why can't we?'

Henry was sceptical—not so I. It was simply a matter of writing a few letters; but first we had to go round to the O.K. Bazaar.

The O.K. Bazaar is the place at which the whole of Cape Town does its shopping. It stocks everything. The food department is self-service; you stack what you buy in a wheeled trolley and pay as you go out.

This time, however, it was not as customers we went in, shopping-list and pencil in hand. I went around, reading out from the labels on the cans the names and addresses of the manufacturers, while Henry wrote them down. We spent a whole morning doing this and came out with seventy-two names and addresses. They included all the South African food-processers.

Back in our own boats, each of us drafted a separate letter that read more or less as follows:

'Dear Sir,

'I am a single-handed sailor, and I am writing to you in the hope that I may be able to provision my boat more cheaply at your factory than at the local grocers.

'I assume that accidents must occur, infrequently, of course, but from time to time, which may cause external damage to the can containing your products, and so reduce the market value without in any way impairing the quality of the contents.

'Such cans, which cannot be put on display in the shops are bought, I presume, at reduced prices by hotels and restaurants.

'May I ask you to have the kindness to allow me to buy them on the same terms and so reduce the cost of provisioning my boat?'

Seventy-two such letters were typed by Mary and Joyce, signed, half by Henry and half by me, and the whole lot posted: a mass-production effort!

Shortly afterwards, we received ten or so obliging replies:

'No we have no damaged cans in stock, all having been recently destroyed. However, we are anxious to do what we can for you and are ready to supply you with our products at factory prices.'

That was indeed a kindness—forty per cent off the retail price.

Then, a little later, other little documents arrived for us. They were notices from the station telling us that they had a parcel awaiting collection. We made a number of journeys, ten at least, and brought back precious packages from the goods office, sent from all parts of South Africa with the compliments of the manufacturers—God bless them—and their best wishes for our success.

On other occasions a delivery van would leave cases of food in the hall of the club, and always with a little note of encouragement: good luck to your next passage, and best wishes.

And good luck to those good friends, too, who gave us so much help and enabled us to leave Cape Town well-stocked and with a little cash to enjoy ourselves in the West Indies. Fair winds and kind seas to them!

My evenings were now spent in writing letters of thanks, in which I enclosed quantities of postage-stamps for the children of the generous donors. Perhaps the pleasure of the kids may have helped the parents to understand the delight and gratitude of the two lone sailors to whom they had been such good friends.

With our huge stock of rice, the cans we had been given or had bought cheaply, we were stocked for more than a year: we had even a two years' supply of porridge thanks to a heartening gift from the Tiger Oats factory.

Mankind has been greatly slandered. People are in fact very much better than they are commonly thought to be. And yet—I was soon to sin, so that it could not be said that I was too like an angel of Paradise stranded in Cape Town harbour. Man, unfortunately, will always remain human.

The occasion of my sin was concerned with dog biscuits. These biscuits were extremely cheap and Henry and I found them perfectly edible. Henry regularly ate them for breakfast: not I. However, as a result of hearing myself constantly described as a fastidious and spoilt bourgeois, I finally agreed that it was perhaps time to revise my opinion of these dog biscuits. They had not killed Henry, and if he had managed on them since Durban without fatal effects I might well do the same.

Accordingly I took a new nib and wrote the following letter to the manager of the excellent factory which made these too-little appreciated biscuits. It was, I admit, a completely mendacious production—but let the reader who has not sinned throw the first stone.

Dear Sir,

'This letter will probably come as a surprise to you; but please allow me to explain the motive that dictates it.

'I am a single-handed sailor, a Frenchman, recently arrived in Cape Town, and in a fortnight's time I am proposing to sail for the West Indies.

'While I was in Durban, I went to a shop to buy some biscuits. The assistant thought I wanted dog food and gave me a large packet of your biscuits. The price was much less than I expected, and I left Durban two days later on my next voyage, which was to take me to Cape Town.

'It was only during this passage that I realized the misunderstanding in the shop; but, not liking waste and being in no position to afford it, I tasted one of your biscuits and found it delicious.

'I should even add that I found the yellow ones tasted better than the red and were more digestible.

'Since these biscuits suit me so well, and since, moreover, they have the advantage of cheapness, can you do me the great kindness of letting me have forty pounds of them at factory price?

'Your assistance in this matter will enable me to leave better equipped in rigging, and I need hardly tell you how grateful I shall be to you for this.

'Yours faithfully.'

Oh Satan, why did I listen to your seductive voice when you whispered in my ear 'Go on, man, and don't funk it! When the boss gets your letter he'll split his sides laughing and immediately send you eighty pounds of his stuff. Just think, you'll be able to gorge for months, and Henry too, and don't tell me that your conscience is going to worry you?'

Joyce, who had typed this disgraceful letter, had not been able to refrain from passing it round in her office. They laughed till they cried, the department manager included. 'Bloody Frenchman, before you know it he'll be asking to marry the boss's daughter!'

The answer came two days later, short, sharp, and to the point.

'In reply to your letter, I must point out that the dog biscuits made in our factory are not intended for human consumption, but exclusively for dogs.

'I must therefore disclaim all responsibility should the biscuits be used for any purpose other than that stated.'

And that was that! Well, I'd asked for it! The boss had not been tickled by my letter. It was now Rex King's turn to laugh, rolling about the floor of *Marie-Thérèse II*'s cabin. I was laughing too, though somewhat wryly, and Henry, who was in it with me. Joyce, however, was furious.

'He might at any rate have wished you good luck and a fair wind for your passage: that wouldn't have cost him anything.'

And so, worse luck, we would have to eat something else instead of dog biscuits. Meanwhile, I had been properly told off, and it would teach me not to abuse the too often libelled goodwill of mankind.

Our provisions were on board and we were now ready to sail. In fact, a boat is never completely ready to weigh anchor even though one can almost always sail at any moment one cares to.

There were still a few visits to be made to those whalers whose names were not preceded by the little cross which meant that they

had already been visited. And there were still a few lengths of that
wonderful thick-as-your-wrist nylon. In that department, we had
enough to last us ten years. As it wore out, we had only to unravel
one of these heavy warps to convert it into halyards and sheets.

The next time we manufactured nylon line it would be under
the shade of coconut palms. 'Right, Henry? Somewhere in the
Caribbean or Pacific?'

All that then remained to do was to fill our water-tanks. Henry,
whose boat had an engine, brought *Wanda* alongside the club jetty.
For my part, I find these harbour jobs most tedious, and I solved
the drinking water problem in my own way.

A friend lent me his fibreglass tender; I cleaned it out thoroughly
with a scrubbing brush and detergent, and then rinsed it out, and
rinsed it again with the hose.

I then lowered it into the water and filled it with fresh water
through a plastic pipe attached to the tap on the jetty. When this
floating tank was full, I towed it with my dinghy and made it fast
fore and aft alongside *Marie-Thérèse II*. I then used a bucket to
fill a four-gallon drum placed on the cabin roof.

The fresh water was syphoned in a plastic hosepipe into each of
my tanks in turn, while I maintained the water-level in the upper
container to keep the syphon primed.

The club members were somewhat taken aback by this rather
revolutionary innovation, but they soon had to admit that there was a
lot to be said for it. There are plenty of water-boats which are used
to supply ships with fresh water in harbour where it is not possible
to draw alongside the quay: so why not a water-dinghy for yachts,
and so avoid all that tedious manoeuvring?

And in a calm bay, I would rather fill a dinghy, previously
cleaned out, with fresh water than carry drums in the same dinghy.
With this system, my tanks were filled at one go, in one journey.
It would have taken eight journeys with my two four-gallon drums
to do the same work.

Henry shook his head: 'Bloody Frenchman!'

'But I tell you, I cleaned this dinghy out properly. You saw me,
didn't you? So what are you worrying about?'

'You call that thing clean? With all the cormorants flying around
the club, don't tell me you can clean it out in ten minutes!'

'All right, all right! A dog-biscuit stuffer like you needn't be so
fussy.'

Everything was now ready, and more than ready. It was time to set sail again and seek new horizons. The next day *Wanda* weighed anchor, followed a day later by *Marie-Thérèse II*. And our destination? In the first place, the immediate horizon; and then, if you want exact details, the West Indies—5,500 miles distant on the other side of the Atlantic. Our rendezvous was Trinidad, the largest of the southern group. Ports of call? No port of call—the direct route.

And if you ask why no port of call, why decide to make this long passage non-stop, I hardly know what to say. Perhaps in order to find myself more at one with my boat than I had been during my two long spells in South Africa. There may have been other reasons, too. But that was how I felt about it. I wanted to drop anchor at Trinidad, in the sunny Caribbean and to do so for the first time since Cape Town. Perhaps, too, there would be time for it to prove a cleansing process.

However—I was interrupted by a call from the club jetty. It was Henry the barman to tell me that I was wanted on the telephone. 'Henry? Where the hell are you calling from?'—for his voice was loud and clear, as though he were only a few yards away.

'I'm on Robben Island. I was practically becalmed off the island and I've put into the little harbour here. Hurry up, old man, and we might be able to hang on here together until the south-easter gets up and then start from here.' (Henry had left that morning, and Robben Island lies just where you come out from Cape Town, seven miles seaward of the harbour).

'Right, Henry: but I can't leave Cape Town until tomorrow morning. I must keep this last evening for Joyce. I'll pull out tomorrow without fail.'

'O.K.' came Henry's voice from the other end of the line. 'But if the wind gets up in between, I'm off. And you can scrap the idea of a non-stop passage. You can't imagine how peaceful it is on this island. It must be the same on St. Helena, and it would be madness to sail by without stopping. Whoever gets to St. Helena first waits for the other. O.K.?'

'O.K. then—St. Helena after all. And I hope you're still on Robben Island when I get in tomorrow.'

Goodbye, Joyce! Goodbye, Mary! and goodbye all my dear friends in Cape Town and South Africa! It is time to set my white sails to the light south-easterly breeze which tells me that I must once again set out for the horizon my boat will never reach. But beyond that horizon lie other countries and other friends, and these too I must come to know a little, before I leave them also. Such is the fate of the seaman, never satisfied, always persuaded that what he seeks lies a little farther, always on the other side.

On this occasion, however, it was with no light heart that I felt my anchor detach itself from the bottom of the harbour; here, the memory of so many friends sought to detain me. Above all there was Joyce, Joyce who was only waiting for the word, just one word, to bring her kit on board and join me.

And yet that was the one word that I had not the courage to utter. I was afraid. Later, perhaps, not now. I would think about it, alone at sea, in the peace and security of the great forces of nature, sun, wind and sea. It might be that the answer to the problem would come of its own accord, unmistakable. Or perhaps those god-like elements, and my boat too, would remain silent, and I would have to find the answer myself even though I might upset some mysterious inner equilibrium.

Goodbye, South Africa, and God bless you!

CHAPTER 7

Cape Town to St Helena:
1,740 miles

It was dawn on November 21st, 1957 when I set sail. The boats slept in the yacht basin and the south-easter would not get up until eight or nine o'clock, as it normally does in fine weather at that time of year.

Marie-Thérèse II was rowed out of the kind haven which had sheltered us for so long. Rex King had come to give me a tow in his dinghy, and I worked at the stern using the invaluable curved stern-oar based on those I used in Asia, with Rex pulling ahead.

Joyce came to wish me favourable winds, calm seas and safe passage. For a long time I could still make out her figure on the jetty, deserted at that early hour. Then she would be off to the office and back to work as usual. Goodbye, Joyce! and may the deities of the sea watch over you, until they have given me the answer to my question.

Rex had cast off the warp from *Marie-Thérèse II*'s stem; a very light breeze had got up and my boat was leaving a gentle, almost imperceptible, wake as she moved towards the harbour mouth. The south-easter remained light and some hours later I sailed into the little harbour at Robben Island. *Wanda* was gone. Henry had left during the night, taking advantage of the favourable wind that had got up. He was now probably heaving on the swell and swearing, because he hates rolling. No matter. If it pleased the deities, who delight sometimes in using us as playthings, we would be seeing one another at St. Helena.

For my own part, I decided to wait for the wind inside the tiny peaceful harbour of Robben Island. I wanted to spend a day at anchor putting everying straight without bothering about my heading or all the little things that crop up during your first day at sea. It was, moreover, so quiet and peaceful there. It would allow me to tidy up my own ideas and the interior of the cabin. The twin stay-sails were carefully furled, each on its boom, and could be set in a minute. Meanwhile they could remain as they were without inter-fering with the normal working sails.

I had a good supper that evening: rice, curried corned beef, and lentils, with enough left over for another two days.

The south-easter got up during the night, dying down again in the small hours. But, wind or no wind, it was time to sail, and in any case it still had sufficient strength. I headed for the open sea, therefore, without waiting for one of those violent north-westerlies that so often rage on this part of the coast. There are currents, too, that cannot always be relied upon, and the winds are inclined to be variable. This was something that Harry Pidgeon learnt: two days after leaving Cape Town he found himself aground a hundred miles further north; his boat was stranded on that ill-famed coast for over a week, and it was a miracle that he saved her. The wind, which had been very light, shifted during the night, driving *Islander*, with her helm lashed, onto the only sandy beach in those parts, while Pidgeon was asleep in his bunk. However, the god who rules the winds was in a kindly mood, and refrained for a week from delivering his mighty gusts, a most unusual concession in the neighbourhood of the Cape.

For me, accordingly, it was the open sea at last, while the wind was still light: as, indeed, it remained for these first days, without disturbing the sea or my stomach, which had not yet readjusted itself to life at sea.

During my first day, the sea-gods spoilt me. I had a royal escort of penguins, cormorants and gannets. It is incredible how swarming with life the sea is in the summer, off the Cape. Shoals of sardines and mackerel, and sea-birds swimming and diving for their hard-won food.

I found the gannets particularly interesting and entertaining. Flying at a great height, they dive down on the shoals of sardines, with gleeful cries, their wings folded, so that they look like a stick of anti-tank missiles released from an aircraft. At times there is a veritable bombardment of these black and white birds, falling from the sky in screeching groups of forty or fifty hungry individuals.

The cormorants are altogether quieter. They seem to me indeed, to be dumb, for I have never heard the least sound from a cormorant. The penguins, on the other hand, are more interesting,

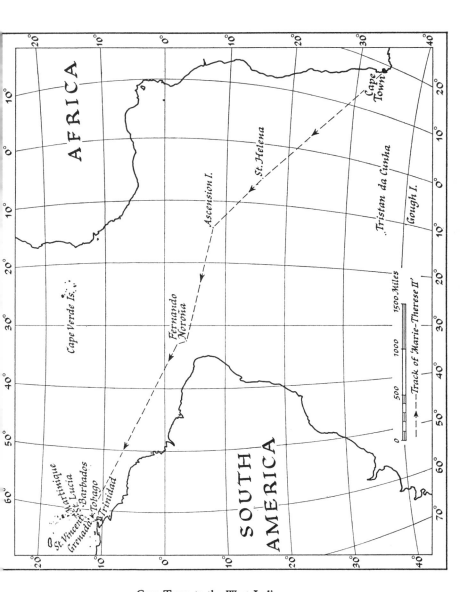

Cape Town to the West Indies

even though they produce no hair-raising dives or spectacular bombings. They swim in compact groups, mostly underwater and raising their heads, all together, only to utter a sort of shy honk, looking at me with their big round eyes: one of the funniest sights I have ever seen.

There were any number of seals, too. They take it extremely easy, floating with their bellies in the sun, flippers folded over their chests, and their nostrils just emerging from the water. They look like great big babies peacefully asleep. You can get within a few yards of them and then they wake up in a fright and dive in a brief flurry of foam. 'No need to worry,' I called out to them, 'my boat is full of food, and in any case I don't know how I'd set about hauling your thirty stone of meat on deck.'

Today, I feel happy, well fed, and full of wonder. I am living intensely and I want other creatures to live too: even the stupid cormorants which skim over the deck and choose that moment to deposit their white contribution—their aim is as accurate as my catapult's!

At sunset my marine companions went home, to Dossen Island— seal island, I suppose—while *Marie-Thérèse II* held on alone towards the open sea, making three knots under full sail, with the Marin Marie automatic steering working wonderfully. If ever anything deserved the name of wonder, that invention certainly does. It takes only a few seconds to adjust it for the required heading; all you have to do is to unfasten a wing-nut to set the vane, tighten it again, and the job is done.

How delightful it is to be able to live in peace, to read, write, cook, listen to music, or simply dream under the stars, while you watch the phosphorescent wake grow as it stretches out astern, governed by this miraculous little rudder which works untiringly and uncomplainingly twenty-four hours a day, in fine weather or foul, with the wind ahead, on the beam, or aft.

Two days with a south-westerly wind on the quarter, Force 2 to 3. Magnificent weather, sea calm, speed three to four knots. But neither fish nor bird, now, apart from the big, sabre-winged albatrosses, and the eternal petrels, tiny sea-birds like swallows, which you find in almost all waters, warm or cold.

I was now back to shipboard routine: porridge and coffee (with milk) for breakfast; position-fix around the middle of the day, from a noon sight for latitude and two equal-altitude sights a little before and after noon for longitude.

This latter longitude calculation is somewhat tedious. It is possible only if the sun is visible for an hour around midday, and this keeps you up on deck when you would prefer to be lunching peacefully in the cabin.

At the time I was using S. de Neufville's *La Navigation sans logarithmes,* which has this advantage over the nautical almanacs and navigational tables commonly used in warships and merchant vessels, that it contains all the relevant information for a period of ten years, almanacs and tables; thus you do not have to buy new almanacs every year, which are expensive and may reach you late if you are in some out-of-the-way place.

Moreover, de Neufville's book is not bulky. It has however, one defect—I could not manage to understand how the author succeeded in working out a position with the diagrams he maintained were so simple.

I had shown the book to Bardiaux in Durban. 'So you have a copy,' he said. 'I have one too. You can have a present of it if you like. Have you got to the bottom of that system of diagrams?'

'No, not yet. And meanwhile I simply work out my longitude from two equal altitudes, before and after noon. It's extremely simple and well explained. There's no need, either, to buy a new almanac every year.'

'And suppose the sun decides to retire after your first altitude, or you're not there at the right time?'

'Well, in that case, it's too bad But it doesn't happen often, because I take four or five altitudes before noon (noting the time by the chronometer for each); and even if it's dull weather I'm bound to get one or two of the five at any rate after noon.'

Bardiaux shook his head. 'In reasonable weather you'll be all right. But in bad weather it can't be much fun spending an hour on deck playing hide and seek with the sun while your boat is trying to drop you into the drink. The method I use is childishly simple. Have you ever heard of Dieumegard's tables? Try and get them sent out to you. They take up half as much room as Neufville's book and you'll understand straight away how to draw a position line without even noticing, it's so easy. There's only one disadvantage: you have to get a new nautical almanac every year.'

That being so, there was no question of my adopting the new

method. Neufville's system, which allows you to keep the book for ten years, seemed to me to answer better the needs of a wanderer in tropical seas. And as for those mysterious diagrams, some day or other I would find an obliging French naval officer to show me how to use them: unless, of course, my own thick head ultimately worked it out on its own. Meanwhile it was all Greek to me.

Later, the mystery of these diagrams was most kindly explained to me on St. Helena, where some officers from the *La Grandière* took a great deal of trouble to make me understand them. At the same time they taught me how to use Dieumegard's extremely simple tables. Bardiaux was quite right. Nothing could be simpler, apart from Neufville's diagrams, which give you altitude and azimuth at one glance without having to work out a second calculation for the latter.

To any reader who owns a boat and is interested in Neufville's method, I can offer only one small piece of advice: get his little book and I can guarantee that you will not have the least difficulty with latitude: nor is there any difficulty in longitude by equal altitude, before and after noon. You will understand it in twenty minutes, and you will be able to work out the simple calculation again without giving yourself brain fever.

But when you come to working out an altitude line with the diagrams, then one of two things will happen:

Either you will wonder how I found it difficult; and in that case well done, and congratulations.

Or, you will wonder how de Neufville can find it easy. In that case, the best thing you can do is to tuck the diagrams under your arm, find a naval officer, and ask him politely to sort out this gibberish for you.

Since naval officers are, on the whole, nice people, the one you choose will certainly be glad to put you right. 'Of course,' he will say, 'let's have a look,' thinking to himself, poor man, that it will be just a matter of a few minutes.

You will then be able to regale yourself with the spectacle of a logarithm-juggler sweating over a problem so simple that he is sure the solution must lie very much deeper. After half an hour he will decide that there must be a mistake somewhere in these accursed diagrams, for he will probably be hopelessly tied up in the terms 'angle at the pole' and 'colatitude', which he has learnt to use in quite a different sense. He will perhaps want you to add or subtract 180 degrees or twelve hours somewhere.

And it is quite possible that after an hour of this you will leave your kind instructor, armed with a number of sheets of paper on which he has scribbled his own type of calculations, practically unintelligible to the vulgar mob to which we belong. And it will be with a fine headache, too, that you will leave this bridge.

Nor am I joking: this happened to me twice, the first time in Durban and the second time in Cape Town. And heaven knows it was not from any lack of goodwill on the part of my two teachers or on my own. However, maybe I am pretty dense.

*

Marie-Thérèse II was now sufficiently far offshore. The wind, which had been fairly light ever since sailing, now shifted to the south-south-east and strengthened. I adjusted the mainsail and mizzen and set the port staysail; the other staysail was lowered, furled on its boom, and we pressed on at five knots, making 240 miles in forty-eight hours, without rolling or pitching, and correcting herself, day and night. The sky was amazingly clear, with every star visible right down to low on the horizon. The sea was phosphorescent. There was not a cloud to be seen. It was sailing to dream of, trouble-free, and with no watches at the helm. If only, I thought to myself, this could go on for ever.

Meanwhile, there was nothing to do but please myself. I could read, listen to music—the latter particularly in the evening when short-wave reception is best—or cook, though cooking is no great favourite of mine.

To my great surprise, I found myself cleaning the shrouds with a wire brush, and then carefully greasing them and wrapping them in canvas bands to a height of six feet from the deck, to protect them from spray—my morale must, indeed, have been high!

That evening, Cape Town radio forecast a violent storm off the Cape of Good Hope. I was then a long way from the Cape and the breeze did no more than drop a little during the night, to freshen again the next day. The sky, however, began to be overcast, with high cirrus and alto-cumulus.

Harry Pidgeon (whose account of his passage I was then reading) was surprised at the constantly overcast sky between Cape Town and St. Helena: so much so that he decided to make his landfall by latitude, as being the more certain; and this had caused him to lose a day or two in order to make sure that he was well to the east of St. Helena before altering course to the west and heading directly for the island.

The Cape Town Meteorological Office had also mentioned to me the almost permanently overcast conditions which prevail in that part of the Atlantic, accompanied though they are by winds that are almost always moderate and dependable. Real young ladies' sailing, they told me, but you may well get no more than a glimpse of the sun.

Using the method of longitude by equal altitudes, this might well make it difficult to fix my position with sufficient accuracy. At the moment, I was getting on well enough, by taking four or five altitudes before noon and the same number after. My excellent flat Omega kept very exact time and, in addition, the B.B.C. time-signals were very clear and would have enabled me to navigate with an ordinary alarm clock.

The absence of sun made the sea a dead grey colour. I missed the little pilot-fish, the tireless travellers in tropical waters. In this area between Cape Town and St. Helena there was nothing, not a boat and still less a fish.

All I could see was some albatrosses, their heavy bodies held up by their long narrow wings, flying at sea-level; they would disappear in the trough of the waves, to appear again just where I would not expect to see them. These birds are associated with cold waters, and seemed to me out of place in this part of the ocean, geographically tropical but at the same time rather cold and quite sunless.

There were petrels, as there always are at sea, not over-familiar, but pretty and graceful, flying close to the boat and skimming over the crests of the waves; they feed as they do so, though on what I have no idea, for I have never seen them actually put their bills into the water. On the other hand from time to time they dip a foot and seem to use the tiny webbing to give a little push and then veer away at a right angle.

Where on earth, I wonder, do these friends of mine sleep? Surely not on St. Helena or on the coast of South Africa, since I can see them even at dusk tirelessly zig-zagging at sea-level.

Would they sleep on *Marie-Thérèse II*? Alas, no: I would have been delighted to be able to invite them on board and tame them. Why not? Sailing in the Indian Ocean in *Marie-Thérèse*, I had made friends with a *margouilla*, the tiny grey lizard found in hot countries whose little paws have suckers which enable it to walk up smooth walls and on ceilings. This creature (who, between you and me, was a little simple-minded) must have suffered from amnesia. He would regularly try to drown himself in the tin of condensed milk which I used to leave open so that he could help himself like a grown-up; I used to have to fish him out, wash him in fresh water to dissolve the sugar and then dry him carefully with a cloth (not my horrible dish-rag).

What was most curious was that he got on very well with an invisible cricket, who had a fine voice but whom I could never find to offer him some condensed milk. I was afraid that I might one day see him dead from hunger, so I always left a few grains of rice in a cigarette-tin lid. I do not know whether my cricket flourished, but the cockroaches and big winged black-beetles certainly put on weight. They made excellent targets for my blow-pipe. There was no close-season in *Marie-Thérèse* during her long passage across the Indian Ocean—and yet people imagine that the single-handed sailor has no way of passing the time. Just think: blow-pipe safari in the jungle of saucepans and crockery, followed by resuscitation of baby lizard (including breathing on him to warm him up), and then a check-up on my little pilot-fish to make sure every morning that none have disappeared during the night into the belly of a poaching shark.

There were four of these pilot-fish ahead of the boat, protected by the bow-wave from the attacks of the voracious doradoes. They never left the bow-wave, except to dart for a moment in pursuit of tiny flying fish, no bigger than a match, which had not yet learnt to fly. They used to leap into the air, some two feet ahead of the stem, sometimes falling back upside down and desperately trying again. My pilot-fish would be on them like a flash and then zip! back to the bow-wave ready for the next lightning attack.

I numbered the doradoes, too, among my friends. In the first place because they were perhaps the most beautiful fish you could hope to see from the deck of a boat; their long bodies, in a shimmer of blue-green and gold, combine strength, flexibility, speed in attack, and beauty of colouring. The second reason is that the dorado is excellent eating, either fried or curried. Moreover, a single fish, averaging a yard in length, will give you food for several days.

However, there was some reserve in the friendship displayed by these beautiful creatures. They were undoubtedly interested in my boat, but not so much in me, after two of them had come to know my harpoon. Exposing their little white scars on their sides, they used always to swim at a respectful distance from the boat. The others also became wary, except just before sunset or at dawn, when they would sometimes come quite close to the side.

And then for some days there were no more doradoes. Had they deserted me for ever? No, they had not: and this was most mysterious. How were they able to find us again after an absence of some days? For it was undoubtedly my own doradoes, recognizable by the scars, that came back.

In this part of the Atlantic, however, the sea is completely empty. What is more, it seemed dead, from the grey colour it was to retain all the way to St. Helena during the eighteen days of this passage. I fell back accordingly, on my old friends in the cabin: all the familiar objects gathered in turn to give warmth to the miniature world in which I had now been living for some years. My books, carefully arranged in order of popularity on the shelves made to fit them with loving care, and then decorated as the fancy took me; the blue curtains, with their pattern of white sails, running round the cabin like a procession of symbolical boats sailing in company with the same wind: the wood-carving reproducing the map of Africa, which Wilf gave me the day before I left Cape Town. All these were familar and friendly things in this floating kingdom, free, and enamoured of the sun and new shores. But when I call it a free kingdom, I wonder whether I may not be exaggerating—anyway, I shall come back to that later. At sea, however, you do find freedom, complete freedom, a vast as the ocean on which *Marie-Thérèse II* is sailing, as lovely and peaceful as the starry world I gaze at during the night.

Nevertheless, the sea was not quite so dead as those first days of sailing had led me to think. Mostly somnolent, it would suddenly wake up at about four or five in the afternoon; the rhythm of its breathing seemed to grow faster, shaking the boat and producing a disagreeable roll. This would continue for some minutes, a quarter of an hour at the most, and then the sea returned to its normal quiet rhythm and sank peacefully back to sleep.

Life on board had become almost suburban. It was a week since we had left Cape Town, a completely uneventful week, like a cruise arranged by a travel-agency. Shortly after our sailing, the south-east trade wind had set in (as noted in the *Pilot Chart*), and it was blowing gently and regularly in nature's familiar rhythm. On the continental masses the year is divided into four seasons; in the equatorial countries or those governed by the monsoons there are only two.

In this area, between Cape Town and St. Helena, I found that the trade wind had two seasons every twenty-four hours. A little before sundown it freshens and *Marie-Thérèse II* pressed on through the night, trailing her iridescent wake. Then at about nine or ten in the morning the wind begins to drop, and by one o'clock in the afternoon there is only just enough wind for us to make two or three knots. The trade wind then recovers and gradually strengthens until dawn, when the log begins to rotate more rapidly. During the first week we logged 640 miles, an average of 91 miles a day.

During the next week we added a further 743 miles, a daily average of 108. Well done, *Marie-Thérèse II,* I told her, you are beginning to get the taste of it. However the spinner of the log had been swallowed by a large fish, a shark, probably, or a barracuda.

My morale being particularly high, I decided to make a new one. I cut a one-foot length from a plank, pointed at each end, to which I screwed two fins of thin brass, judging the angle by eye. I attached this contraption to the log-line and lo and behold it revolved like a real log.

I could not, of course, calibrate it correctly, for I would have needed a second log as a control before I could carry out that delicate operation. It was sufficient, however, to compare the results given by a the new spinner with my noon-positions for several days, to establish the ratio: 93 miles by the log corresponded to 112 miles made good. There was, it is true, a slight favourable current but so slight that I did not take it into account. Until I lost the original spinner, my calculated positions showed a difference of only three miles from the log-readings: accurate enough without splitting hairs.

It was becoming increasingly difficult to obtain an accurate fix. The sky was nearly always covered by high cloud, making it only just possible to distinguish the sun with the sextant, without using the shades. Seven or eight pre-noon altitudes gave me only two or three in the afternoon, and that involved an hour and a half on deck.

Back in the cabin to work out my position, my right eye (used to sight the sun through the telescope of the sextant) could no longer distinguish green from grey. My colour vision returned to normal after an hour or so, but this worried me rather, and I felt that it was high time for the sun to show itself properly, or there would not be much chance of making St. Helena. Still, better miss a port of call than ruin your eyesight.

I took the precaution of noting each day how long it took for my colour vision to return to normal. So far, it does in less than an hour, with no variation in the time; so that for the moment my optical mechanism seems safe enough. However, I shall have to watch it, because it is not a thing you can afford to take chances with.

That silly albatross that I have seen every day since Cape Town is still here, and is beginning to get on my nerves. It is probably he who is bringing the clouds and the dull weather. In cold waters, around the Cape, albatrosses are part of the local colour, and one would be sorry not to see them, with the seals and penguins. But fancy meeting them in the middle of the tropics, a few hundred miles from St. Helena.

We are now quite close to St. Helena: 160 miles to go and I shall be there, provided I can obtain an accurate noon position tomorrow. If not, I shall heave to at night and sail only during the day, and so avoid an unpleasantly abrupt landfall.

The next day was Monday, December 10th and the sun kept the appointment. The sky cleared nicely and I was able to take three good observations and work out my position quickly and neatly: only 60 miles to sail before I drop my anchor in the road-stead at St. Helena. Moreover, I shall arrive this very night, as indeed, I expected. Singapore, the Chagos, Durban, Cape Town, and now St. Helena: it is always the same story—and my landfalls, good and bad, take place at night.

This time, there could be no doubt about it. The wind, which had been rather light for the last two days, began to freshen considerably and *Marie-Thérèse II* was showing her best speed. For once I could have wished that the wind-god would moderate his good will, and allow me to have a good night's sleep and arrive comfortably about ten or eleven in the morning: though he might have done still better and blown more heartily for the last two days, so that I could have made St. Helena this afternoon.

It was, however, no time for me to complain. When you have had seventeen days of fine weather, completely trouble-free, never having to reef anr never becalmed, then you should be grateful to the gods of the sea and not grumble because you arrive at night and have missed your full allowance of sleep only on the last day.

I shall be saying my thank-you this evening before sunset. For in spite of myself, a faultless landfall is still something of a mystery to me; there is still something unreal about that little dark blue smudge that gradually emerges above the horizon at the very spot where one expected it, without daring to be over-confident, and then gradually takes on the shape of an island.

It is stupid, I know, but I cannot help it. It will always be something of a miracle to me, to see an island emerge after I have been several weeks at sea, in a place where an hour earlier I could see only water, waves, clouds and the unbroken, eternal, line of the horizon. Each time, I feel the same mixture of astonishment, love and pride as this new land is born which seems to have been created for me and by me.

And, just before sunset, when I was already beginning to feel a little niggling of doubt, St. Helena rose gently from the sea.

I spent the night hove-to, ten miles to windward of St. Helena, waiting for daybreak. In the morning I could see the fishing pirogues just behind a headland which shuts off Jamestown Bay. Then I could distinguish the little church mentioned in the *Sailing Directions*. I picked up my binoculars and recognized a familiar mast. So Henry had arrived before me. *Wanda*'s deck was deserted, but the dinghy was made fast astern. I was delighted, although, between ourselves, I would have been better pleased if *Wanda* had sailed into the harbour a few hours later.

I sounded my fog-horn and Henry's head emerged for a moment from his cabin, to disappear again immediately. Then came three shots: Henry must indeed be pleased that our rendezvous had worked out, to waste three of his Colt 45 cartridges. He then jumped into his dinghy, pulling like a madman, and came on board. We selected a mooring together, as close as possible to the shore, near *Wanda*, where the squalls coming down the valley are less violent than offshore. I dropped anchor at seven in the morning.

'Seventeen days and twelve hours for *Wanda*. How did you get on?'

'Eighteen days, exactly.'

'Tell me, did you have it overcast all the way to St. Helena as I did? I thought you must have dropped the idea of putting in here. I very nearly did. If I hadn't had a perfect sun-sight the last day, I would have skipped it.'

'The same with me. What's more, I wondered more than once whether you hadn't gone quietly on to Ascension Island, considering the dull weather and the difficulty of getting a fix.'

'It's a good job you managed to find the island. The locals are first-rate. What about breakfast, anyway? Come on board. Fried mackerel and "Mardi Gras". O.K. for breakfast? You've only to throw a line out and you'll have all the mackerel you can eat. I'll take you over in my dinghy and then I'll give a hand to erect that thing you have the face to call a dinghy. You'll see, the boys here are a wonderful crowd.'

'And the dollies?'

'Plenty!'

CHAPTER 8

On St Helena

Seen from the sea, St. Helena has the appearance of an enormous fortress, massive, hostile, with the cliffs falling precipitously to the sea, and the rocky scree lining the narrow valleys; the wind is funnelled into the latter and builds up its speed, so that it seems to have torn away from the rock anything that has struggled to take root. There is some green growth in the valley bottoms, though very little, and from seaward St. Helena looks just like the dry rock that witnessed the end of Napoleon, as our history books describe it.

But once the visitor leaves the austere grandeur of the shoreline he is amazed and delighted by what he finds, a landscape of rich green vegetation, full of colour and sweetly scented.

Napoleon, it is true, was a prisoner; any man is a prisoner as soon as a line is drawn around him beyond which he cannot venture. There is a world of difference, however, between the way in which a prisoner was treated two centuries ago, and the way he would be today.

The climate on St. Helena is delightful, and its healthiness is reflected in the faces and character of the islanders and in their behaviour, which are instinct with good will and kindness towards every living creature, human or animal. I had not yet been in the Pacific, on my visit to the Tuamotus Archipelago, and I would have liked to be able to make a comparison. And while I have at the moment no idea where I shall ultimately lay my bones, I have often, since that call on St. Helena, dreamt of that peaceful island, beautiful and kindly, and of its inhabitants, hoping that one day I may meet them again.

The first friend we made was Sidi Youg, the dockyard foreman. He had lived all his life by the sea, and had met all our predecessors on passage since Gerbault and Pidgeon, the latter twice.

He had been born on St. Helena and had never left the island except for a few days in a fishing boat. For Henry and me Sidi

Youg embodied the essence of St. Helena, and he helped us to understand the island.

He was a born story-teller, and could bring back to life for us the sailors he had known and loved, so that we had a complete picture of them: the single-handed sailors in particular. And this he did with a tactful sympathy that was at once simple and penetrating.

In an ordinary British colony, an Englishman would have referred to Sidi as a 'native': not so here, where the English call the people born on the island, as Sidi was, 'St. Helenans'.

Sidi and the others adopted us from the outset. We became full-fledged members of their big family. How rare it is, and how comforting, to find a small community where they say 'this is your home' and mean it.

It was rather like Mauritius, although there can be no comparison between the two islands. Both are beautiful and blessed by the gods; but while Mauritius is a glorious bunch of roses, St. Helena is a single, simple carnation, and I love them both equally in spite of their difference.

It was a miniature Paradise we had found.

We decided to stay for Christmas and a few weeks longer. Moreover, in the New Year, the *Jeanne d'Arc* and *La Grandière* were both expected. This would give Henry an opportunity to meet the Franch navy; and for me it would be a chance once again to enjoy the frank and free atmosphere of the wardroom, of which I retained such pleasant memories from the time, some years earlier, when the *Jeanne* and *La Grandière* called at Mauritius.

I was, however, a little worried about *Marie-Thérèse II*: when she had last been hauled up the slip at Cape Town, some days before sailing, I had noticed a small damp patch on the hull, which had been drying for a day. This was unusual for a new boat.

I scraped it carefully a little with a screwdriver, and the wood crumbled! In a fever of anxiety, I scraped a couple of inches further along, with the same result. The wood was soft, as though it were rotten, just by the frame.

This was peculiar and irritating, and rather depressing, too, but not really serious, because the timber on either side was perfectly sound. I had only to cut out the defective part and patch it. It would be a matter of a couple of hours, including caulking, to replace the few square inches with sound wood.

At the same time, there was something odd about those few square inches of rot. And the rot had attacked the wood, opposite the frame, stopping only at the next plank, just at the strake. Could it be that—but, no, surely not, heaven couldn't have played me such a nasty trick!

I laid the edge of the screwdriver against the next plank, pressed a little, and it went in as though it were cardboard. My blood ran cold, and at that moment I must have known what a father feels like when the doctors tells him that his daughter has caught leprosy: for my boat was part of my own self. Into her creation had gone my whole mind, heart and energies. I had witnessed her birth, watched her grow and change and become more beautiful, as one watches one's daughter grow into womanhood. And suddenly I learnt that she was a leper: and, there could be no doubt, through my own fault, through hurrying the work, and using the timber I bought at the little local shop because I had not the patience to wait till better timber could be had. Some had been expected in a month's time and it would have cost me no more at the warehouse of one of my Mauritian friends.

A month seems a long time to wait when you are sitting idle; longer still when you have had to accept from the outset that, with the limited capital you have managed to save, it is going to be a gruelling race against time.

Moreover, when I began building *Marie-Thérèse II*, there were so many elementary principles of which I was ignorant; among others, the importance as a preventive against rot of thoroughly coating the timbers and frames with creosote or a similar substance. Even paraffin would have served, if only I had known. I had learnt all this later, in Durban and Cape Town, when I met the shipyard workers and Henry and all sorts of other people.

Even so, before beginning the work, I had asked my father to send me a book I had heard of, about building wooden boats. Unfortunately, I found it quite unintelligible, and so did another competent friend of Mauritius to whom I gave it to read. He gave it back to me with the comment, 'This book is useless. The writer has tried to make boat-building so impossible to understand that the amateur won't risk building his own but order it from a shipyard.'

It is true enough that there are very few good books about building wooden boats, I mean books for the non-expert. And when I say building, I do not mean simply putting the boat together but everything covered by the word. This includes measures to preserve the timber, which is one of the most essential aspects of the construction. Henry had found the same, that there was nothing of this sort published in English.

However, there is in fact a book which covers everything. It is published in America, and it contains a full treatment of everything you need to know: wood-preservation, methods of construction, caulking and so on. I read it—but much later. It is a great pity that it has not been translated into French, and that I had not heard of it when I was on Mauritius. Still, this is what happens so often: you make the initial mistake, and then you have to pay for it. And it is only then that you hear about what would have saved you all your troubles.

Now that I have got that off my chest, I can take you back to Cape Town, three days before my sailing, when a complete check disclosed that four planks were affected, all opposite the same frame. This was extremely serious. I was in desperation, and felt that I simply could not summon up any more energy, for it was clear that it was that frame which was the source of the trouble. And, what was even more disturbing, it included a floor-frame. Replacing a timber is not much fun, but putting in a new floor-frame is quite another matter and much more irksome. I would have to take out the masts in order to remove the carlings bolted to the floor-frames; and before that, I should have to break up and remove all the concrete inside ballast. Then change the faulty floor-frame, put everything back and finally replace the four planks: two months' work, at the least. And in any case it would cost more than I had.

There followed a council of war with Henry: two doctors in consultation about a desperate case. We finally decided that the work would be done in the West Indies and that Henry would give me a hand. My spirits recovered a little.

We carried out the emergency patching together, preceded by a first examination to determine exactly how much was involved. All the affected parts of the planks were removed along the length of the floor-frame, and we found that the latter was perfectly sound. It was a timber between the floor-frame and the planking which had developed rot, and this had spread to the four planks. The framework, however, was sound, and only the planks needed replacing: and that could be done in the West Indies, in the shade of the coconut-palms.

I experienced the relief of a man who was about to have a limb amputated and finds that it is only a bruise—as I had found with my right foot.

The temporary repair was carried out, with sound timber, well soaked in creosote. We then re-caulked, and *Marie-Thérèse II* returned to her native element, resigned to leaving it again as soon as we reached the West Indies.

However, we had no sooner arrived at St. Helena, than I noticed something on the quay; a crane.

When I asked Sidi about it, he told me that it was used to lift out of the water the two big fishing boats moored in the roadstead, boats twice the weight of mine. They were simply lowered onto the quay, painted with anti-fouling, and returned to the water: provided, that is, that the sea was calm, for you sometimes get very large rollers on St. Helena.

Our plans were decided after a new council of war. I went to see the harbour-master and explained what I wanted: to use the crane to lift *Marie-Thérèse II* out of the water, and leave her on the quay for a couple of weeks while I replaced the faulty planks. He agreed, and told me that it would cost a thousand francs to lift her out and return her to the water when I had finished the work, plus fifteen francs a day while she was on the quay. In other words, a gift!

There was timber in a government store: good African timber, and incredibly cheap, somewhere around five or six thousand francs for all I should need. It was giving it away, and work would be a pleasure on such an island.

'In exactly a week,' Sidi assured me, 'you'll be on the quay. There are three small boats that need urgent repairs first, but that will soon be fixed.'

Henry was delighted with the good news, and that there would soon be an end to what had been such a terrible worry to me. 'We'll both get to work on that sieve of yours and we'll soon put it to rights, you'll see.'

*

It is characteristic of Henry that faced with the prospect of any sort of work, he cannot bear to remain idle.

'Let's go ashore at once,' he urged me, 'and sort out some timber in the government store.'

'What about the measurements?' I asked. 'Let's wait at any rate until she's out of the water and we can see properly.'

'And suppose somebody else wants some wood and gets away with all the good planks?'

That seemed sensible, and so we went round to the store and picked out a dozen or so planks which they kindly put on one side for us. We would not be needing them all, we explained, but we wanted to be on the safe side.

The manager understood and agreed. 'Don't worry,' he told us, 'there's some excellent well-seasoned timber stacked in a corner of the store. I put it on one side for my uncle's boat, but I'll tell him about yours, and he'll let you have it. He's in no hurry for the work on his own.'

With the problem of wood settled, we got talking about this and that. The conversation then turned to underwater fishing.

'Fish? Plenty of it! Not very big, at least not in the bay. But you'll find any amount by the wreck of the tanker, some fathoms deep, to the left of your anchorage. It's odd, but you'll find more at the stern of the wreck. Chiefly parrot-fish.'

They'd be a change from the mackerel we'd been gorging on for the last few days. There were compact shoals of these out in the bay and around our moorings. It was a simple process: Henry gave me a shout at lunch-time and I pulled over to *Wanda*. The primus was lit, oil poured into the frying-pan and Henry handed me the mackerel one after the other at a few seconds' interval. You had only to put the line out to catch one. I had to clean them, because Henry was always rather squeamish about gutting fish, a thing that never bothered me.

'How many can you manage? Two? Three?' I gave my order, and when it was made up, they went into the frying-pan. There was no need to catch any more to save for lunch: just one, for luck, and then we would mount the same operation at midday and in the evening. But it would be agreeable to vary the menu with a parrot or two (fish, I mean, not birds).

'What about the wreck?' we asked. 'Anything worth having there, apart from the parrots?'

'There were some cases of whisky, but they were found too late; the sea water had ruined it and it was undrinkable. There's still the bronze propeller, but unfortunately there's no diving gear on St. Helena. In any case, how could one detach it from the shaft without an oxy-acetylene cutter? We're not equipped for that sort of work here: a pity, considering the price of bronze.'

Henry and I looked at one another: we were both thinking of the same thing, the diving gear I had tried out in Durban and then improved and made easier to handle in Cape Town. Henry had been interested in it and we had often discussed the possibility of perfecting it.

The system we used in Durban consisted of a container which served as an artificial lung. A four-gallon drum was opened with a tin-opener. Several weights, amouting to at least forty pounds, were then attached to the open end. These made it possible to insert the drum in the water, open end down, so that it retained the air, like a diving bell. The depth at which this artificial lung rested in the water was controlled by a line.

A plastic hose was inserted into the drum from the open end, the end of the hose almost touching the upper end of the drum, running, therefore, to the top of the air trapped inside. To the other end of the tube was fitted the mouth-piece of an underwater swimmer's syphon. It was a crude contrivance, but easy to make, and I found in Durban that the four gallons of air it contained enabled me to breathe normally at a depth of six feet for a minute. (On Mauritius I had used a forty-gallon metal drum which allowed me to stay twenty minutes under water; but it was much too cumbersome.)

The problem was then the re-filling of the reservoir of air. Henry inclined to the idea of an air-pump and his mechanical genius had suggested a number of solutions. I favoured a completely different idea from that of the conventional pump, which Henry had found impracticable.

Whether it is water you wish to transmit or air, you have a number of different ways to choose from. One is to drive the liquid or gas through a tube with a force-pump. Another way is simplicity itself and as old as the hills—all you need is a bucket: and it is particularly applicable when you have to use the means to hand; you can get hold of a bucket easily enough, but a pump has to be bought or made.

In the end Henry came round to my idea. We would recharge the artificial lung from another drum, turned upside down, which would carry the air under water, like a diving bell.

The simplest way, in theory, would be for someone to lower the second drum at regular intervals, beside, and a little below, the artificial lung. The diver would then only have to tilt up the second drum just below the opening at the bottom of the first and the air would spill out from the former and fill the latter.

The diver, however, had not gone down to twiddle his thumbs and watch the fish. He was there to get through some work, but in practice he would have had to spend his time in recharging the artificial lung. What we wanted was to have this done automatically, with only the help of the man on deck who was looking after it. This would enable the diver to get on with his work, inside a radius limited by the length of the breathing tube connecting him with the air-container.

This is how we succeeded, using only materials we had on board.

The first thing we needed was another tube. Various odd lengths were found in *Wanda* and *Marie-Thérèse II* and joined together with couplings cut from the ends of copper pipes (curtain-rods are extremely useful in a sailing boat—or you can sometimes find a couple in the Cape Town Yacht Club's dustbins).

We then had about twelve feet of hosepipe, one of whose ends was fastened just inside the opening of the artificial lung. It was through this pipe that the latter would be refilled from the second drum.

The other end was inserted into the second drum, which was to carry the air under water, and which was then lowered so that it rested deeper than the artificial lung.

And then—the miracle failed to materialize: the air in the second drum refused to pass obligingly into the artificial lung—an elementary mistake on the part of the half-wit who thought himself a genius and had forgotten a little law of physics that every schoolboy knows.

Henry was delighted and made no attempt to disguise the fact. 'You and your lousy system!'—but soon he realized why the apparatus had failed to work. 'Look, we're a pair of idiots! Of course it won't work like this—if it did, there'd have been no need for some bright spark to discover how a syphon works!'

Henry now took charge. 'The hose must start from the top of the drum. And then the air will flow towards the artificial lung as soon as the filler containing the air is lower than the lung. Got it, stupid? However, your idea of feeding the air into the lung from a second diving bell was not such a bad one after all. A good job you had me to sort out the details for you, you bloody French bastard.'

'O.K., O.K., I'd have fixed it all right without you, you bloody English tramp.'

This exchange of French bastard and English tramp, qualified by the prefix 'bloody', indicates that we are beginning to see daylight.

We made a coupling from a copper plate with a hole cut in the middle, to which we soldered a length of copper tubing (this is where the curtain rods come in) with a blow-lamp and a stick of solder. We cut a hole in each corner of the plate and the coupling was bolted to the upper end of the drum and made watertight by a washer cut from a piece of inner tube.

This time the apparatus worked properly, and I went down four feet for my first dive, with Henry in charge of the refilling drum.

When you are breathing under water, there is always something wonderful about watching this submarine world, calm and caressing, which Cousteau has so rightly called 'the world of silence'.

I hung in the water, fascinated by the sight of my boat lying in this unreal setting, admiring the strength and grace of her lines.

A generous mouthful of sea-water brought me back to the surface.

'Anything gone wrong, Henry?'

'Look, you bloody Frenchman, I've been sweating on deck for the last ten minutes. What about me having a turn below?'

I felt that I was going to enjoy myself, because, although Henry can do a great many things, I very much doubted whether he knew much about diving. I had seen friends of mine on Mauritius swallow quite some mouthfuls while playing at fishes with this system: for it is a mistake to imagine that it is easy to use this apparatus, simple though it is. After a little practice there is no trouble, but for the inexperienced it can be a surprise.

I reminded Henry of the essential rules: 'You go down at the same time as the artificial lung, and once you've reached your depth, you move only in the horizontal plane. Right? If you're unlucky enough to rise a little, even a very little, the air-pressure delivered from the lung will be higher than the pressure of water on your rib-cage. The air will then reach your mouth under pressure, you'll lose your head, and I'll watch you surfacing with the tube in your hand and swearing by all the saints that only a maniac would mess about with such a contraption.

'And if you move deeper than the layer of air contained in the lung, you'll find it difficult to breathe, because the pressure of water on your rib-cage will be higher than that of the air in the lung.

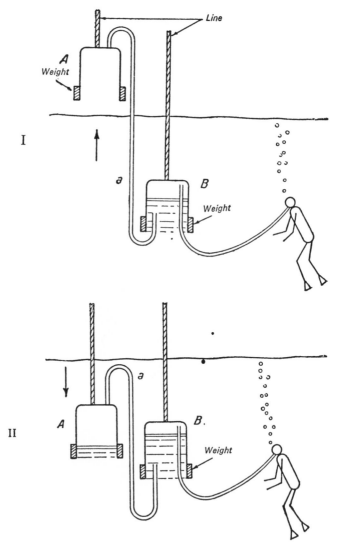

Fig. 7. Home-made diving bell.
I. A is hauled clear of the water.
II. A, refilled with air, is lowered again into the water.

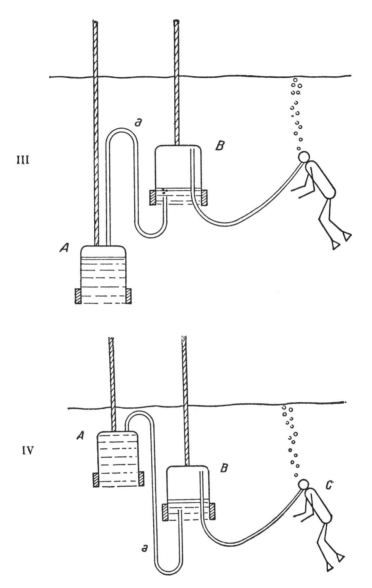

III. Air flows from A into B. The lower bend of the pipe *a* must be above the level of the drum A.
IV. B has now been refilled with air, and A is drawn up to start again at stage I.

'If that happens, come up a little, but very gently, so as not to rise above the level of the lung, which would send you straight back to the surface. And a final warning: make sure that . . .'

'O.K., save your breath. I'll manage quite all right on my own. Just keep awake and concentrate on delivering the air-supply.'

Henry began his dive, while I gently paid out the end of the line attached to the lung. Not for long, however. He was already surfaced, coughing, spitting and swearing.

'Got a bone stuck, Henry?' I asked him. 'I was trying to tell you to blow into the pipe so that you wouldn't swallow any water that might be in it.'

Henry gave me a dirty look and blew into the pipe to expel the water.

He dived again: four seconds, this time. He was coming on. No swearing this time; no doubt Henry had exhausted his vocabulary.

'Tell me straight, Bernard. Do you really believe the common herd can use this contraption, or do you have to be a South-east Asian swimming champion first?'

'Of course they can—anyone can. The great thing is always to keep at the same level as the diving bell. Look, take my weighted belt and hang on to the drum while I lower it. And you can console yourself by the thought that every one who has tried to use the thing has begun by surfacing at speed as you did. Just relax and you'll get the hang of it.'

Henry brightened up a little and dived for the third time. And lo and behold, he had got the knack. I saw him let go of the drum and then cautiously move about to one side of it. Another minute, however, and he surfaced again, coughing and spitting.

'Lazy bastard,' he complained, 'you've been mooning on deck instead of sending air down!'

I apologized, but added, 'In any case, my dear Henry, you were marvellous. I've never seen anyone learn to use it so quickly' (which, indeed was quite true).

At the fourth attempt, Henry got on like a fish, while I kept up the air supply every thirty seconds.

He, too, was fascinated by the new feeling which possesses an earth-bound creature when it masters the world in which the fishes are at home.

Henry stayed under water for twenty minutes. When he climbed back into the boat his eyes were shining with delight. But I was far away, lost in a dream.

In my dream I saw a big tender anchored in the tepid waters of a tropical bay. On the deck a bronzed figure was busy supplying air to four of his companions who were breathing through tubes connecting each of them to a single artificial lung made from a forty-gallon metal drum. They had even improved further on the system Henry and I had just been using, by adding a valve (Cousteau-Gagnant) incorporated in each tube. The artificial lung could thus be lowered slightly below the keel of the boat and the divers could move both horizontally and vertically without their work being incommoded.

But what were they working at? At the moment they were scraping the bottom, and with four men this would not take long. Then would follow the caulking of defective areas, and stopping with the cement-plaster-and-clay mixture the parts that had been touched up. (In parts of Indonesia the fishermen use a clay and cement mixture to stop the strakes. Jean Gau told me that on some South American coasts cement and sand is used for this purpose, as that is the only material which will resist the marine life in those muddy waters.) This was a matter of a few hours' work. All they then had to do was to give the bottom a coat of a special anti-fouling paint. This was a new product designed for us under water!

*

My dream faded. Henry was making hot coffee in the cabin of *Marie-Thérèse II*; and, sitting on the coach-roof, I was thinking about what would be involved here and now in bottom-scraping a tender of fifty or sixty tons in the tideless seas found in the West Indies and the majority of Pacific Islands. There are two methods.

The first is to haul it up onto a slip. There are not many of these, however, in less advanced countries, and you have to wait your turn. Moreover, shipyards so equipped are few and far between, and correspondingly expensive.

The other way is to careen the vessel. This involves emptying her of all her contents, including the inside ballast, and then laying her over on her side with the keel clear of the water, heaving with tackle attached to the masts. For this you need an anchorage in deep and completely calm water.

On some islands, careening is carried out with two boats, one serving as a fixed mooring for the other. When the first boat has been laid over first on one side and then the other, and the maintenance or the repairs to the wetted surface have been completed, the roles are reversed; but when everything is in order, the inside ballast, stores, equipment, etc., have to be reloaded.

This is work that not only requires care but takes up a great deal of time. Too often, accordingly, it is put off as long as possible because of the loss of profits due to the simultaneous immobilization of both boats. As a result of this delay, the fine schooner, only a few years old, begins to be attacked by borers; the stout wooden keel will soon have long galleries driven into it, some of them as thick as your finger, and a fine new boat will remind you of a young athlete who has over-strained himself. His heart is damaged and he can no longer stand up to a stiff test.

We (Deshumeurs and I) had had experience of such damage in *Snark*. Coming back from our Indonesian cruise, Deshumeurs was at the helm, at night, off Pulocondore, about 150 miles from Cape St. Jacques.

Old *Snark* was groaning and creaking in the short, heavy seas, broken by the southerly current which rounds the Camau headland and runs across the south-west monsoon.

I was asleep in my cabin when Deshumeurs came in and shook me.

'Time already?' I asked him. 'What time is it, anyway?'

'I don't know, and I don't bloody well care. Come and take the helm, Bernard. Something's going on that doesn't sound too good to me. I've just heard the keel cracking.'

'Are you daft?'

'Perhaps I am, but come and take the helm anyway, just for an hour or two even, while I calm down a bit. I tell you, the keel gave a great crack, believe it or not, and my guts practically turned inside out when I heard the bashing she's taking—it was just like a scream of agony.'

I went to the helm. Nothing unusual happened. Heavy, vicious, seas—that was all.

Deshumeurs gave a few strokes of the pump, as we used to do when changing watch. I was wondering why he was still pumping, because I had handed over to him only two hours earlier and it seemed to me that that was a lot of water to have to pump.

'Look, Bernard,' he called across to me, 'there's something very odd here: with what I've pumped out she ought to be quite dry by now.'

Deshumeurs continued pumping for another ten minutes, each stroke of the handle bringing up half a bucketful of water. He was only too right, something must indeed have cracked, and it must have been pretty serious, because since that moment and until our arrival, we had to spend a great deal of our time off-watch at the pump. We had developed fine biceps, I can assure you, by the time we made Cape St. Jacques; but we were heartily sick of *Snark* and the Gulf of Siam and everything else.

It was only after we had entered the Saigon river that the trouble cured itself: mud was carried in with the water through the gaps in the seams; it settled on the sides and gradually plugged the innumerable leaks, including those in the keel.

Two days after dropping anchor in the river harbour of Saigon, we were pumping out only four or five buckets of water a day.

All we could then do was to sell poor *Snark,* riddled with rot from truck to toe, hull, frames, and all: devoured, unhappy vessel, by borers. We were not carrying even a canoe on board, to save our wretched lives had things come to the worst between Singapore and Cape St. Jacques.

This was the prelude to an invaluable conversation with an old Vietnamese fisherman, while *Snark* lay in peace, sleeping her last sleep, stern-on to the quay, in the Saigon river.

The fisherman had witnessed our sailing eight months earlier. Without, it is true, much confidence in us; for apart from a few close friends, no one believed that we would make it.

On our return, the old man was a little less sceptical, although he still had some reservations: but in the whole story, which by and large was pretty uneventful, he found only one thing really interesting: the leak, or rather the large number of leaks, which might have cost us so dear.

'And so: you didn't mind having to pump like galley-slaves? What about bran, or don't you know that trick? If you have no bran, sawdust will serve practically as well. But neither of them are a patch on cowdung; dried in the sun and powdered and then mixed with a couple of buckets of sawdust, that will cure the trouble for you.'

'Come again?'

'Don't tell me that you've lived all your life in Indochina and don't know that dodge. Ah, but of course—you used to sail with the fishermen in the Gulf of Siam, and they probably don't use such a childishly simple method. The people are quite different on the Annamese coast.'

'I still don't follow you.'

'Your old tub was making several tons of water a day between Singapore and Saigon, wasn't she? And you've now been here two days and she's making no more than a couple of bucketsful a day. And why? Simply because the mud that's held in suspension in the river water has made its way in and sealed the leaks.'

'We know that well enough, Ong Gia' (a term of respect used in addressing an old man) 'without having it explained. We realized immediately what the mud was doing.'

'Then you've only to do a little more thinking and you'll understand the rest. If mud held in river water can seal leaks, then there must be other substances that will do it as well, or even better.

'On the Annamese coast, we use cowdung, dried and then crushed to a powder between two stones. You have only to dive below the hull with a tin of this powder, and apply it to the suspect part of the planking. the cowdung enters with the water through the defective caulking, sets inside the hole, swells, and in half a minute it will plug the smaller holes.'

'But supposing the water is coming in everywhere, as in *Snark?*'

'In that case, you need to use sawdust, because you'll need a lot of it and it's cheap. With cowdung, you have to collect it, dry it and then reduce it to powder; bran, you have to buy; but you can go to any carpenter's with a shovel and fill a sack of sawdust in half a minute.

'Using sawdust, the technique is a little different. You fill a drum or a half-gallon can, and empty it about six feet below the keel, at the same time stirring up the water so that the particles of sawdust are well dispersed. They rise towards the surface and as they do so come in contract with the hull; then they are sucked into the leaks and act in the same way as the cowdung; the water makes them swell and in a minute or so they form a seal.

'If the boat is at anchor, this will last well, but when sailing the durability varies from some hours to some days according to the circumstances. Is that clear, paleface?'

Perfectly clear—although at that time Deshumeurs and I thought the venerable old fellow was rather over-emphasizing the cunning of the Annamese fishermen and wanted to persuade us that a make-shift remedy was a panacea.

And yet he was right, and abundantly so. For later, in *Marie-Thérèse*, when I was sailing in the Indian Ocean, on more than one occasion I lowered a large can of sawdust below the boat. The Vietnamese fishermen's trick worked wonderfully, and not only for small leaks.

I need hardly add that a sack of sawdust, stowed in a corner of the forepeak, is now an integral part of my boat's equipment: together, moreover, with the invaluable cement and clay (and, since Cape Town, plaster) mixture, which is the very latest in first aid for leaks, large or small. It constitutes the medical kit for the hull.

We soon ceased to bother about the wreck. The bronze propeller could stay where it was, for it was not really important and never had been. The great thing had been the construction of the diving gear and its control from the deck of a sailing vessel. More-over, the sea at St. Helena is not very warm—not exactly cold, even so, but on the other hand not warm either. And this, considering the geographical position of the island, well in the tropics, is surprising. The coolness of the water is due to the Antarctic Current, diverted by the southern extremity of Africa, which slowly makes it way to meet the great Equatorial Current which originates in the Gulf of Guinea.

It was cold for two such tropical birds as us. Nevertheless, we found we had to hunt for our food under water with the spear-gun, for the mackerel were beginning to leave the bay, followed by the St. Helena fishermen.

*

Sidi was as good as his word. On the day he promised, the whalers under repair on the quay were returned to the water, and *Marie-Thérèse II* took their place. The sea had been calm since our arrival, having decided to postpone its little periodic crisis of bad temper; without this concession, it is impossible on St. Helena to lift the boats out of the water. They have to wait until everything has settled down, the sea is calm and the crane can be used. With ten men to help, the latter hoisted *Marie-Thérèse II*, very slowly.

Henry and I remained on deck during the operation; I was feeling pretty nervous, because I am not too fond of seeing my boat suspended at the end of a wire cable, however thick it may be. Finally, after an hour's work, she rested on the quay, held by four timbers.

The work went quickly, and that same evening all the doubtful planks had been removed. Henry was horrified by what we found.

'Instead of all your talk about *Snark*, about what a miracle she was, riddled with rot and leaking like a sieve, and yet floating, you have a better example right here. How on earth could you have had the nerve to sail in this tub?'

I, too, was wondering how I had been able to survive the heavy weather off the Cape with these five cardboard planks. If only I had known when I was building her, there would have been coat upon coat of creosote, of paraffin; there would even have been rock-salt inserted in small holes bored into the top of the frames. Rot is without a doubt a wooden boat's worst enemy; it is worse than an enemy, a vile, underhand fifth-columnist trying to insinuate itself wherever the paintbrush will never be able to reach again, into joints, and into the most inaccessible parts of the hold where light and air cannot penetrate.

It was in Cape Town that I learnt the trick of inserting rock-salt into the tops of the frames. It originated, apparently, from an American in the heroic age of wooden ships, who noted the tendency of rot to start in the upper surfaces of the frames where you cannot paint again once the deck has been laid. He had the inspiration, as a preventative, of boring a vertical hole some inches deep in the top of each frame and filling it with rock salt (not common salt, which has too great an affinity for water).

It would also appear that in these big sailing ships (now almost disappeared) they did not waste time in replacing portions of the framing that were attacked by rot. Replacing a plank is simple, but it is quite another matter to replace a floor-frame, the keelson or the stem.

In these cases, a small wooden container was mounted on the affected part, filled with rock salt, and sealed. As the salt absorbed the damp it acted as a concentrated antiseptic, checking the otherwise irresistible spreading of the rot.

Fortunately, there were only five planks to be replaced. The number might well have been much higher. The frame was found to be unaffected and the work did not take long. All the exposed parts were thoroughly washed with plenty of water, scraped and scrubbed. The extremely dry atmosphere on St. Helena would dry the wood very quickly and allow the creosote to penetrate thoroughly. The two garboard strakes (these adjoining the keel) were removed, which enabled us to do the same to the floors. These, and the underside of the floor-frames, were similarly treated with creosote. After several weeks in hospital, *Marie-Thérèse II* would be fit again; but it was none too soon.

So we set to work. The second day was spent in marking the first plank, and cutting it out with extreme care, stopping the plane half a millimetre from the line in order to leave ourselves a small safety margin.

When the first plank was ready (cut out and ready for nailing) I thought it better to wait and allow the frames to dry more thoroughly. To assist this, I used up a few pints of paraffin in the blow-lamp which for several days in succession had been applied to all the exposed surfaces. It was essential that the timber should be perfectly dry if the creosote with which it was going to be impregnated was to penetrate thoroughly.

After a week of this treatment, the boat was ready to receive the first new plank. This was a day's work. We had begun with the easiest plank, so that we could get the hang of it as we progressed. Cramps, wooden wedges, levers, and a few round oaths were brought into action. And the plank took up its position without protest.

In a fortnight's time the hull had regained its normal appearance. We had worked away quietly, without any damage to the boat or to our own persons—but parrot-fish was beginning to run out of our ears. In the waters off St. Helena there was any amount of them. First thing in the morning, to freshen up, we dived into the cool water—parrots everywhere, nothing but parrot. We would catch a couple of fair-sized ones for breakfast.

At about midday, I used to go on board and put the saucepan of rice on the stove. Then Henry and I dived overboard again; we looked in vain for something worth eating—the parrot-fish were practically nibbling our flippers. We took no notice of them. They then started their antics a couple of feet away from our harpoons. Still we turned up our noses. We wanted to get our teeth into anything that was not parrot: we were *completely fed-up* with parrot. We would willingly eat a moray eel, covered in spines, even raw. We would eat anything at all, so long as it was not parrot.

In the end, we had to resign ourselves to parrot after all. Work is all very well, but still you have to eat. And six fools of parrots were spitted, with rage.

The same scene would be repeated about five in the afternoon, dinner being equally as important as lunch. After all, on an island abounding in fish we were not going to open a tin to get a meal.

This game lasted for the whole month *Marie-Thérèse II* spent on the quay, and even during the week following her return to the water, for, unhappily the mackerel had put out to sea.

*

The days passed in St. Helena's characteristic serenity. Then came Christmas, a Christmas that was at once quiet and gay, as all Christmases are necessarily in this corner of the world.

After Christmas came a big event: the *Jeanne d'Arc* and *La Grandière* put in to spend three days in the roadstead: three days of celebration for the St. Helenians, and three profitable days, too, for the isolated island.

St. Helena used formerly to be frequented by ships rounding the Cape, but since the Suez Canal offered a shorter and less costly route, they have ceased to call.

In these days the island's economy is governed first by the price of flax on the world market, and secondly by the ships that choose to put in. Since the price of flax is low and very few ships call, life on St. Helena is unhurried and lonely, but government subsidies, the philosophical attitude of the inhabitants, and the tropical sun ensure freedom from care.

The visit of the *Jeanne* and *La Grandière* was accordingly a godsend. Quantities of souvenirs were sold: necklaces, shell-work, water-colours, lace napkins and table-mats, etc. All the cars were converted into taxis and drove the crews along the islands roads (which are first-class) and for three days there was a completely new atmosphere on St. Helena.

As ill-luck would have it, however, the rain coincided with the visit: a fine, penetrating rain which began on the day the two training ships arrived, and stopped, miraculously, the very day they left.

I can still hear, and remember with a pang, the remark of one of *Jeanne's* officers: 'Napoleon didn't die: the English murdered him by shutting him up in this hell of rain and drizzle.'

When I think of the delightful climate that prevails here, the air dry and fresh, free from storms and squalls, except on the very rare occasions when for some incomprehensible reasons, the local gods wear a frown, then I say to myself, oh no—Napoleon was not murdered, not, at any rate, by the climate of St. Helena.

Meeting my seafaring fellow-countrymen, and enjoying their warm hospitality, made the visit of *Jeanne* and *La Grandière* three days of real gaiety: the caulking could well wait until later.

The midshipmen were uncommonly interested in this little sister perched on the quayside, and they were frequent visitors to my cabin, sitting on the bunks with big mugs of coffee in their hands and puffing the good old *Gauloises* whose taste I had almost forgotten.

As for the wardroom officers, while they were certainly interested in *Marie-Thérèse II,* most of their interest was in the combined man-boat entity; and it was expressed in a practical and unmistakable way.

'Come and lunch on board today,' they invited me. 'We'll take you with us now. Anyway, you're welcome in the wardroom any time you please. Bring your navigation tables. You seem to have some trouble understanding the method you're using, and we can have a look at them together.' (We had, naturally enough, been discussing navigation in my cabin.)

It was a most agreeable lunch, a heart-warming example of true French gaiety. I was deeply moved at finding myself straight back in France, a few hundred yards off a little British island in the middle of the Atlantic.

The navigation lessons went splendidly. I was, moreover, ready to get the full benefit of them and at last to understand (none too soon, indeed) how to work out Neufville's mysterious diagrams.

They also explained Dieumegard for me. This reminded me somewhat of the way in which we replaced a strake in *Marie-Thérèse II.* I was supported by two of *La Grandière's* officers, who pushed me quietly along, firmly held, just as though I were the silent plank, and nailed me in position as we progressed. In a few minutes, the plank was neatly in position again: and I have never ceased to be grateful to the officers in *La Grandière.*

'Cadets,' my obliging new friends were at pains to point out to me, 'are not allowed to use this method. You see, it would be too easy! When they have a couple of rings they can do what they like, but until then they have to do it the school way.

'Have you everything you need in the way of charts?'

'Yes—or practically so.'

'Still, we may as well have a look together.'

After we had this look together, it was unanimously decided that I could do with being better equipped, and I spent a day tracing charts with the help of a petty officer, the most obliging fellow you could wish for. And, as though by happy chance, he had duplicates of some charts which he begged me to accept without further ado.

Chart-wise, I was now ready for anything—if one can use an expression which has no place in the seaman's vocabulary; for in a small sailing vessel one can never speak of being 'ready'. To be 'ready' one would have to spend one's life in harbour and would in the end have to build a bigger boat to hold all the equipment.

Dr. Aury, the *Jeanne's* senior medical officer, a man with a passion for scientific research, personally saw to making good some deplorable shortcomings in *Marie-Thérèse II*'s safety equipment and her skipper's knowledge He is a friend of Bombard, and deeply interested in anything that concerns survival at sea.

We spent two hours together in his cabin, and I came out with valuable notes about the main principles for saving my worthless life, if some accident should consign me to the sea more rapidly than anticipated. Among other things, I learnt that one must not eat coloured plankton because it contains the dangerous poison curare, which paralyzes the nervous system.

After the *Jeanne* and *La Grandière* had sailed, we finished the caulking. We had then only to apply hot pitch to the seams and give her two coats of anti-fouling before returning her to the water.

Then Henry sailed. Our call had lasted long enough. We were to meet again at Ascension Island or Trinidad, if not in hell.

Soon *Wanda's* twin staysails were out of sight, driving the little vessel towards new and even more distant shores.

Two days later, *Marie-Thérèse II* was back in her own element, just in time to avoid another month on the quay; for the day after she had been lowered from the wire cable the sea began to get up. Although there were none of the notorious breakers of which the *Sailing Directions* speak, the seas would have been too heavy to risk returning her to the water, so close to the adjacent rocks.

Alas, everything was still not perfect. An hour later I heard the glug-glug of water in the hold, the noise so dreaded by every sailor. The water was already up to the floor of the cabin. Was the caulking defective? Impossible, because I had put a lot of time into it and the job had been really well done. Was it the frames drying and causing the strakes to open up slightly? That might be more likely, but I had re-stopped all the fissures in the hull. So what could it be?

I spent the night pumping every hour. But I had been able to locate one large leak inboard, behind a frame.

At dawn I put on my diving goggles and went down to inspect the hull. It took me a good hour's search to discover the cause of the leak.

If you have any compassion, reader, I beg you not to read what follows—turn over the page—it is too embarrassing. I had simply forgotten to drive a nail into a hole I had bored to receive it. At any rate, it was fortunate that I found what the trouble was. And incidentally, it was by rubbing my head against the suspect area that I felt the sucking of my hair. Thank God for the age-old wisdom of the East!

With a screwdriver and a strand of caulking cotton, I made it watertight, and then applied my clay-cement-and-plaster mixture so that the borers should not penetrate the cotton as a preliminary to attacking the timber.

I then carried out a final underwater inspection of the hull. It was as I feared. In spite of the serving and all our other precautions, there were three places where the wire-rope slings used to lift the boat and return her to the water had damaged the anti-fouling.

I drove some copper pegs half-way into the parts that had been stripped and applied the familiar mixture. The hull was now safe from worm.

As for the leak, it ceased to be a serious problem. The big one, at least, was cured. A little water, it is true, did make its way in through other cracks in the hull, but this is no more than one would expect when a boat has been high and dry for six weeks: particularly in so dry an atmosphere as that of St. Helena.

The sack of sawdust was then stowed on deck, and with a few tins of the precious remedy not a drop of water found its way into my boat.

Everything was then ready for my next stage, to Ascension Island; but I wanted to get to know St. Helena better, for I had been so busy with my repairs during my stay that I had seen little of the island. My friend Dr. Ocorski, the government-employed doctor, accordingly took me with him for some days, as he made his rounds in the interior: a countryside of green vegetation, flowers and fragrance. It is astonishing how the landscape changes with the altitude. On the plateau everything, in spite of the low rainfall, is green. The plants contrive to absorb water through their leaves and transmit it to their roots; and then, through the lowest tendrils, it comes into contact with the mineral salts that supply the plant with food. The salts are dissolved and then rise up with the sap towards the sunlight.

My friends the Ocorskis had a record-player, some good records and comfortable armchairs in which to listen to them. It made me think of what I still lacked to make me completely 'at home' on board: a small record-player (battery-operated, if such exist) that I could hang in gimbals with a good collection of L.P.'s. This is what I would aim at next time, in Venezuela—or anywhere, for that matter.

I thought too, of Joyce's last letter, and my answer: 'O.K.—meet you in Trinidad.'

And so, on the eve of my sailing, I felt completely at peace with the world.

CHAPTER 9

St Helena
to Ascension Island:
700 miles

It was January 22nd, 1958, and the trades were blowing gently. Not that I complained about the lightness of the wind, because I far prefer to put out to sea in fine weather, and from that point of view this day was ideal. Nevertheless, I felt one regret—it was the word which I had not had the courage to say before I left Cape Town. For the first time since I had been sailing, I experienced a feeling of guilt; and it tended to spoil the luminosity of this day, which, to make it perfect, needed only the company of another human being, dear to me and unafraid of this type of existence.

For the first time, too, I was feeling alone at sea. Once the anchor had been weighed, I had never had this sense of solitude. I had sometimes known it on land, but never at sea.

'Pull yourself together,' a voice told me. 'The die is cast, and you are committed. Have you not, anyway, arranged to meet her in Trinidad? How foolish of you to be down in the dumps on such a glorious day.'

Marie-Thérèse II was indeed being an angel. She did not generally speak to me so frankly and kindly. Perhaps she had developed a more conciliatory frame of mind since I had made such a special effort for her on the quay at St. Helena.

Three hours after my sailing, the island was only a blur to the south-east: a thin veil of mist, indistinguishable from land, which seems permanently present in this latitude, had interposed between the island and my boat. I was back to my cruising routine. The twin staysails were set as soon as I was far enough from the land for the wind to have become more regular. There was no doubt about it: *Marie-Thérèse II* was in a very good temper—not a word of reproach for my omission to fit blocks

185

to the ends of the booms, which would have enabled me to set my two extra jibs, down to water level, as in Henry's system.

The Marin Marie self-steering gear was working wonderfully, as usual. How is it that it can work in so light a wind? It may be as a result of Henry's idea: a rudder compensated by an extension of the lower part of the blade, forward of the stock.

I glanced into the hold: no water, which meant that the sawdust had been effective. Life was good, after all, and peace soon repossessed the little floating world that was sailing on a north-westerly heading towards another little world, Ascension Island. However, unless the gods who rule the seas wake up from their sleep, it will be a month before I drop anchor again among the other boats lying off the beach of Ascension.

The sea, however, was still fast asleep, and the trade wind was hardly more wakeful. At the most, there was just a slight increase in the rhythm of its breathing during the first half of the night.

The mysteries of the ocean are most strange. You would think that an invisible frontier divided the part that lies to the south of St. Helena from that which lies immediately to the north. Between Cape Town and St. Helena I was sailing under a completely overcast sky over a leaden sea, without fish and with no birds except petrels and a few occasional albatross.

Here, only a little further north, flying fish appeared on the very first day after my sailing. Their wings flashing in the bright warm sunshine, they flew at first in scattered groups, and some days later in compact shoals of a hundred silver bodies, under an open sky of a deep tropical blue which seems to give the sea a sort of intimate life, peaceful and relaxing.

The domain of the flying fish is shared by the dolphins, friends of man and of boats. Trustful and gay, they play with a sailing vessel just like a gang of laughing high-spirited children. They compete to see who can spin the most times before belly-flopping onto the water again with a great splash. The exhibition lasts for between five and twenty minutes. I could see them coming from a distance, in great leaps, intercepting our course. When level with the boat, they change direction and play follow-my-leader, gambolling just like children who have found a fascinating new toy. Then, when the game is over, the whole gang returns to its initial course, to reappear sometimes during the night.

This first visit from the dolphins made me think with shame of the harpoons which Henry and I had made before we left Cape Town: murderous great contraptions, specially designed for dolphins. And I thought of our conversation about them:

'So your thick head has at any rate grasped the fact,' he said, 'that tinned food means a good spell of work, and that means prostituting ourselves in harbour. So, we might as well be guilty of a slight transgression by knocking off an occasional dolphin and thus do our best to avoid the prostitution of having to work in the next port. Doesn't a couple of hundred pounds of grub drying in the shrouds make your mouth water? And what's more, didn't the God who made the sky and the sea tell our first parents that all living creatures were there to serve them?'

'I quite agree, Henry, but there's something different about dolphins. They're so friendly and companionable. I don't know how I'd have stuck the monsoon in the Indian Ocean without them. One day perhaps you'll understand what I'm trying to get into that bone-head of yours.'

'You stupid French bastard! Why don't you be honest and admit they were too big for you? You'll never make me believe that you'd hesitate to kill a common dolphin: one only has to look at you, and besides, you're always starving: especially in the Indian Ocean, where all you had was rice and canned sardines.'

And yet—when I met Henry on Ascension Island, the subject was to come up again.

'Did you see any dolphins, Henry?' I asked him, 'or did they keep a respectful distance from your lousy boat?'

'Of course I did: lots of them. But what surprises me is that they visited your boat as well, because dolphins like speed!' (Henry had had the advantage of a better wind, and had made the passage in seven days, whereas I had taken nearly nine.)

'How did they taste?'

'Didn't try them—too friendly!'

*

On January 26th, we had covered 280 miles, on a line which should have placed us some fifty miles to the east of Ascension, under the influence of the westerly current which, according to the *Sailing Directions* and in particular, the *Pilot Charts*, prevails in these waters. I had no trouble in working out my daily position, for the sun was visible all day. There was only the same light mist still obscuring it at sunrise and sunset.

Like someone who has just learnt a clever card trick and insists on doing it again every couple of minutes, so delighted is he at always getting it right, the sun no sooner appeared than I started indefatigably bombarding it with my sextant. I would then return to my cabin and, handling Neufville's admirable tables with an increasingly offhand confidence, draw altitude lines all day long; these lost their miraculous aspect as the first day's timid gropings were gradually replaced by the completely automatic reaction of my hands turning the pages without hesitation, to lay the stub of pencil on the exact spot which gave me both an altitude and an azimuth. When I think of the time it took me for the penny to drop!

The tropical birds were arriving. It began with the morning visit of two bo'sun-birds, one of the most familiar species I know, after the sea-swallows of the Cargados-Carajos.

After a few turns round the boat, they try to settle on the masthead. 'Too much movement up there, my friends,' I tell them. 'Others have tried that and failed.' You need to have sampled a masthead perch to realize how much it rocks even in the best of weather.

Another two or three turns around the boat, followed by a farewell skimming dive, and my two bo'sun-birds are off again for St. Helena. I shall see no more of them until my next call.

Although the south Atlantic bo'sun-birds resemble those of the Indian Ocean in all respects, they do not seem to me to be such great travellers as their counterparts. The latter accompanied *Marie-Thérèse* for over two months, from north of Sumatra to the Chagos.

Other birds, however, came to replace the two deserters. These were the little, noisy wideawakes, who came in groups of twenty or more, creating enough din to wake the dead. Their curiosity satisfied, they withdrew to a distance, screaming and screeching, making me think of the Chinese proverb to the effect that the smallest birds make the most noise.

The gannets, again, which are so vocal around Cape Town, are much quieter here; you might even say completely silent. 'The fishing, I suppose, is not so good between St. Helena and Ascension as it is off the Cape; and that's why,' I suggested to the gannets, 'you're so stand-offish and won't come and play with me! Off to Cape Town with you, where you'll find all the sardines you can eat. Or are you frightened of long journeys? Ah, I understand! You don't like the cold. Neither do I, which shows that we have something in common.' (I have always hoped that hell will not turn out to be icy-cold. They tell me that it's hot, but I'm not so sure, and I can't say I really trust them.)

However, this is no time for such irreligious talk, when everything around me is so agreeable, apart from the wind, of course, which too often goes to sleep. Nothing unhappily, is ever really perfect, and when, as today, things are to all intents and purposes perfect, one nevertheless finds some way of criticizing the gods who are befriending us.

And to make it quite plain to me that everything is perfect but nothing is really perfect, the same gods are whispering in my ear that this is an ideal day for a spell at the truck of the mainmast: that I would be able, for example, to enjoy the view, always new and always equally moving, of the loveliest boat in the world, seen from above, drawing behind her, with no-one at the helm, her three-knot wake on the calm waters of the Atlantic. For my boat is to me the loveliest boat in the world, just as *Wanda* is to Henry and *Kurun* to Jacques-Yves Le Toumelin.

So here I am at the top of the mast. Alas, alas, you cursed gods! Could you not have waited until the Caribbean before dealing me this cruel blow? There is rot in the masthead! I am past swearing, I am past blaspheming. I am, quite simply and plainly, utterly and completely *sick* of it, and I feel this ghastly nausea right deep down in my guts. I almost wish I could have the relief of bursting into tears. But no: here I am, at the top of the mainmast, limp, disgusted and on the point of vomiting.

Slowly, then, I come down, with my two arms clasping this rotten mast; go into the cabin, and throw myself down on the bunk. If only Joyce were here, she would know what to say to put new heart into me. She would say, for example, 'Come on, it's not so serious as all that. In fact it's even a bit of luck, because you're always saying that *Marie-Thérèse II* carries too little sail. We'll find a good mast, the two of us, in the West Indies, taller, and brand new' (for a song, of course), 'and then I'll help you cut out and sew a lovely new sail for it to carry. It's quite simple, you see, isn't it?'

But now I am feeling all alone, terribly alone, looking at this mast which is pointing to the sky and seems to be saying to me, 'It serves you right, chum; how often have you thought about my care and maintenance? Once, when you made me, and soaked me in linseed oil, and then once again before we left Mauritius and you slapped a coat of cheap paint on me. And since then? Not a thought, not one! And yet, haven't you noticed all these cracks that are ruining me. When you were in harbour, you were careful to impregnate the deck and hull of your boat with salt, but not for a moment did it occur to you to spare a little time for me and treat me with linseed oil every six months to save me from rot. What has happened serves you right.'

Whether it is my own fault or not, I am still fed up—and even more so today than when I discovered the rot in my hull at Cape Town. For suddenly an awful feeling strikes at my heart: *I no longer have confidence in my boat.*

I was now beginning to realize how dearly I should have to pay for the hastiness of my work on Mauritius, and that the two years I had spent slaving in South Africa in order later to be able to devote myself to what really mattered to me, had all been wasted. There would never, I saw, be any real freedom in the free life of which I had dreamed: not, at any rate, with this boat, not when I had to spend my time in every harbour in large-scale repair work, in order to keep alive a hulk that was gradually but inexorably on her way to join the dead crabs in their final resting place.

This was to be a landmark in my life. For I was already thinking of my next boat: a really strongly built craft, carefully protected from rot, without a blemish: a boat that I would really love, and that would not be a constant worry to me.

I remembered an idea suggested to me on Mauritius by Bardiaux: a stainless steel boat. And in my mind I was already drawing up the plans for it. It would be thirty to thirty-five feet overall length, with watertight compartments, water-tanks and provision-lockers welded directly to the hull, shallow draught, to enable me to sail practically anywhere, and with sufficient ballast in the keel to ensure that she righted herself if a breaking sea should capsize her.

Yes, what I needed was a boat built once and for all, at the cost of prodigies of work, heroic privations and an expenditure of energy that would leave me completely exhausted when the work was done. The result, however, would be a floating home that would last for the rest of my life, that would require the minimum of maintenance—practically none—and would so allow me to devote myself more wholeheartedly to whatever I liked doing, instead of being obliged to prostitute myself as soon as I put into harbour.

It is natural enough that a sailor should reserve some part of his time for the finest boat in the world, and, from the spiritual and emotional point of view, it is even essential. For a boat is not simply the end product of so many hours' work in building; in the integration of hull, rigging and sails, there exists something more than wood, wire-rope and canvas. A boat has a personality and even (or is this going too far?) a soul. Every sailor is conscious of this soul—he has only to look at his boat, whether sleeping peacefully on her mooring in the shelter of a quiet harbour, or under sail and tracing her route towards the horizon.

A stainless steel boat: practically no maintenance or expense, once launched, and with sails of synthetic fibre. No topsides painting, and, maybe, no anti-fouling even. There is such a vessel, the *Seven Seas,* some thirty-five feet, based on the design of Harry Pidgeon's *Islander,* i.e. hard-chine bilge.

Her owner, an American, had lived for some weeks with a friend of mine in Cape Town during his stay in South Africa. He was extremely satisfied, it would seem, with the boat; it had given him no trouble at all during his world-cruise, partly single-handed and partly accompanied by his wife.

He did, however, say this to my Cape Town friend Moekli: 'I rather think that it'll be a long time before I see another stainless steel boat sailing. It would be terribly expensive to build—and I know what I'm talking about.'

Even so, I could not stop myself from dreaming of such a boat: dreams, at any rate, cost nothing and are some consolation for a rotting mast and a boat that is beginning to disintegrate.

There might, perhaps, be a compromise solution—a wooden boat, with a complete fibreglass skin, hull, deck, and cabin; but it would be better to wait a few years until the experts have brought out a completely reliable product, without the tendency to develop cracks, as has sometimes, unfortunately, occurred. Even so, there are, apparently, methods of manufacture that have given faultless results. It is still expensive, no doubt, but if what you get is really perfect, then I believe it is well worth the extra cost. It means no more painting, no more topsides maintenance, and, if you are a bit short of money, you might even dispense with anti-fouling. It would be enough to give the bottom a good scraping, followed by a scrub, just before you leave, and then you could sail without more ado, provided you repeated the operation from time to time at sea.

You might think that this is hardly a serious suggestion, but it is nevertheless perfectly feasible. I have done it often enough to *Marie-Thérèse* in the Indian Ocean, in order to get rid of the countless goose-barnacles which are quite undeterred by anti-fouling paint. As for barnacles and other marine crustacea which are the bane of habours and moorings in the tropics, they hardly ever attach themselves to the hull in the open sea. So along as the boat is moving they present no problem.

*

Marie-Thérèse II was still sailing quietly and peacefully.

On January 27th, I saw my first pilot-fish. I have no idea where it came from, but it seems to be happy in the company of its big sister, swimming a few inches ahead of her stem. Is it the tropical waters extending their welcome? It must be so, because we have now reached them: a golden sun, a sea that has become much warmer since St. Helena, and, to crown all, my striped pilot-fish, no longer than a pocket-comb, to show me the way: and this he has no trouble in doing, for we are not making more than three knots.

I know what my pilots live on: but how do they sleep? I had often wondered about this in the Indian Ocean, when they had accompanied *Marie-Thérèse* for over two months, without ever being absent at reveille.

It was when I was later reading Bernicot, I believe, that I thought I had found the answer to this question, which all who have spent some time sailing in tropical waters have asked themselves. Bernicot, however, if I remember rightly, was speaking of doradoes. It was full moon that night, and from *Anahita*'s deck he could distinguish a white shape, motionless in the water, lying against the hull. Later the dorado (for Bernicot had identified it as such) was left astern, as his boat sailed on at a speed of some knots.

Several times in the course of half a minute *Anahita* overtook a sleeping dorado, lying on its side. It was the same fish as had woken up after being left behind by the boat and had darted after her to regain its position at the bows; there it would go back to sleep, lying alongside and safely protected by its prettily named big sister from the possible rapacity of a marauding shark.

As the moon was nearly full that day I decided that I would try to see my pilot sleeping alongside: not, you may be sure, in order to play a dirty trick on him—for I would never treat a friend so—but simply to find him and watch him.

When night came, I strained my eyes in an attempt to pick out my fellow-traveller. I could see nothing at all, which was not surprising, since he might well be there without my being able to distinguish him from the flecks of foam thrown up by the stem.

Just in case, I had taken the harpoon: not for my little pilot, but you never know—I might see a white shape, a yard long, lying flat on the surface of the water, neither pilot nor dorado.

Finally, I made my way to the bowsprit with my rubber-cased electric torch and shone it on the bow-wave.

'No sleep, little fellow? Not tired? Don't you want a little nap? Nothing you want?'—for there he was, in the place he had picked out when he arrived that day, sheltered by the bow-wave.

It was, perhaps, too early for him to go to sleep, and I thought it would be interesting to check this: but as I was able to find out later that night, and again on the following nights, my pilot had his own sleeping-technique. Day and night, he was always in the same place, adjusting his speed to that of *Marie-Thérèse II*.

He must obviously, I thought, sleep at some time, for, each in its own way, all living creatures sleep, the period of sleep varying from several months in a hole scooped out of the snow, for the marmot, down to a few seconds for the rabbit and the dorado.

How much sleep, then, do the pilot-fish need? A fraction of a second every fraction of a second? If they keep at it, they could put in twelve hours sleep a day, and still be awake for the whole twenty-four hours—and I know one person who would like to do the same!

On January 30th we had covered practically the whole distance from St. Helena to Ascension Island. It was a fine day, with a calm sea and blue sky. The wind had been strengthening a little for some days and my noon fix that day gave me a position some fifty miles from Ascension.

Providing, of course, that my calculations were accurate (and in such fine weather you would be hard put to it to make a mistake) I should see the top of Green Mountain appear before sundown. And, as usual, the sun set without a vestige of land.

The island finally appeared, all at once, at 11 p.m., like a child playing peep-bo: *Marie-Thérèse II* was hove-to (mainsail sheeted home, staysail balancing it, and helm a-lee) to wait for daylight, for

G

there is no lighthouse here (any more than on St. Helena). Moreover, an extensive sandbank, with underwater rocks set in it like huge teeth, runs along the shore some hundreds of yards west of the normal anchorage.

At about four in the morning, drift and a fairly gentle current had brought us some miles closer and we were under way again in an almost dead calm. It is always the same: from one continent to another you average eighty miles a day and complain at not getting on faster, and then it takes hours and hours to cover the remaining five or six miles before you can drop your anchor—as I did now under the amused gaze of Henry.

'Hi! bloody Frenchman! How many days from St. Helena?'

'Eight and a half, you tramp!'

'Call it nine?'

'Fair enough. How about yourself?'

'Seven, you lazy bastard. What kept you so long out there?'

'No wind. How did you find it?'

'Much the same as you, but *Wanda* doesn't believe in hanging about.'

'So you say. We'll see how it goes on the next leg.'

'Cheer up! *Phoenix* took fifteen days between Cape Town and St. Helena, and then another ten from St. Helena to Ascension.'

'What are the locals like?'

'Pretty good: but they're all madly busy on this island, the Americans with their guided missiles and the Cable and Wireless people with their telegrams. And I rather think the Cable people are a bit suspicious of passing yachts—they must have seen plenty of bums in their time. But come on board and have some breakfast; I speared a few extra fish when I saw you arrive.'

'Mackerel?'

'No—not a mackerel to be seen. These are black, and go about in big compact shoals; they clean the hull, eating everything that has managed to cling to it, sea-weeds and shell-fish. And I warn you, they don't mind *what* they eat.'

'Well—neither do we!'

CHAPTER 10

Ascension Island
a lunar port of call

What is peculiar to Ascension Island and distinguishes it from the majority of its tropical sisters, is the incredible dryness that prevails on its coastline. The only green vegetation to be seen is on the summit of Green Mountain, the island's highest point. All the rest is rocky, but in a way that goes beyond anything you could imagine. Wherever you look you see an expanse that is broken up by huge round stones, spreading out in every direction, in the valleys, along the roads and on the hillsides. There is not a blade of grass, not even a vestige of growth to give evidence of a past vegetable life: just stone, nothing but stone—a sight that makes you want to leave it as quickly as you possible can.

To the left and right of the jetty, however, in front of Cable and Wireless's little group of buildings, there is a very large beach of white sand. This faces the anchorage, and seems to invite the traveller to stay for a little while, long enough to get to know the place. There is another voice which offers the same wise counsel, that of the countless wideawakes, as noisy as they are small, whose eggs must undoubtedly cover a good stretch of ground, to judge from the constant racket to the west of the anchorage.

Henry had formed the same impression when he arrived, but had nevertheless spent a week doing odd jobs in his cabin. 'Nothing of interest in this dump,' he told me, 'apart from Green Mountain, perhaps. I'd have liked to go for a walk there but it was boring to go alone: do you like walking?'

'In a tropical forest I do—but I'm not so keen on walking over rocks, particularly if I'm climbing, too.'

We finally decided that we would walk up Green Mountain together the next day, a ten-mile uphill scramble, and that on the way back we would pay a courtesy visit to the wideawakes' 'reservation' with a four-gallon canister to collect eggs.

Then with 'operation ovum' fixed, we would go and say hullo to the turtles, who at that time of the year lay their eggs on the beach—a useful saving of our canned food.

'Meanwhile,' I told Henry, 'come on shore; and don't forget your passport. Mr. Harrison, the manager of Cable and Wireless, acts as governor of the island as well and he will ask you to hand it over to him until we leave.'

'Why should he keep them, instead of just checking them and giving them back straight away?'

'I've no idea, but that's how it is. I have the impression that on Ascension they're a little suspicious of types like us.'

'With a mug like yours, you can hardly blame . . .'

'Wait till he sees yours: his worst suspicions will be confirmed!'

*

We launched my little dinghy and went ashore. Making the jetty called for much more elaborate acrobatics than on St. Helena, and it is on such occasions as this that you are glad to possess an ultra-light dinghy, one that you can carry quite easily at arms' length. Once ashore, we lifted it into the jetty, out of reach of the waves.

Mr. Harrison gave us a friendly welcome in his office and immediately asked us home to lunch: very bright and attractive, very homelike. The English know how to live in the wilds as comfortably (or more so) as in their own country. It is indoors that really matters to them. Once you are inside an English colonial home, a curtain seems to exclude everything outside the house, or rather outside the garden.

Another miracle: although every drop of fresh water on the island has to be carefully rationed, the little English colony still contrives to keep a fresh green garden around each house.

As it turned out, the unflattering remarks that Henry and I had just been making about one another's appearance were certainly without much foundation, for the Harrisons seemed pleased to see us. Like most of the Cable and Wireless personnel, they belonged to a nomad clan and seldom stayed more than two or three years in the same place.

They had already had a spell on Ascension eighteen years earlier, and it was there that the ravishing young lady (their daughter) was born, who sat between Henry and me.

'When we were here before,' Mr. Harrison told us, 'there was very little green because of the wild goats who ate up every scrap.' (I looked at Henry, who was eating away steadily.) 'However, during the war, the British and American troops stationed here found a consolation for their loneliness in hunting goats; and they must have wiped them out completely, because nobody has seen any for years —a blessing for the vegetation, which is spreading considerably on the slopes of Green Mountain. We have noticed this since we came back recently. Tomorrow I have to make a tour of inspection with my wife and daughter. Would you like to come with us?'

I put up my hand, only too happy to have the opportunity of seeing this curious place at closer quarters without having to pay for my curiosity with a ten-mile climb on foot and the same distance coming down, and not a vestige of shade during the whole outing.

Henry was delighted at the kind invitation, but he seemed to be sorry at missing his twenty-mile tramp in the sun. I was teasing him about this when Mr. Harrison continued, 'Don't worry about that; you'll get some walking, because even if the jeep can get to the top, or nearly there, there will still be a good few miles to cover on foot for my inspection.'

We then broached the question of turtles. Ascension Island is, in fact, well known for the number of sea-turtles which come there to lay the eggs on the beaches. They seem even to have very largely deserted St. Helena, which is not so safe for them because of its relatively large population. As everywhere where red meat is scarce, the inhabitants would not miss the opportunity of rolling one of the enormous females onto its back before converting it into steaks for fifty people, with second helpings for the greedy.

Ascension, on the other hand, has always been a desert or practically a desert island, inhabited only by the twenty or thirty Cable and Wireless staff and a handful of St. Helenians employed by the company. And this means that the turtles can rely on being able to return to the water without interference.

With the establishment of the American base things might have changed. But the Americans got their frozen meat by ship, if not by air, and the turtles were left in peace—the more so in that to kill a turtle you have to have permission from the governor—in this case Mr. Harrison.

Henry, who had arrived a week earlier than I, and heard about the reluctance with which permission was, on rare occasions, granted, had advised me to be extremely diplomatic.

He was quite right. The subject was no sooner mentioned, than Mr. Harrison's face clouded. Henry and I retreated as one man: 'Eat turtle! Good heavens no! We did eat it once on St. Helena, just to satisfy our host,' we admitted shamelessly. 'Just think of it—some hours after the flesh of the poor creature had been cut up, you could still see it moving on the kitchen table! It was heartbreaking.' (I was thinking to myself of the loads of 50 to 150 turtles that I used to send over every month to Mauritius and the wonderful meals I had of the delicious meat when I was Raphael Fishing's manager on the Cargados-Carajos.) We quickly added, 'It's the eggs we'd like to sample. We're told they're excellent.'

Mr. Harrison recovered his good humour. 'Excellent is hardly the word. Let's say they're eatable' (I know from experience that turtle eggs are revolting, and I'm not fastidious) 'but if you want to try, go ahead and help yourselves. The best way to get them would be to be on the spot when they're laying, in a few days time, so that you'll have the advantage of the full moon.' (Turtles lay at night on the beaches at any time, irrespective of the moon, but you need moonlight to pick them out.)

Later, Henry said to me, 'You see, Bernard, that this man of iron is basically good and kind. From what I've heard, he loves and respects every living creature. Didn't you notice his tone when he was telling us about massacring the wild goats when the British and Americans were stationed here? I'm sure he'd never had allowed such slaughter had he been here at the time. Goats have a right to live even if they do make inroads on the vegetation.'

After settling the turtle question (as Mr. Harrison believed at any rate, though he did not know us very well) we went on to coffee, and the conversation, as it happened, turned to the group of ornithologists sent to Ascension by some British organization to study the different varieties of sea-birds.

The wideawakes are the most numerous of the island's winged population. Small (but highly vocal), they scream night and day, in the air, on their nests, and even, I do believe, in their sleep. They are not afraid of man and to liberate an egg you often have to take it from under a noisy female.

Unlike turtle eggs, the wideawakes' eggs are excellent, in spite of a slightly fishy after-taste: but what is more important, and was irresistible from our point of view, there are infinite numbers of them.

Mr. Harrison came to see us, but this time with a kindly smile: 'I shall let you each have a permit,' he told us, 'to collect four dozen eggs' (you have to have one for birds' eggs also). 'It's not many, but the eggs don't keep, and it would be waste to take too many.'

'Moreover,' he added, 'the St. Helenians who come here under contract are only allowed to send two dozen eggs each to their families when the regular ship calls. Without this rule, which I admit is rather strict, the wideawakes would establish themselves somewhere else. So you'll understand that to allow you to take more eggs could cause jealousy among the contract labourers. And in any case, as I told you, there's no point in doing so because the eggs don't keep.'

If there is one thing that Henry and I really do know it is that eggs keep fresh for at least six weeks if you take the precaution of coating them with some fatty substance, to fill up the pores of the shell. There are many other methods, some of which enable you to keep eggs for months on end. The Chinese have even contrived to keep ducks' eggs for some years, but I must confess that the result is not the height of palatability. Those who have lived in Asia and know the 'century eggs' will certainly agree with me.

Apart from these technical considerations, the point was that we two evil-doers were quick to remember the teaching of the Bible when it suited us. Did not the Lord of Heaven and Earth tell our first ancestor that everything that swims, flies or walks on four feet belonged to him and to his posterity? The neighbour's fowl, it is true, belong to the neighbour and not to evil-doers. On the other hand, turtles and sea-birds which spend the greatest part of their lives at sea, in waters that belong to nobody (until further orders), are thereby common property.

And if this question seemed settled to Mr. Harrison, it was by no means so to Henry and me. He looked at it from the point of view of an administrator responsible for the orderly running of the island he was in charge of, while we two saw it from that of sea-rovers, citizens of the world, whose chief concern was to live—and, to live, you have to eat (even though some misery-mongers maintain that all you have to do is to work), and eat without bothering too much about meaningless laws that they took no notice of: not,

I may add, that we thought it necessary to say so in so many words.

As you see, there was complete good faith on both sides. That was the great thing, from the moral angle. As for the more practical side of the matter, the great thing centred on one point— we must leave Ascension with a half-turtle and some hundreds of eggs in each of our boats without our host's knowledge. And so everyone would be happy.

Anyone who thinks we were being cynical should put himself in our place: and if Mr. Harrison should chance to read this, I hope he will forgive us. In any case, could he have any quarrel with two fellows who have shown themselves to be so fundamentally honest —with themselves?

That same evening, while we were dining with 'black-fish' as our main dish (a change from the parrot-fish of St. Helena, but not so good), we drew up the main outlines of the plan for operation bird's-egg-and-turtle. We would have to wait until the day before leaving in order to get back our passports. We would then each fill a four-gallon canister with eggs and bring it back at dusk. Once we had the eggs on board, we would need a few hours to coat them with vaseline and pack them carefully in cardboard boxes. (Vaseline does not give the eggs an unpleasant taste, as grease would.)

Then would come our visit to the turtles. This second operation would be more trickly. We would have to spot the turtle (not difficult in moonlight) and then slip a double sling around its forefeet. The slings would be hitched to a 15-yard line which would be used to lead the turtle to the boat, as in the method used by the fishermen in the Cargados-Carajos.

It is astonishing with what docility a three-to-four-hundred-pound turtle will allow itself to be towed on a line behind a dinghy once it is in the water, while on the beach the same animal would pull several men without difficulty, at the same time throwing up sand into their faces with a violence that could cost them an eye.

The only at all serious difficulty would be getting through the line of surf which breaks directly onto the beach, in a dinghy with a turtle in tow. With a little luck, and one or two attempts, we thought we might manage this without too much cursing and swearing.

Moreover, the sea was not running strongly just then.

The next morning, we were in good time for our appointment at the Harrisons, and set out for Green Mountain, in a dry and desolate landscape. I wondered how anyone could bear to spend three years on end in such surroundings.

However, it was not long before I understood. As the jeep approached the top, a new countryside was gradually disclosed as one looked down, a landscape one would have been happy to gaze at from sunrise to sunset. It was a sight that I could never have imagined and which, nevertheless, I had already seen somewhere. What I was looking at, I had already seen when looking at the moon through the powerful watch binoculars in the sloop *Gazelle*, when I was doing my naval service. Then, I had seen just the same craters, the same shadows, the same volcanic landscape, infinitely desolate and infinitely beautiful, of another desert world, divided from our own by a distance which at that time only our dreams could span.

Faced with this new revelation, I could not refrain from thinking of the stupidity of the life I was leading. I realized, more forcefully than ever, how completely I was enslaved to my boat, whereas I ought to be the master of my life. I was surprised to find myself already modifying in my mind the dimensions of my future stainless steel boat (or my wooden boat, with fibreglass skin, for one should not ask for too much): it would have to be as small as possible, while at the same time being as big as possible.

As small as possible, in order to limit my bondage to the bare minimum: less maintenance, less expense when I had to replace shrouds, sew a new sail, or repaint. As small as possible, so that it could be hauled out without difficulty and left high and dry for a while if the country was agreeable and one could live there for nothing, or practically nothing (as here, for example).

But at the same time it would have to be as roomy as its limited dimensions would allow, because you need to be able to house plenty of provisions and ship's stores if you want to spend any length of time in peace.

The tragedy of this sort of life (as one must honestly admit) is that after several years on board, one is often pretty fed up with it. At sea (when the weather is not dirty), life is full and you hug it to you to get the full savour of it.

But when you are at anchor—when you are in some marvellous spot (of which there are so many), one which whispers to you, 'Stay here, lad, pitch your tent on the beach or anywhere you please. You are free, and when you have had enough, you may move on without regrets'—it is just then that your boat calls for your attention. For a boat is a weakling, even in the calmest bay. She is afraid of the wind which may knock her down, after smashing the moorings; she is afraid of other boats, who may run into her (as, indeed, happens too often, unfortunately); she is afraid of the tides, which chafe the warps and foul the anchors; she is afraid of rot, so much more a menace in harbour than at sea. In a word, she is one great phobia.

At anchor, then, your boat is a weak creature who has to be constantly protected from every sort of evil. You cannot say to her, 'Wait for me like a good girl, I am off to stay a week, or a month, or a year, with a friend of mine.' Or again, 'I am going to put up a tent on Green Mountain so that I can have my fill of gazing at this lunar valley which I cannot share with you; but I shall be back in a week, and then we'll move on together—unless of course I stay for a month.' Or it might be, 'I am leaving you for an unspecified length of time, because a friend, a traveller for a big firm, has offered me a trip across South Africa in his dormobile: now, be good while I'm away; it may be a long time because I shall have to hitch-hike back. But cheer up: I'll bring you a really nice present when I come home, a nylon staysail or stainless steel shrouds.'

Alas, I cannot say any of these things to *Marie-Thérèse II*. She would die, not understanding the importance of 'conjugal holidays' —something I am beginning to appreciate.

The jeep soon reached the mist-laden area and we were swallowed up in green growth. It is not like a tropical forest, it is true, but bushy, extremely dense, green and damp. It is the humidity in the air, on the high ground, which is absorbed by the leaves, transferred to the roots and converted into sap, as happens on the St. Helena plateaus. The process is more marked here, however, because rain is almost unknown. Even the drinking water comes from the dew which falls at night on the walls of a huge artificial tank built into an extinct volcano, the inner surface of which has been lined with concrete flagstones. The water is collected and stored in a pit dug in the middle and then pumped by a windmill to a cistern from which a pipe-line carries it to the administrative block.

After checking the water-level in the cistern and seeing that the windmill was working correctly (we had left the jeep and had been walking for some hours through the luxuriant vegetation), Mr.

Harrison's inspection-tour led us to an English-type market-garden. Beans, peas, lettuces, radishes, and the whole range of vegetables eaten by the little colony that lives by the sea-shore, are grown in this permanent atmosphere of mist. The cultivator is a pink-checked Englishman, exuding health and good humour, as do the members of his little family; at once isolated and closely-knit they live for their plants and their key-tapping friends, roasting on the stones some miles away.

The jeep then drove slowly down again, stopping now and again so that Henry and I might gaze at leisure on this strange landscape: something that we would probably never see the like of again, unless through an astronomical telescope.

Back at the Harrisons', I told them of my new appreciation of these thousands of uniformly shaped stones stretching out of sight, for I felt ashamed and guilty at having at first used such adjectives as 'desolate', 'monotonous', 'arid' and 'inhuman'.

'In the space of a few hours,' Mr. Harrison told us, 'the landscape could assume another quite different appearance. All this stone, which looks quite dead, is only asleep, for it is full of latent life which is ready to wake at the first downpour. Rain is most unusual here; but when a storm does break, as happened during our previous spell, there is a most astonishing change. Everything, as far as you can see, becomes green. The grass grows at a fantastic rate, insects are born in a few minutes, invade the houses, eat up the vegtation, reproduce themselves, and then, their work done, disappear.

'Between all these stones, countless seeds and larvae are dormant, waiting for the great day. They can wait for years and years. But when heaven sends the rain then for several days there is an explosion of life.'

'Have you any idea,' went on Mrs. Harrison, 'of the intensity of this animal life? Let me tell you what my husband and I witnessed many years ago.

'The Cable and Wireless staff had organized their regular monthly dance. It was that night that the rain decided to come down. And in a matter of minutes swarms of cockchafers had stormed the dance-hall, flying into the room, running across the floor and getting themselves squashed to death in hundreds. It was really an incredible sight. It was no good shutting doors and windows; they came in everywhere, making their way through the tiniest cracks, and in thousands. We had to abandon the hall, only to find that our houses, too, had been taken over by armies of these insects, devouring everything from house-plants to linen.

'But next morning—what a wonderful sight! The whole island was a delicate green, soaking the damp soil and the vegetation in fragrance, and flowers covered the new landscape with countless little splashes of colour.

'Then in a few days it was all gone. First the insects, and then the plants. Nevertheless, they are still there, under those sun-drenched stones, quietly waiting for the miracle of water to allow them, in a few months time, or a year or ten years, to have a new few days in which to bloom. It makes me think of Selma Lagerlöff's story—you know the one, when little Nils finds the town which emerges from the waves once a century, to live intensely for only one night.'

*

During the next two days we did not leave our boats: we were busy with odd jobs in the cabin and on deck. Such work is an integral part of the sailor's life, and I even wonder whether it would not be truer to say that the sailor is an integral part of his boat—rather like the housewife who spends her time clearing up, polishing, and cleaning, only to start again tomorrow.

However, I took advantage of my momentary good intentions to fit blocks to the ends of the twin staysail booms, which would enable me to set the two extra sails.

I carried out another useful (morale-wise, at any rate) piece of work. I climbed to the masthead, wrapped the rotting section of the mast in sacking, and soaked the sacking in creosote, praying aloud that the creosote might thoroughly penetrate the wood and save the part that had not yet been affected.

Every morning, accordingly, I shall climb the mainmast, creosote-bottle in hand: not a great deal of fun, but highly sporting and—revolting. Because I come down from the mast every time covered in creosote, under the amused gaze of Henry and the black-fish.

These black-fish are uncommonly useful, a veritable larder ready to hand. If they move off on a somewhat longer excusion, you have only to summon them by stirring the water with the harpoon-shaft, and they come swarming back in hundreds. A few jabs with the harpoon and dinner ceases to be a problem.

There is another problem which these voracious fish, no bigger than your hand, solve to the satisfaction of all concerned, and with a conscientiousness that is worthy of the highest praise—and that is cleaning the bottom. *Wanda,* after arriving at St. Helena with a great deal of sea-weed below the waterline, was completely free from it two days after dropping anchor off Ascension. And the lighters moored at their buoys boasted astonishingly clean hulls, thanks to these vigilant and ever-hungry fish.

Time drifted by under a warm sun; but the roadstead was beginning to show rather disturbing signs of movement, for the swell from the north had strengthened since the previous night. Henry and I accordingly held a conference on an important subject, 'Operation Eggs'.

To get the eggs back on board, we needed a really moderate sea so that we could put off from the concrete jetty without smashing the lot. Anticipating that the swell would continue to strengthen, we decided to carry out the operation that same night.

Landing was difficult. With sandals and clothes in plastic bags slung around our shoulders, we went ashore in swimming trunks. There was nobody on the jetty to give us a hand up. In one way, this was all to the good, because the quick reactions of a man looking out for himself are generally more effective than the united efforts of a number of willing helpers, all pulling at cross purposes.

With our dinghies safely up on the jetty we had a look around: 'Hum ... with a sea like this,' Henry muttered, 'we may very well have as much as thirty or forty per cent of our eggs broken.'

'We'll manage O.K., Henry,' I told him. 'You leave the jetty first, and then I'll dive in with the canister of eggs and pass it to you twenty yards or so from the dangerous part.'

'However we manage, it's going to be quite a sporting affair—what fools we've been to have left it until today. We should have fixed it as soon as you arrived, while the sea was calm.'

'I don't like Mr. Harrison's holding on to our passports. How are we going to get them back if this swell develops into rollers—we'd find it impossible to land, even by swimming.'

'Anyway, "Operation Turtle" is off: there's no question of getting away from the beach in the dinghy. We'll make up with wideawake eggs.'

And so we set out, heading for the laying-ground, each with a four-gallon canister, walking in the glaring sunlight which reverberated along the road that ran beside the rocky fields. It was three miles walking there, and three back, with our load in addition. The man who invented the bicycle knew what he was about.

A truck passed us and stopped. 'You going down this way? Jump in! My name's Bob.'

Bob dropped us after making a detour to bring us as close as possible to the eggs. During the journey we had become the best friends in the world. He had told us his life-story and we had told him ours in return. He was taking a degree in history while earning his living as a truck-driver at the American base. No expenses, no distractions, no cares: ideal conditions for a student. Needless to say, he was fascinated by the life we were living and was anxious to help us.

'Well, Bob, as it happens, you might be able to do us a good turn. We have on board four soldered drums each containing five gallons of powdered milk, in other words four years' milk for each of us.' We had bought these eight drums for the modest sum of two or three pounds (sterling) from the government of St. Helena, who wanted to get rid of them. Nobody wanted them because American aid supplies the population of the island with free milk.

Bob had already understood. 'You'd like to exchange one of these drums for something else.' (With a wink) 'Vegetables or meat?'

'Meat, if possible. We've practically no corned beef on board. If the canteen-manager at the base is short of milk and has more bully than he needs. . . .'

'He can't possibly be short of milk; but I imagine he doesn't know what to do with the bully, because no-one cares for it. You go and collect your eggs, and I'll be back late in the afternoon to help you take them back to the jetty. Meanwhile, I'll tell the canteen-manager how you're fixed.'

And so Bob drove on: excellent fellow, only too ready to help two chance friends to realize the dream that so many men cherish in their hearts, of sailing towards unknown shores, leaving behind the constricting ties of life and society.

At the same time, I wonder whether Bob would have done for one of his own kind, starving and freezing on the pavements of New York, what he was so willing to do for us. I cannot escape a feeling of guilt for all the kindness I have met with since I first set sail in *Snark*. After all, what have I done to deserve it? Is it not a scandalous confidence-trick on my part? 'By the sweat of thy brow shalt thou earn they bread.' True, I have had to sweat to keep my boat afloat and fit her out; but are not there not any number of men who sweat much more than I have ever done, and nevertheless are still starving?

'Dammit Bernard! What are you loafing for over there? You don't imagine I'm going to do all the work myself?'

'I'm thinking noble thoughts.'

'Thinking up a new way of filling your fat belly! Anyway, I take my hat off to you for the corned beef dodge. If it works, you'll have earned the biggest share, you hypocritical French bastard!'

The laying season was nearing its end. There were not as many eggs as we hoped and we had not sufficient time to use a well-tried method which guarantees their freshness. This consists in drawing a big square marked with a peg at each corner and then collecting any eggs already laid inside and piling them up at the edges. You then come back the next day and collect the fresh eggs laid meanwhile. A little cruel, you may think: may be, but not too cruel, because the wideawakes hatch out only one egg at a time, and if anything goes wrong they are capable of laying one or two more.

Time, however, was short, and we had to be satisfied with a less infallible but still satisfactory method recommended by a St. Helenian who worked for Cable and Wireless.

You pick up an egg at random and break it, to the accompaniment of a volley of curses spat out by the mamma wideawake you have had to separate from her treasure (in a few days she will have the joy of laying another). If the central embryo is already developed, you try another sector, and repeat the experiment a little further afield until you find a new laid egg. This is what we did, and then gathered up eggs, and went on gathering them, more and more, breaking an egg from time to time to check that we were still in a good sector.

In less than an hour we were through, and our canisters were full: hoping, too, that they would still be full when we were back on board.

Bob remembered his promise, or rather both his promises. The truck arrived late in the afternoon, with bottles of ice-cold Coke and cans of beer. 'I thought you'd be thirsty—these are from the guys at the American base. And this case is from the cook with best wishes for a good passage. Unfortunately he only has these big cans, which are not very practical for a single person.'

Bob lifted the cover of the case and we feasted our eyes on the sight of six huge cans of corned beef.

'Fantastic!' exclaimed Henry. 'We'll only have to curry the meat and it'll keep for a week after opening the can. At a can a month, that'll last a nice long time.'

'Hold on,' said Bob, 'there's this too. The boys thought that sooner or later you'd perhaps arrive in New York, and that's not exactly in the tropics.' And he handed each of us a fine, strong, thick, new flannel shirt.

We were back at the jetty a little before sunset.

The swell from the north had not strengthened, as its behaviour in the morning had led us to fear. Henry's dinghy was lowered down the steps and launched in a flurry of foam. Poor Bob, who in spite of our warning, wanted to help, was soaked from head to foot in a matter of seconds. As for Henry and me, we were back in swimming kit, with our plastic bags across our shoulders holding our shirts, shorts and sandals.

The two canisters were then placed in the dinghy, without any breakages, and Henry followed them. We could only stand and hold our breath as our eggs were safely rowed out to sea—all in the same basket.

As for the case or corned beef: at one moment I thought I would have to dive in and fish it out again, but it was satisfied to swim in my dinghy, half filled with water. When the cans were safely on deck we would have to rinse them with fresh water and smear them with vaseline.

Henry went straight back to *Marie-Thérèse II* to leave the eggs there. 'Your cabin,' he said, 'may be badly arranged, but there's more room than in mine for the two of us to finish the job. You pass the eggs to me one by one after coating them with vaseline and I'll pack them four dozen at a time, in separate boxes, so as to limit the damage in case any are broken.'

'Good idea; but just let me put the rice on the stove. It'll be cooked by the time we're finished and then we can eat.'

'And talking of eating, Bernard, let me renew my congratulations on the powdered milk/corned beef exchange. But supposing the cook had accepted the deal? What would we have done then?'

'He wouldn't have accepted, even though he's never been hungry in his life.'

'Hum. . . . In that case, it's given me a wonderful idea. These cans, you see, are much to big for us, and to open one would be a wasteful extravagance. On the other hand, supposing we meet the cook of a ship anchored in some harbour in the West Indies, we might suggest to him to exchange them for smaller ones: one six-pound can for six one-pound cans. What do you think?'

'I think you're hardly any more honest than I am.'

'That's what I'm beginning to be afraid of. But I've just had another idea, Bernard.'

'Some even more certain road to damnation?'

'Not at all: you've seen these turtles all over the place, and all these fish? Now, why have we never brought back a turtle on board? Simply because we wouldn't have known what to do with it once we'd killed it. It's true we'd have begun by making a vast curry which would keep for five or six days. But what would we have done with the rest? Salted it, or made it into strips of dried meat as they do in South Africa?

'The salted stuff is generally foul, and the dried meat is not much better. And what's more, it calls for constant care and even so ends up by making the whole cabin stink and finally gets thrown overboard. It's the same with salt fish. It's not too bad for a week or so, and then you get sick of it, not to mention the smell below.' (We had been eating it regularly for more than a month since Cape Town, and that was quite enough.)

'You're quite right, Henry,' I answered. 'If it hadn't been for the tricky problem of keeping it, we'd already have a turtle on board, prohibition or no prohibition, breakers or no breakers. But what sort of idea are you hatching out?'

'Some day, to make our own canned foods.'

'You don't feel you're beginning to go a bit round the bend?'

'A little, perhaps. But just think, all the same, and you'll realize that although it may not be easy, it's certainly possible. After all, what is a can of food? It's nothing but a metal box containing meat or fish or vegetables that have been sterilized under pressure. After cooking, the food is put into the open cans and the whole goes through the sterilizer again. While the cans are still at a high temperature, the lids are put on and sealed mechanically. Now, I'm sure that I've read somewhere that a domestic model of this sealing machine is produced in America, where some housewives do their own canning. As for the sterilizing, we've already got on board what's needed, the pressure cooker. So all we would have to do would be to get hold of the can-sealing apparatus and a stock of cans—unassembled, so that they won't take up too much room on board. We'd be able to buy them from any canned food manufacturer.'

'We could even,' I suggested, 'try to get taken on in a factory so that we could learn a bit more about the technique. I'm told that if you don't do it properly the cans may explode.'

'That might be so with mass-production, perhaps. But if we do it carefully ourselves, there will be no risk in that quarter. What makes a sealed can swell is fermentation caused by faulty sterilization of the contents or the container itself. There'd be no such danger if we cooked the contents under pressure and sealed the cans while they were still hot.

'Just think of how independent we'd be if we used this method! All these black-fish preserved, and a load of canned turtle as well! When we put in, we could exchange it for fruit and fresh vegetables.'

'Yes,' I added, 'and then put to sea without waiting for the explosion. However, I'm only joking, Henry, because there really is something in your idea. If it works, it will mean that we'll no longer be guilty of the sin of hypocrisy, offering to exchange powdered milk for big cans of bully, and big cans of bully for something else, and. . . .'

'Don't worry, Bernard, we'll certainly find some other way of making up for it, and somehow find our way to hell: like you, I only hope it'll be nice and warm.'

When the eggs had all been packed, Henry went back to *Wanda* with his share of the booty carefully stowed in cardboard boxes. Each of us had almost four hundred eggs, and at the rate of ten a day this would give us practically six weeks without having to touch our stock of canned food. (Wideawakes' eggs are about two-thirds the size of an average hen's eggs, and our livers were pretty robust.)

Our landing the next morning was an epic sight, and we only just managed to get up on the jetty with our precious dinghies: a wonderful vindication of canvas stretched over a flexible frame. Canvas resists tearing much more than you would imagine. And if it does tear in the end (which it does with difficulty, but it sometimes happens) it takes only a moment to sew a patch over the torn place.

Our passports were returned to us, and then Mr. Harrison took us to the bakery, where we collected the bread he had ordered for us the day before. But how were we to get it on board? With such a sea beating on the jetty, this was another difficult problem. As a precaution, we divided it into four lots, in separate sacks, to lessen the danger of an enforced immersion.

The regular ship was due to arrive in a few hours and we were waiting for our mail from—from Cape Town, and elsewhere, while discussing birds with one of the ornithologists. He asked me to undertake a small assignment for him: to keep an eye open and make a note of all the birds I saw between Ascension and our next port of call, the Brazilian island of Fernando-Noroña, indicating the geographical position of sightings. I was to send back the information from Trinidad.

At last, we were handed our mail: not much, but it contained the main thing—news from my family and from Cape Town.

'Well, Bernard, are things still working out all right for you in Cape Town?'

'Yes: she's put her name down on the waiting list. It's time to move on to Trinidad, with a brief call at Fernando-Noroña, or else she'll arrive first and may have trouble with the Immigration office.'

*

We went to say goodbye to everyone and entrust our mail to Mr. Harrison, who would not hear of our buying stamps. He would send our letters by air to New York at his own expense. It was the same with the bread, 'It's a little present, so just take it as such: you've shown yourselves extremely "independent" while you've been here, in the way you managed by yourselves in your journeys between your boats and the jetty. That was most admirable, and we shall retain very pleasant memories of you both. You got your eggs all right?'

'They've been on board since yesterday. A few breakages, but we anticipated that and collected a couple extra' (we hardly like to tell him that we'd also allowed for possible bad eggs).

We both made our way on board our respective boats, but not without some difficulty on that occasion. A vicious sea flung Henry's dinghy against the jetty and the first two sacks of bread floated gaily in the bottom of his half-filled vessel. Henry warmed himself up with some good round oaths. And, to avoid me occasion for jealousy, another sea treated me in the same way. However, the precious bread was brought safely on board, there to be cut into slices and dried on the coach-roof during the first days of our passage.

CHAPTER 11

Ascension to Fernando-Noroña
a 1,100-mile ocean race

Shortly before daybreak on February 6th, our anchors broke out from the bottom of the bay. *Wanda* and *Marie-Thérèse II* set their sails in company to the moderate trade wind, heading for Fernando-Noroña, 1,100 miles west-north-west, on their way to the West Indies. For the first time, however, a new wind animated the crews, the wind of the racing spirit.

In a normal trade wind (which is generally extremely irregular) I would probably have let *Wanda* sail before me, in order to avoid any temptation to compete in performance. To me, the cruising mentality is as far removed from that of racing as is that of a rider hacking through the woods from a rider on a race-track.

But with a trade as out of the ordinary as this, which had brought us here without a single day of calm or a single squall, one may be allowed a little light-hearted relaxation, so long as a minimum of respect is retained.

As soon as we were clear of the coast and the big bank which extends it to port, the two staysails were set, with *Marie-Thérèse II* controlled by the automatic steering-gear. I then set the two extra jibs on their booms, and was under full sail.

But no, not yet: the spare mizzen was extracted from the fore-peak, bent onto the mizzen halyard, and sent up to the head of the mizzen mast, the foot free, with a sheet on either side to hold it in an oblique position. This would assist the forward sails in driving the boat, and at the same time, because of its angle in relation to the vertical, tend to ease the stern of the boat. That, at any rate, was my own personal idea which I had been turning over in my mind for some days.

I soon wanted to improve on this, because *Wanda* had succeeded in outdistancing me in spite of my new and, as I thought, extremely clever and effective system. I accordingly transferred, section by section, all my spare chain (part of which was aft) as far as possible forward, together with a heavy spare anchor, which was normally lashed at the foot of the mizzen mast.

The idea of all this shifting was simply to weighten the bows, thereby lightening the stern, and so obtain the utmost hydrodynamic benefit. Some captious minds will probably consider this notion rather absurd, on the ground that to add extra weight forward in a boat running before the wind may well make the bows dig in, and that, in addition, it makes it difficult to maintain her heading.

That is perfectly true in a rough sea and a strong wind. On this occasion, however, the sea was calm, the wind Force 3, and we maintained our heading perfectly. It depends on the boat. In any case I wanted to try it out as a matter of interest, which in fact is often the way one ultimately solves quite a number of problems.

At sunset *Wanda* seemed to have maintained her lead of three or four hundred yards, and I changed five degrees to the south to prevent a possible collision. That would be altogether too ridiculous. Contrary to my usual practice, I hung the lantern in the bows. I then saw that Henry had had the same thought: as night fell his little light was flickering between the waves.

It was a quiet night. We were making four knots, caressed by a warm wind, leaving behind a phosphorescent wake, dead straight, sharp and clear. Here and there I could see large phosphorescent patches, which shone for a few seconds and then disappeared. You would have taken them for light-buoys. I tried in vain to determine what produced these numerous transitory phenomena. Was it the track of large fish? No, because in that case there would have been a phosphorescent trail and not this local illumination. But what, then, was the explanation of this sudden burst of blue-green light, with no apparent reason? Plankton, it is true, often comes up to the surface at night time.

The dawn came with an unbroken horizon. And once again I was alone with my trinity of Wind, Sea and Sun. In other words I was not, in fact, without company. My striped pilot-fish, moreover, was playing at the stem. Was it the one who had fallen in love with *Marie-Thérèse II* between St. Helena and Ascension, and had disappeared when we put in at the latter? It might well be the same.

I threw him some bread-crumbs but he pretended not to see me. To tease him, I threw him some larger pieces just in front of his mouth—and he immediately went and sulked astern, against the rudder. 'Come on,' I told him, 'back to the bows: that's the place for a pilot-fish, and don't sulk.' He quietly obeyed, with the shaft of the harpoon to help him understand, and went back to his station at the stem.

The noon position placed us 97 miles from Ascension, a bit slow. (By constantly complaining about things being a bit slow, I shall end up getting more than I bargained for.) A few bo'sun-birds and wideawakes were fishing a hundred yards from the boat. I made a note of them for my ornithologist friend on Ascension. I would like to be able to send him a worthwhile report when I reach the West Indies. It would please both of us: him, because it would mean that I had not forgotten my promise; and me, because I should have kept it and I knew that he would be glad to know what his birds were up to at sea.

In the meantime a new trouble had appeared this evening in the cabin. Searching among my books, I found three small cockroaches, who got away. So here we are: a new invasion is starting. Since Durban, these stowaways, familiar to so many sailing vessels, had deserted the ship, or rather, thanks to several canisters of gas, had been exterminated. The aim of that operation was not the destruction of the cockroaches, but the much more important destruction of an extremely prolific insect which attacks the wood and in the course of a few years will convert it into sponge. The only indication of its presence on board is a trail of yellowish powder. I need hardly add that I paled at this discovery, and all the more so in that I had already discussed this infliction with a friend on Mauritius.

This friend owned a *Colombine*-type boat, with a central drop-keel, and had been obliged to use the only possible solution for getting rid of these accursed insects, after having tried a number of products, all equally ineffective, including paraffin and creosote. His solution was to sink the boat for ten days in a sheltered bay. That finished them. The insects had not been able to resist this desperate treatment.

It was not possible to use the same method for *Marie-Thérèse II*, at least not until everything else had been tried. Only three frames were affected, and I tried to kill the insects by applying a blow-lamp to the wood.

For ten days I thought I had won. There was no more yellow powder trickling from little holes (about the size of the eye of a fine needle). After ten days, however, it started again. I tried again, this time adding a good soaking with paraffin after using the blow-lamp. The result was no better, and I began to be seriously worried.

I consulted Raymond Cruickshank, who told me that the South African government takes wood-borers (as they call them) very seriously. Some years earlier he had witnessed the complete destruction by fire (on Government orders) of a house infested with the pests.

Almost out of my mind (and with good cause) I took a day off from work and went the round of the firms that specialize in wood-preservation. The first two I called on only had products designed to prevent infection.

'But suppose my house is already attacked by these filthy creatures?' I asked. (I said 'house' rather than 'boat', because it might be reported and the police would be able to trace me—you never know).

'In that case,' they told me, 'the only remedy is to take out all the affected beams and planks, burn them, and put new ones in their place.'

My heart sank: Blasted boat, I thought, if it's not one thing it's another! The third firm had some consolation for me. They showed me a new product. 'It's a liquid which vaporizes as soon as the tin is punctured, and it gives unexpectedly good results in the curing of timber attacked by wood-borers.'

The salesman had an honest look: I felt that he would not let me down, and knew what he was talking about. I gave him all the details of my own predicament.

'Yes,' he said, 'that ought to save your boat. We've never tried it except for furniture which has been moved into a separate room for treatment. But if you can hermetically seal your cabin and paste paper over all the joins and cracks the result should be equally satisfactory.'

He gave me ten tins. These were to be laid on the cabin floor and punctured, using a nail drive through the end of a stick, through a port-hole which would then be closed from outside. I would have to start by puncturing one tin every half-hour, and then one every three hours for the last six tins.

Two days later, the cabin was opened up and aired. The gas had done its work as promised and that was the end of the wood-borers. But another miracle accompanied the first: the cock-roaches also disappeared for nearly eighteen months, and it appeared that their eggs brought on board later (they generally come with provisions) could not hatch. The wood had been impregnaged with the insecticide and it protected it from any further development of parasites for a very long time. I am sorry that I lost the note I kept with the name of this product.

During the morning of February 8th, there was great excitement in *Marie-Thérèse II*. *Wanda* was in sight. It was hardly credible, this meeting of two sailing vessels, forty-eight hours after leaving a harbour on a 1,100-mile passage.

I climbed the mizzen mast to enjoy our victory more completely; for *Wanda* was three or four miles astern. I wondered whether Henry, too, was perched on his masthead, swearing that God's goodness is a myth, while I am cock-a-hoop.

It is, of course, rather a ridiculous feeling, but I cannot help it. I then climbed down again, to fiddle about with the sheets, making an improvement in one place and an adjustment in another, doing every-thing I possibly could to gain a little more speed. I hauled in the log, and coiled the fishing line in the stern, which would cut out its slight braking action.

In any case, the log is not much use in such splendid weather, which makes it possible to draw position lines at any time you please. The fishing line, in any case, seemed to be possessed by an evil spirit, for I had never had a bite: though I should add that I have little talent as a fisherman.

It was a feverish morning, idiot that I was; but Henry had so often mocked at the slowness of my boat, on the ground that his own had taken twelve hours less than mine for a passage of 1,740 miles that I was anxious to show him that *Marie-Thérèse II* was not so slow as he maintained.

About noon, I thought there was a greater distance separating the two boats; but I spent a good half-hour moving as much as possible forward in order to lighten the stern a little more. I was even tempted to empty overboard one of my twenty-five gallon fresh-water tanks to save more weight.

As afternoon became evening, *Wanda* was still in sight though a little further astern. The sun was in the west (and so behind me as I looked astern) and enabled me to make a more accurate estimate of the distance between us—five miles, perhaps, I thought.

Marie-Thérèse II was holding her course well, with practically no rolling; I had removed as much weight as I could from the stern, so that the water could flow by more freely, with the minimum of friction. (This is an example of a law of hydrodynamics which can be verified by observing fish, for example. The rear part is always more streamlined than the head. Another example can be seen in the shape of a sounding lead; the end attached to the line is narrow, while the base is wide. If the line were attached to the wider end of the lead, you would find that it sank more slowly. The braking action applied to the bows of the boat is accordingly less, over an equal area, than the suction operating on the stern)

I set small extra booms (a broom-handle and harpoon-shaft, as it happened) at the stern to stretch out as far as possible the sheets of the two lower staysails.

Whistling, I went below to get supper.

I found another cockroach (the third in eighteen months) scuttling away from the tin of condensed milk. Still, this is often the way in which a full-scale invasion starts.

There was a time, in fact, in *Snark,* when we (Deshumeurs and I) had a terrible experience with an invasion of cockroaches. The memory of that epic period was making me laugh, while the coffee was heating in the percolator: and my mind, well satisfied by the work done that day, was wandering off at random, far, far away, to the little Indonesian village of Toboali.

Snark was at anchor in the bay of Taboali and the village Chief of Police, believing that we were two completely harmless, if slightly cracked, young men, advised us to make fast to the quay. We did this, only too pleased at this stroke of luck which allowed us to patch up our aged *Snark* at low water, while waiting a decision from Jakarta.

With the boat made fast, Deshumeurs and I went below to the cabin to make a jar of Ovomaltine. However, instead of our peacefully drinking our Ovomaltine and crunching Chinese biscuits, it was we who were nearly devoured by cockroaches.

They had gone completely mad at feeling the proximity of damp soil (for it had just been raining), unless it was that their antennae had detected the presence, in the many cracks in the stone jetty, of another variety, friendly or hostile.

In a matter of half a minute, you would have thought that all the cockroaches in the world had arranged a rendezvous in our cabin. They were flying in every direction, running over our bare shoulders and chests, over our faces, and biting, while we could only rush out of the cabin with disgusted cries, leaving biscuits and Ovomaltine to the cockroaches.

*

I was up at dawn and glanced astern. Nothing in sight. A little anxious, I examined the horizon on either side, and even ... ahead: you never know, that brute might have been racking his brains to find some way of overtaking. Still nothing to be seen.

However, the distance between us had not increased during the night. *Wanda* was, just then, up sun from me, and so I could not see her.

I made a few more slight adjustments so that the sails would hold the wind better (another concession to the racing fiend) and took an altitude. This would allow me to possess myself in patience until the sun was high enough not to blind me when I scanned the eastern horizon.

A short spell at the masthead after the noon observation showed that *Wanda* was still in sight but a little further astern than the day before. And this was three days out from Ascension! This must be most unusual in ocean passages. She was not, however, on the same bearing as before but further north. Hell! We both seemed to have had the same idea; for yesterday, seeing that *Wanda* was dead astern, I had thought of a possible solution which might perhaps allow me to arrive first—to take advantage of the currents.

According to the *Pilot Charts*, the favourable curents would be stronger at the latitude of Fernando-Noroña. On the other hand, valuable though their information is, these charts are not infallible. Even so, as Henry stood, his best chance of being first lay in a detour of a hundred miles which would put him in the current. If the *Pilot Chart* was right, he would easily make up the lost time and arrive first. If it was wrong, and the information was incorrect, then he would have gone out of his way for nothing and would be a day late.

At sunset Henry's tactics were apparent. *Wanda* was off north to find the current. *Marie-Thérèse II* was continuing on the same course. So it was a toss-up: funny if in the end we were both to drop our anchors together in the bay of Fernando-Noroña, quarrelling with one another over a matter of seconds!

Our 'round-pond' sailing continued, with nothing to impair its quiet delight, made up of the whisper of water, the slight creaking of blocks, the scarcely audible sound of the trade wind caressing the sails as the boat covered her regular hundred miles a day, preceded by her faithful striped pilot all alone in the shelter of the bow-wave.

For some days, a small dorado has been paying us a visit just before sunset. Is it looking for the protection of its big sister? If so, it is making a big mistake, because I am without feeling when it is a question of something just the right size for my frying-pan; and so the dorado meets the end of its journeyings—a change, for a day, from wideawake eggs.

I opened the belly of the dorado, for I have a mania for knowing what the fish I catch live on. I had known for a long time what is the dorado's normal food (the flying fish know this, too); but the curious thing is that all the flying fish I have found in dorados' stomachs have had the head neatly cut off, just at the root of the lateral fins they use as wings. In other words, the dorado snaps up the flying fish, cuts off the head as smartly as one could with a knife, and then lets go of its catch for a fraction of a second before gulping it down 'without chewing it properly', like a badly brought-up child.

A number of flying fish, of course, were present in my dorado's stomach, most of them half-digested. One of them, however (the biggest), seemed to have been only just swallowed, for, apart from the head, it was quite intact, and for a moment I wondered whether it should not join the rather skinny dorado in my frying pan. (Come to that, even the head of a flying fish provides calories, and I for one would not reject this part of its anatomy.) In the end, it went overboard: I find the head of a fresh fish more appetising than a fish already swallowed by another.

There was, however, a surprise for me inside the stomach of this dorado. If was fifteen or so tiny 'balloon' fish packed together among the normal flying fish: and I would have betted my life that this variety of fish, which blow themselves up in the presence of danger, live only along the coast, among the coral and rocks in which they can hide from their enemies. And yet there must be shoals of them in the middle of the Atlantic, half-way between

Africa and America: a very odd thing for these defenceless fish which cannot bite nor fly, and can only swim at a couple of knots however hard pressed. I should add that these were tiny children and in their disobedient way they may have been wandering where they had no business to be.

One thing, even so, is certain: the dorado now frying in the cabin must have fallen in with a dense shoal of young balloon fish for me to find so many in its stomach—and it must have happened a very few minutes before being speared, because its victims were still intact.

*

February 12th: The trade wind is still between Force 2 and 4 Beaufort scale, from the east-south-east. It has been dead astern since my sailing, without the least shift, unlike its behaviour between Cape Town and Ascension.

The sea, on the other hand, has reverted to a pattern familiar to me: a moderate swell, overlaid by secondary undulations from a direction different from that of the prevailing wind. These are distant evidence of the north-east trade which dominates the wind system of the tropical belt north of the equator, beyond the doldrums.

At the moment, we are not very far from the doldrums. They lie (at this time of the year) between 3° and 4°, and 5° and 6° N., at the longitude of Fernando-Noroña, which is itself still in the trade-wind zone, on the third parallel south.

It is only after calling at Fernando-Noroña that we shall have to cross this area, which so many sailing ships have cursed for its long periods of calm interspersed with violent squalls and gusts. A ship without an engine can spend days and even whole weeks there, completely becalmed, the sails hanging lifeless from the spars, or, by contrast, under bare poles in squalls that threaten to dismast her.

There are times, however, when the doldrums cover a very narrow area. This is generally the case in the vicinity of the coast of Brazil, though it has even happened that ships sailing from Cape Town to the English Channel, and crossing the doldrums as far as possible from the coast of Brazil in order to cut down the distance, have passed from SE. to NE. trades in one short squall. The point is that it is towards the middle of the Atlantic, and particularly when close to the African coast, that the doldrums are at their widest and accordingly their most formidable. The Cerberus of the equator, patrolling his domain, must have been uncommonly surprised at seeing his prey escape like a flash, too delighted at its good luck even to glance astern.

Fortunately, however, all the little afflictions that had been showered upon me when crossing the Indian Ocean in *Marie-Thérèse* were to be spared me in her successor.

The *Pilot Charts* are quite definite on this subject. The doldrums are practically non-existent in the part of the Atlantic which stretches from Fernando-Noroña to the coast of Brazil; and when the *Pilot Charts* are really definite, you may pretty well take their word for it.

On the other hand, there is a little detail which these excellent publications do not mention: the wind system off the Amazon. It is understandable because the charts (which are American) cover half the Atlantic and they cannot include all the smallest details, or they would be illegible. In any case, I have no intention of flirting with that ill-famed coast, whose mud-banks are strewn with vicious rocks that sometimes stretch so far offshore that some ships, after running aground, have completely lost their bearings, out of sight of a mainland with no prominent features.

*

Midday position: longitude 23° 55′ W., latitude 5° 39′ S.

Distance covered since Ascension: 595 miles in six days, a daily average of 99 miles. Pretty poor. But I always think it is too little (between you and me, if I had averaged 120 or 130 I should have had no complaint).

A cloudless sky all the way, but there must be a light mistiness floating in the atmosphere here in spite of its apparent clarity, because I have never, since a few days after leaving Cape Town, witnessed either sunrise or sunset.

I am still living the life of Reilly. Nothing to do. You could not wish for a more restful form of sailing. The boat does her own work without needing any human help, while the man is free for his own business, which means doing nothing that he does not want to do: reading, dreaming, sometimes writing a letter, but mostly contemplating the domain of which he is the centre, which belongs to him, and to which he belongs heart and soul.

Still, the man has to do the cooking, and that is not so pleasant. And the washing-up, which is even less so. It sometimes happens that he polishes and tidies the cabin when *Marie-Thérèse II* begins to grumble too openly. It is hard to get down to this work, but once it has been begun under protest and is well under way, it seems to become so natural that the time passes pleasantly. It is rather like gymnastics: you start in a listless, hangdog way, but as soon as your muscles have warmed up you want the session to go on all day.

For another two days we continued to log mile after mile, and the positions drawn on the chart formed practically a straight line from Ascension.

Then, without warning and without any increase in the wind, there followed two days each of 130 miles. An average of over five knots.

The *Pilot Chart* was right. We had sailed right into the Equatorial Current, which starts in the neighbourhood of Guinea, runs parallel to the equator in a belt which includes Fernando-Noroña, and then comes up against Cape Recife in South America. The cape splits this great oceanic current, one half continuing up the coast towards the Caribbean, while the other follows the coast of Brazil and Argentine as far as the Cape Horn area, before it again turns east under the influence of the prevailing current in the Antarctic belt.

February 16th, noon. Still sixty miles to cover. Another night landfall, for the wind is holding well, Force 3 to 4. At sunset I handed the two main twin staysails and furled them on the booms, while *Marie-Thérèse II* sailed on at reduced speed under the two lower sails.

I would have liked to take a final longitude at sunset, but, as had happened every day since Cape Town, the usual veil of mist hid the sun too soon. A star-fix would have been useful. This is another important detail in which I am not well equipped, since I have not the *Nautical Almanac* for the year, which is indispensable for working it out. I shall have to make good this lack at the first opportunity, in the West Indies.

A star-fix is much quicker and more accurate than a sun-sight. Three star-sights can be taken in a few minutes, and from them, by a little calculation that is as simple as with the sun, you can draw three position lines. Where the three intersect gives you the position of the boat. Thus a position worked out from star-observations can be obtained in a matter of twenty minutes or half an hour.

In the absence of a latitude calculated from the noon altitude of the sun, another position line can be drawn, at least three hours after the first (to give the sun time to change its azimuth).

Perhaps these theoretical explanations of mine are not very clear?

I am afraid that this is so; but with Neufville's or Dieumegard's tables, or the good will of a naval officer giving you practical examples (i.e. from the log) all that I have said can become crystal clear—provided you have a little good will too.

*

Sleep, of course, is out of the question tonight. Did some malign spirit cast a spell on my boat at her birth? Perhaps I ought to have burnt some sticks of incense and sacrificed a cockerel on her stem so that the invisible gods and goddesses assembled round her cradle might shower gifts upon her. Of one thing I am certain: some sort of wicked fairy must have waved her wand over the innocent babe and prophesied 'When land you sight, 'twill ever be night.'

At about one in the morning, the beam of the light-house swept across the sky, dead ahead. The two lower sails were handed and stowed in the forepeak. Then the mainsail, staysail and jib were set and the boat hove-to, the forward sails sheeted on either side, the mainsail sheeted home and the helm-a-lee. The ground tackle had been ready since sundown, the anchors shackled to the chains.

At three o'clock, the light-house was visible above the horizon, and I got under way. It was very unpleasant. The forward sails were masked by the mainsail and the boat rolled. I had become unused to the motion for, oddly enough, although *Marie-Thérèse II* rolls easily at an anchorage that is the least bit choppy, she does not do so under twin staysails with the wind aft. *Wanda,* on the other hand, who behaves perfectly at anchor, sometimes rolls from side to side, with the deck awash, when she is sailing under twin staysails, even in the ideal conditions we had enjoyed in the Atlantic. Different boat, different behaviour. That is why it is sensible not to make categorical judgements about whether one should heave to or not heave to, run or not run with the wind aft in a heavy sea, or adopt or not adopt Bermudan rig.

One sailor will maintain that a high life-line is an essential to safety at sea. Another will say that it is an excellent way of throwing yourself into the sea, and that a life-line should be as low as possible because you do not walk on a deck, but slither along it like a lizard; and finally a third will tell you that you can keep your bloody life-line—he's never had one on deck. Yet all these three are right (or wrong: it comes to the same thing, and the earth will go on turning anyway).

I rounded the north-eastern island of the group at dawn. The tide was running against us, producing a very pretty miniature tide-rip. It was like the undulations running down the back of a purring cat.

The breeze, fortunately, was anxious to please. It drove us gaily from astern after having rounded the island itself. Wonderful! We could have sailed almost into the anchorage under twin staysails, making a south-easterly course, even though offshore the trade wind was blowing from that direction.

The anchorage marked on the chart soon came into sight: a fine beach, big, sandy, dazzling white, a light swell from the north-east sinking to rest on it as though exhausted by its long journey from far away, across the doldrums.

And then, hidden until that moment by a huge rock standing up alone in the bay like the stump of a great tooth, there appeared a familiar pom-pom headed mast. Oh the brute! *Wanda* had won.

My blasts on the foghorn brought out a bearded head; Henry jumped into his dinghy and pulled across to me, while *Marie-Thérèse II* swooped in close-hauled, in the trade wind now blowing in short gusts across the inlet formed by the hills on either side of the bay.

I caught the dinghy as it went by and tied it up astern. Henry stationed himself by the anchors, ready to moor. We fetched up fifty yards from *Wanda*, where *Marie-Thérèse II* would be able to doze at the end of the chain shackled to the C.Q.R. anchor, in the utter peace of this tropical bay.

'I thought you'd decided,' said Henry, 'to carry straight on for Trinidad when I didn't find you here yesterday evening.'

'What time was that?' I asked.

'Just before dark.'

'Well done, Henry: you've won the first round.'

'I went north to find the Equatorial Current. I might have lost a day looking for an imaginary current: so it was double or quits.'

'Let's have another try on the last two thousand miles from here to Trinidad? If you get there first, you've won the rubber.'

'O.K. What's more, this'll be the real test because we'll have to sail a good part of the way under working sails.'

'What are the locals like?'

'Haven't had time to go ashore yet.'

'Have you had breakfast? No? Then stay on board and have some. The porridge is ready and then, just for a change, there are hard-boiled eggs. After that we'll go and find out if the natives are friendly.'

CHAPTER 12

Fernando-Noroña

The Fernando-Noroña group of islands is almost unknown to sailors. In all the accounts of voyages I have read, and if my memory serves me correctly, only Harry Pidgeon's has a brief description of them.

Islander entered the narrow channel which separates the main island from its little sister, lying steep-to a good deal less than a hundred yards to the north-east. Pidgeon, however, did not stop because, I believe, of the cyclone season then approaching in the neighbourhood of the West Indies.

I would like to know what Pidgeon would have had to say about this group of islands, stretching out in a line some ten miles in length, set with rocky 'objects' which are neither mountains nor hills nor large rocks, but a sort of combination of the three.

There are some landscapes that leave you unsatisfied because they seem to keep their own counsel. And this group will always remain an enigma to me: not forbidding, and not genial, just a riddle. There is nothing familar suggested by the colours of these rocky masses. The purple here is not purple, the yellow is not quite yellow and the green is not like any green I have seen. It is not really green at all. What colour is it, then? I cannot say. It is simply different.

Perhaps I am experiencing here what happens when a Western ear hears Indo-Chinese music and tries to relate its strange tones to something already known. It proves impossible, because the music of the Far East is made up of notes that do not produce the same number of vibrations as those to which the West is accustomed.

To return, however, to practical questions.

In the first place, Henry and I have decided that our stay will be a very short one. There is no need to assemble my dinghy. Henry's will do for pulling to the beach and back. We swallowed breakfast, put on shorts (and nylon singlets which we later pulled off before they were soaked in sweat), and set off in the dinghy, with our sandals slung over a shoulder and our passports tied to them.

We landed without incident, and two hours later, the village came in sight, lying below a bend in the road. We had chosen the longest way round, in spite of the almost painful heat. At sea, real heat (I mean unpleasant heat) is extremely unusual. There is almost always a light breeze to make it bearable. It is very different on land; if the countryside is at all dry, without sufficient tall trees to give shade, the heat attacks you from two sides, from the sky above and from the heated ground below you.

Here, there was not a vestige of shade all along the dusty road that was already scorching our bare feet. We were carrying our sandals so as not to wear them out, and would put them on before we reached the village.

In spite of the unpleasant conditions, we had loitered on the way, because lizards are fond of the heat at the roadsides; and perhaps they would like to add cockroaches to their diet and enjoy in addition sunbathing on the decks of our boats.

It was Henry, most of all, who needed shock treatment for his stowaways. A couple of lizards should clear up my invasion, which was still only in the early stages of development.

And so we turned for a time to lizard catching. They are from four to eight inches long, their scales small and smooth, with greenish-grey reflections: jewel-like and a gay adornment to a cabin. Moreover, if it is true (as I think I have read) that they eat every day their weight in insects, *Wanda*'s cockroaches' days are numbered, while my own will be struck off the crew-list in a morning. All I shall have to do then is to leave the tin of condensed milk open and from time to time fish out my new lodgers.

Catching lizards may be less dangerous than shooting rhino in the African bush, but I doubt whether it is any easier. You see, these attractive and friendly (but not over-familiar) little creatures can snap up a fly in an instant: there is not much chance, accordingly, of the clumsy mammoths we are in their mischievous little eyes being able to pocket them without difficulty.

However: love's vows are sworn in the open sunshine by this race of climbers (they can climb like lightning) and it was by our mercilessly taking advantage of the few seconds while our love-struck victims were gazing into infinity, that they followed one another, two by two, into our pockets.

Three couples would be enough: two for *Wanda*, and one for *Marie-Thérèse II*. The right-hand pocket of my shorts would serve as their temporary prison until they came to know the pleasures of ocean sailing and the emotion of seeing a new land gradually emerge from the waves of the sea.

Pocketing the charming little animals was not too difficult, but persuading them to behave was quite another matter. Perhaps we should have remembered the English saying, 'two's company, three's a crowd'—all the more valid in this case, since there were six in one pocket. I used my singlet as a stopper, hoping that the poor things were not allergic to nylon.

We had then to find a solution more compatible with the arbitrary demands of social life, because you cannot appear before a police chief as though you were advertising a new fashion, well-bronzed torso, nylon singlet dangling from a pocket bulging with lizards: not in Brazilian territory, anyway.

As we entered the village, we tried to question the only human being in sight. As it happened, it was a girl. She fled without further ado, as though we were Casanovas or plague-bearers. And yet we had put on our singlets, and used Henry's handkerchief and my own to block the exit from the lizards' quarters.

'What a country!' I complained. 'They're a miserable lot here, aren't they?'

'Bloody Latin mind!' was Henry's comment. 'And you tell me to go anchor off Cannes some time!'

'The French,' I pointed out to him, 'are not exactly Latins. A pretty French girl would at least have tried to answer, and if she couldn't understand your gibberish (as would probably be the case) she'd have a smile to console you.'

' "Police" and "passport", surely, are international words.'

'Let's try the old woman sitting on her doorstep over there.'

Heavens! Does she take us for two gangsters? The old woman went back into her house and slammed the door.

We went on through the deserted streets, pulsating with heat (it was almost the siesta time). As we went by, doors opened behind us and heads appeared.

This was too absurd. We turned and knocked at a door.

The door opened, and disclosed a bearded and smiling giant: the sort of man you want to take by both shoulders and look at him and say, 'Yes, you've a grand look about you. I like you, and we are brothers.'

Behind him his children were crowding, shy in spite of their bright, impish eyes. But they were not shy for long: they noticed my right-hand pocket and were trying to stifle their laughter as they looked at it. I looked too, and pushed back one of my lodgers who was already half out of his dungeon. Poor little thing, upset, I suppose by the smell of Henry's handkerchief.

Once let loose, the children became friends—rather demanding friends, as children of ten become when the ice has been broken. First they wanted to see the lizard. We explained to them by signs that that was difficult because the others might escape. So there were others. And all the children rushed at us. One of them put his hand to his mouth, in the international gesture, to ask us whether we ate lizards. How does one explain by sign language that the lizards were going to eat our cockroaches?

One thing struck me in the behaviour of these children (who had been joined by others from neighbouring houses): the boys seemed delighted to learn that we ate lizards, but the girls were almost in tears: to judge at least, from the expression in their big round eyes, which seemed to plead, 'No, it can't be true: you don't eat them! You couldn't be so cruel, could you?'

To reassure them, I drew a boat on the cement door-step with a stone; and then an insect which might have been a cockroach or a spider, or even Henry. I drew the insect in the middle of the boat with the lizard just behind it.

Our little audience probably understood something quite different from what I was trying to explain: and it must have been something very funny, because they all burst out laughing. But it was certainly a success, and the children adopted us.

We then had to turn to serious business.

'*Dové* Police?'

The giant showed his teeth in a huge smile; but he did not understand. Anyway, it was Italian, or was supposed to be.

'Let me do it, idiot!' said Henry. 'Police! Passport!' waving the passport in his face.

Another smile. These good folk do not get many visitors, but, even so, surely those words are the same all over the world?

Suddenly, I remembered the right (or practically the right) word: '*Carabiniero!*'

A score of little hands then took hold of our shorts, our singlets, our arms. It was a chattering mob, growing as we proceeded, that led us to the building which housed the chief of the *Carabinieri:* for they realized, too, that it was the chief of police we wanted and not his under-strapper.

The chief was a charming man of about thirty, extremely friendly. He had a luxurious office with carpet, curtains, and comfortable armchairs in which I would have enjoyed a short siesta, for the room was wonderfully cool.

He hardly glanced at our passports. 'You are French?' He could speak French pretty well, but was using English out of politeness to Henry.

It is strange how far afield France produces the same reaction. In all the countries I have visited, France always raises a kindly, slightly mocking, smile; but at the same time it is a country infinitely respected and admired as a symbol of civilization and freedom.

His eyes filled with emotion, he began to discuss Gide with me and wanted me to tell him how much I, too, like Gide. He wanted to know whether I understood him in the same way as he did. Had Gide opened new horizons for me? When I read him, did I feel the impact, the shock, the ecstasy of a revelation?

A minute later, it was quite another shock I felt. I was looking at Henry, and I noticed that his eyes were fixed at a particular point on me. Mercy! One of my lodgers had again escaped from my pocket. I felt that Henry was about to dissolve in laughter. But our host had not noticed anything: he was still lost in a Gidean nirvana. And as for me, I was on tenterhooks.

So long, I thought, as neither Henry nor I made some foolish move; I moved my hands gently downwards towards my knees in what I hoped was a natural gesture. As they passed my pockets, I brushed the lizard. Curses! He did not move, and I was afraid he might bite me. It would not hurt, but it would certainly trigger off Henry's uncontrollable laughter. That would be the utter end: Gide mocked at, and the Brazilian police insulted.

Meanwhile my fingers were stroking the lizard, and I was trying to answer our host's questions and at the time keep a straight face. 'Be off with you! miserable scum of a reptile!—And yet what a curious animal it is, even so. You can only catch it by cunning when you want to cage it, and now that it has got out it refuses to leave me.

Ah, at last it decided to move. I felt it climbing down my bare leg, while I looked at the ceiling and made a confession to the admirer of French culture which came close to making him choke.

'...Gide: ah, yes: what a pity that I have never been receptive to the riches he has bequeathed to the thinking part of mankind. I have, in fact, tried three or four time to read *Nourritures terrestres:* the first attempt was when I was 24, the second when I was 26 or 27, and the last one was quite recently, between Cape Town and St. Helena. But with all the good will in the world I have never been able to get more than halfway through that masterpiece. You see, I'm not receptive to Gide.'

'You should have read him for the first time at sixteen or seventeen...a pity.'

By now the lizard was on the carpet, outside the Chief's field of vision; he was looking around in every direction, quite overwhelmed by the luxurious set-up. A pity he got away; he was already quite tame and we would have become great friends on board.

El Señor Carabiniero made a telephone call.

'I have a friend,' he told me, 'who would like to meet you. He will be over in a moment; he is very keen on underwater fishing, and spends all the time at it that he can spare from running the only hotel on the island.'

At the word 'hotel', Henry and I pricked up our ears, quite unconsciously, no doubt, just as an automatic reaction. You cannot control such reflexes. The single-handed sailor has a sort of instinct that sniffs out the delicious savour of a ready-cooked meal waiting to be put on his plate.

The friend soon came in: a delightful man, on very familiar terms with the chief, and a fluent English-speaker.

Our instinct had obviously not lost its keenness.

'Where are you going to have lunch, you two?'

'Oh, we'll leave that until the evening. The fact is that we both had a huge breakfast before coming ashore this morning. That is what we generally do when we're off for a day's exploring.'

'Nonsense: you'll lunch with me. And what's more it's about time, so I'll take you along. My friend tells me that you want to change two British pounds into local currency for your shopping in the village? I can do that for you: so come along now.'

The hotel was only a few steps from the Police headquarters.

'Whisky?'

'No, thanks: not in this heat. But a Coke would be fine.'

We stretched out in long cane chairs, so comfortable that you wondered whether you would ever be able to get out of them. The blinds were lowered, and the big room, tastefully decorated with pin-ups and little fishes painted on the walls, was as cool as a cellar.

Poor lizards! They must be dying of heat in my pocket. I felt gentle. Odd—could they have melted? I carefully withdrew the handkerchiefs—and one curled-up survivor was lying in agony at the bottom of my pocket.

The casualty was immediately set free under a bush, his nose against the earth over which I had previously poured a glass of water to moisten it. This reminded me of my holidays in Indo-China, when I used to go out barefooted (I was about twelve or thirteen then) to shoot birds with a catapult. My bag used to be plucked, drawn and roasted on the spot, between three stones I used as a fireplace. The birds which were only knocked out were laid on the ground with their bills against the damp earth, from which, as though miraculously, they drew the mysterious force which restored them to life. Then I used to tame them. The squirrels also, in particular, could become very tame. But if the little creatures had been laid not on the damp earth but on a bed of soft grasses, the result would not have been so magical, and many of them would not have survived the shock of the stone striking their fragile little bodies.

The great mythological contest between Hercules and Anteus may perhaps have originated from the ancient Greeks' very correct appreciation of the astonishing power of Mother Earth. Thus the sea is not the only great recuperator.

However, enough of this chauvinistic talk.

Lunch was a gay meal, and we had nothing but compliments for Brazilian cooking. Since we did not wish to abuse the hospitality of our host (believe it or not, but it is true) Henry and I politely refused any expensive alcoholic drinks, on the ground of the heat we had to face outside, and asked for water.

'Mineral water? What sort? I've several brands.'

'You're too kind: but we only want ordinary plain water—you

know, the sort that comes down from the sky. It's the best of the lot.'

'Certainly, if that's what you really want. A little more meat?'

Our host served us automatically, disregarding our protests, which were perfectly sincere, for we could manage no more. When at sea, the sailor is constantly nibbling, night and day, at little snacks; and as a result his stomach must shrink somewhat and prevent him from eating a large meal when the chance comes.

Henry and I had already noted this distressing fact, which used to prevent us from doing full justice to our hostesses' cooking when we were invited out in habour. Behind every effect there must, of course, be a cause, and once that has been discovered you have only to find the antidote. (This is the basis of all real progress.)

The time came when Henry's brilliant brain produced an inspiration. (The glutton must have lain awake thinking about this problem.)

'Tell me, Bernard, have you noticed how little we eat when we're asked out by friends?'

'It's not surprising; our stomachs have shrunk. For example, after *Marie-Thérèse* was wrecked on the Chagos, I could only just about manage half a plateful of rice for dinner, and yet I was in perfect physical shape.'

'Have you ever thought about what the answer is?'

'The answer to what?'

'To eating more, of course, when our friends have the honour of entertaining us. I think I've found the solution, a wonderful device.'

'Stuffing the food into your pockets, I suppose, or developing a pair of cheek-pouches like your ancestors?'

'I'm not a bloody Frenchman, to dream of behaving like a guttersnipe.'

'Watch your language, honourable representative of perfidious Albion! Anyway, let's hear your idea: it must be pretty hot.'

'Have you never thought, you brainless ambassador of a decadent nation, that if our stomachs have shrunk we could swell them out again before turning up when we're invited? Come on, try—think!'

'No good—not a clue.'

'And yet it's perfectly simple. All we have to do is to swallow a gallon of water and keep it there for half an hour, so that our stomachs will develop (and keep) the shape of a nicely rounded gourd.'

The trouble with Henry is that one never knows when he is serious and when he is joking.

We staggered back to our comfortable chairs. Three cheers for the king of sluggards who invented this miracle of comfort, the long cane chair. He must surely have been born under the tropical sun.

Our host, the underwater-fishing devotee, showed us photographs of the giant cod he had speared when fishing with his friends, on the coast of Brazil. We discussed the ideal weapon. This was rather like the differences of opinion expressed by sailors about boats, rigging or nautical tables. He advocated the spring-gun as being very accurate, while I prefer the ordinary rubber-spring spear-gun, extended by a length of broom-handle, as being simple and strong and floating when not loaded.

I asked him whether he had heard of the *Moana* expedition.

Not only had he heard of it, but he had a copy of the first part of the book. 'It's the fullest and most straightforward book I've read on underwater fishing and the shark problem.'

'And Cousteau?'

'Yes, he's a great character, too, is Cousteau. Moreover, he and the *Moana* people each supply what the other lacks. Cousteau is a sort of scientist, an investigator, transparently conscientious and honest. The *Moana* quartet, for their part, have investigated the practical side of the problem with the same single-mindedness in the pursuit of truth, presenting the facts and analysing them with extreme caution, without trying to cover anything up. I take off my hat both to Cousteau and his crew and to *Moana's*. It's a pity that I have only the first part of Gorski's book, and in English at that. One of my old crew-mates sent it to me from England. I'm waiting for the second volume, because that, you may be sure, will be really interesting.'

In spite of my abandonment of chauvinism, such compliments to my countrymen from a little island lost in the south Atlantic gave me great pleasure.

Coffee was served.

'A little cognac, just to help it down?'

'No thank you. It's extremely kind of you, but it wouldn't be a good idea, with the heat out of doors.'

'Come, come, you're not little girls.'

Not liking to hurt the feelings of our host by too uncompromising a refusal, we accepted a drop of brandy before going to do some shopping in the village; just some onions and bread.

He then gave us some local paper money, accompanied by—the bill.

Yes, the bill! including even the drop of brandy!

A number of sailors mention surprises of this sort, when going ashore in Spain or Portugal. Reading about it, I had been greatly amused, little thinking that exactly the same experience would be coming my way. 'Come and lunch with me: it'll be a change from your skilly.... Another glass?... There's some tart left—no sense in wasting it.... Surely you can manage just this little bit....'

And then—click! up comes the bill, with a charming, unaffected smile: and that's because in some countries, that's the normal way to behave.

At the same time, I must add this qualification: the behaviour of some hotel-keepers in Spain, Portugal or Brazil, does not mean that everyone in the Iberian peninsula and Latin America behaves in the same way.

*

Mr. (or Mrs.) Lizard, now fully recovered, had disappeared without further ado when we went to inquire how he or she was feeling. Too bad. We abandoned our lizard catching. They did not know what they were missing: fine fat cockroaches, condensed milk, and a unique experience of ocean sailing.

The next morning was taken up by all the small jobs that one gets through (so far as possible) before sailing: a glance at halyards and sheets, a drop of oil on the axles of blocks and shackles, a tidying-up of the deck and the forepeak, coiling down the mooring warps, stowing things away, and finally sweeping and swilling down.

For our next leg could not continue to be the paradise we had been enjoying since Cape Town. The north-east, or rather the easterly, trades would soon replace the regular south-easterlies which had brought us to Fernando-Noroña. In the north Atlantic, the trades are more irregular than they are south of the equator. Squalls are more frequent and the sea can get up under the influence of the strong current which runs up the coast of Guiana to the West Indies. Finally, the proximity of the mouths of the Amazon, off which we should have to pass, meant that we should have to check our rigging with scrupulous care. Off that huge complex of deltas, many sailing ships have encountered weather that was a very different proposition from the benign south-east trades.

Henry, moreover, wanted to refit *Wanda*'s screw on its shaft. He had removed it before sailing from Cape Town, in order to avoid its braking action, and also in order not to be tempted to use his engine. The engine was not necessary in ocean sailing, but it might give useful assistance in the West Indies.

With a few minutes' work under water, *Wanda* was again a sailing vessel with auxiliary engine. The screw was held face-on to the shaft, driven home by stout blows with a sledge, with a baulk of timber between the two, and finally keyed. So that was fixed. In warm waters, such work is a pleasure: I ought to add that Henry did not make use of my good will nor my aquatic skill to help him—which rather annoyed me. He obviously wanted to show me that I was not the only one at home in the water.

By the end of the afternoon, everything was ready. Our sailing was fixed for the next morning.

'So that's agreed, Bernard? If I get to Trinidad before you, I've won the rubber. If you arrive first, we're all square. Right?'

'Yes, in principle. But I can't push *Marie-Thérèse II* too hard if we have rough weather, because of the rot in the mast. [The mast was in fact perfectly sound, except for the rot just short of the top, but there is no checking rot once it sets in.] And what's more, you have your engine now.'

'True, I've got an engine: but your boat is nearly a metre longer than mine.'

'See you in Trinidad!'

*

CHAPTER 13

Passage to the West Indies

We sailed on February 19th. Everything had been ready since the day before, even to the porridge for breakfast. This would only have to be heated when the sails were hoisted up the masts and stays to catch the south-easterly trade.

Yet it was with a feeling of regret that I saw the beaches and rock formations of Fernando-Noroña slide by to port: for it is really rather wicked, after a stop of only two days, to leave behind a spot which breathes such an air of mysterious beauty. The chart showed a long beach which stretches for nearly a mile to the south-western tip of the island. I was strongly tempted to drop anchor in the big deserted bay it enclosed—but I had to be content with wishing.

Wanda and *Marie-Thérèse II* sailed along the sheltered coast, over an almost dead calm sea, crossed by long, hardly perceptible undulations. A line trailed behind our boats, but it was only Henry's spinner which interested the small barracuda. This was no surprise to me. Never has a fish deigned to take my line, except once, by chance, in the Indian Ocean. I really seem to have no talent at all for fishing.

Wanda then came in closer, and Henry tossed me a barracuda as a consolation.

At sea at last now, for the last 2,000 miles that lie between me and Trinidad—and Joyce.

The staysails and lower running-sails were set, and the two boats, after a brief hesitation about the course to steer, left side by side, heading for the West Indies, for the palms and the primitive rhythm of Caribbean music.

The trade wind was steady, Force 3 to 4, driving our boats at over four knots over a sea that was still calm, while the land gradually disappeared behind a veil of mist. At sunset *Wanda* was in the lead—again. For my part, I was furious at the prospect of a difficult task that was waiting for me in the morning.

I had wanted to improve the performance of the small automatic rudder, and at Fernando-Noroña, accordingly, I had increased the size of the trim-tab which projects forward of the blade. In the calm bay, I had only to unship the rudder, make the alteration on deck and then replace it: a quarter of an hour's easy and pleasant work.

But it is best to let well alone: when I came to use it, the tab proved to be too big. I would have to saw away, under water, the excess length, because, if I unshipped it so as to do the work on deck, the rolling would make it impossible for me to replace the whole rudder at sea. Have you ever tried to saw, under water, through a piece of wood whose movement you cannot control? As a consolation, however, for that unpleasant task, I had learnt a useful fact: contrary to what common sense would suggest, a balanced rudder, the projecting portion of which amounts to more than a quarter of the total area of the blade, will give most disappointing results when the boat travels at more than a certain speed. Why? It is a mystery to me. For, after all, how do you explain why, if the forward projection of a balanced rudder gives perfect results at a speed of two or three knots, the situation is completely reversed as soon as there is a slight increase in speed? And yet it is so. Above a given speed, a too-well balanced rudder swings to and fro. Hydrodynamics is full of such surprises.

The swell increased during the night. The sea had already returned to its normal aspect that you find when you are well offshore and there is no land close enough to check the advance of the waves that travel across it. Moreover, the current was with me, which always puts the ocean in a good humour.

Henry's riding light, slung above the double wind-vane astern was playing hide and seek among the waves.

Marie-Thérèse II, however, was steering badly. With the increase in speed the self-steering rudder tended to swing to and fro, and acted as a brake. As a temporary solution, I lashed a length of line to the end of the little slotted bar, to limit the angle of swing to about thirty degrees. This was an improvement, but I should have to operate (in the surgical sense) in the morning, for my boat was imitating the rolling gait of a drunk.

A dangerous coral reef, almost awash, lies some thirty miles from the direct line between Fernando-Noroña and Trinidad, and I accordingly made a sharp northerly correction to my heading. A morning altitude, intersected by a second at noon, would give me my position.

Meanwhile, I would have to be careful, even though a light-house stands in the centre of the reef, a witness to numerous ship-wrecks in the old days when in a dead calm (for the doldrums are close at hand) sailing ships were driven onto it by the current, which runs very strongly in that area. However, the wind remained steady all night, Force 4, and the light-house was not sighted.

The alarm clock roused me from my bed every hour after mid-night. Lost in contemplation of my re-found gods I had not been able to lie down until that late hour.

What a pity, I thought, that Joyce was not with me, because this sea-level reef has some advantages to balance its dangers: the chart shows a fine sheltered inlet, with an anchorage indicated by a little anchor. There is even a narrow channel leading to a huge basin sheltered from the wind from all quarters, where it would be pleasant to spend a few days, or even weeks, at anchor.

We could have assembled the dinghy, and pulled across to say hullo to the light-house keeper and his family: fine people, you may be sure, because that is always true of the people I meet.

In fact, however, the keeper might well be all alone, with his sea birds and turtles, on the bank that overlooks the south-eastern edge of the reef. We would certainly have made friends. We would have visited his quarters and have shown him ours. He would have said, 'Stay here as long as you like; collect all the eggs you want, dive in the basin which shelters your boat and my fishes, which are just as much yours as they are mine. And when you have been refreshed by your stay on my territory, then move on as you came; and from the top of my light-house I shall watch your sails out of sight and pray to the monarch of the oceans to bear you along for many years to come.'

I was sorry not to have the time to linger there, if only for a week. But I told myself that further on there are other lands and other people. True, but still, I would have liked to meet that man and see his reef. A pity!

'You should have decided on that at Cape Town' (this was my boat's comment). 'Because the idea of time has at last come home to you.'

'True enough, *Marie-Thérèse II*, and it can't be helped this time. We'll get back to normal after Trinidad.'

As soon as it was daylight, the staysails were lowered and the mainsail hoisted to heave to. This would reduce the rolling. Then the small rudder was lashed in line with the main rudder, and, armed with a small saw and a certain amount of optimism, I dived down below the keel.

It took nearly an hour of frustrating acrobatics to cut through a piece of wood no more than six inches wide and three-quarter-inch thick. On deck the same work would have taken me half a minute. But under water the saw kept jamming, while the stern of the boat swayed around in every direction. I had not even the consolation of being able to swear properly. Fortunately, everything comes to an end some time, and at last I was again able to set the sails for the following wind.

She was steering perfectly, and I had got rid of the earlier braking effect.

Once again I was possessed by the racing urge to which I paid tribute by busying myself with the numerous tricks which had distinguished my previous lap: moving the weight forward, setting the extra sail as a mizzen staysail, with the foot free, so that its oblique position took pressure off the stern.

The wind held, Force 4. And *Marie-Thérèse II* swooped along, with a fine white bow-wave, showing the trade wind five well-filled sails.

As though that were not enough, I unbent the working jib, released it from its stay, and hoisted it into the empty triangle between the twin staysails. So now there were six. This was becoming a vice. I then began to laugh, thinking of what would be the reaction of Slocum, that patriarch of the seas, if he saw us sail by with our whole wardrobe spread to the wind. Once he had got over his initial surprise, I imagine that Slocum would have called out to me, 'Carry on, son! Take all the advantage you can of this fine wind, because it won't last for ever; and if you can squeeze out another couple of miles every twenty-four hours, that will make twenty miles in ten days, and thirty in fifteen. Good luck, and may the divinities of sky and sea bless your white sails!'

Meanwhile, those divinities are in a good humour. The sea is dotted with whitecaps glittering in the sun, and the trade is driving us along at nearly five knots. With the added help of the current we shall have logged fine progress in this twenty-four hours.

At our midday position, we were well clear of the reef. We had cleared it by no less than a hundred miles. As for the coast of Brazil, and still more of Guiana, I had no intention of approaching closer than a hundred to a hundred and fifty miles. Out at sea, I should have less advantage from the current but we should be clear of shipping routes, and also of the often disturbed conditions at the mouths of the Amazon, where strong winds and peculiar currents are often in conflict.

For three days now, the trade has been at Force 3, dropping a little in the morning as though for a breather.

The nights are star-studded, the phosphorescent sea lighting up both sides of the boat, which is leaving a dead straight ribbon, bluish-green, behind the rudder. With the added fifteen to twenty miles a day contributed by the Equatorial Current, this is giving a daily average of a hundred miles, in ideal weather.

Are the doldrums going to miss the rendezvous, or shall I meet them further north? It would appear to be the latter. On the fourth day, cumulus appears in the hithero clear sky, and the trade wind grows lighter. We have covered only ninety miles in the last twenty-four hours.

Then the wind, which was dead astern when we started, gradually backs to the east. This enables me to set the mainsail and mizzen on the starboard tack, while the port staysail is lowered and lashed to the squared boom. Thus everything will be ready should the wind shift aft again, and I can set the port staysail in five seconds.

This method of sailing under main and mizzen on one side and staysail on the other was often adopted by *Omoo* in her circumnavigation. It allows you, when the wind is on the quarter, considerably to increase the sail-area, because the mainsail generally offers a very considerably greater area than one of the twin staysails; in addition, you get the full benefit of the mizzen because it does not blanket the mainsail in a quartering wind.

The only disadvantage of this rig is that it is necessary to serve the shrouds where the sail will chafe against them and wear through much more rapidly than you would believe. Jean Gau and Bardiaux (and many others, I presume) used an extremely simple and effective form of anti-chafing. In *Atom* and *Les Quatre-Vents* the after-shrouds that might chafe the mainsail had been enclosed in a plastic tube before they thicken out at the base. The result was a perfectly smooth surface which could not chafe the sail, offered little resistance to the wind, and needed no maintenance. And finally, no soot or coal-dust as you get in habour with conventional servings, to make the sails filthy.

*

No: we still had not reached the doldrums.

That same evening, the wind increased to Force 5, driving from the sky the clouds which had appeared in the morning. *Marie-Thérèse II* pressed on during the night at over five knots, leaving behind her a long phosphorescent trail, while the spray was filling with salt the invisible cracks in her topsides.

This was the north-east trade, or one of its cousins at any rate, for we were not yet in the north-easterly wind-zone.

The twin staysails were lashed to their booms, so that they looked like the booms of tunny-boats. For *Marie-Thérèse II* is now sailing with the wind on her beam under her normal working rig. There will be no difficulty if we have to set the sails again for a wind on the quarter or aft; I shall only have to unfurl the staysails and set them without wasting time and without having to bother about the booms, which are already in position with sheet, guy and lift. I do not know whether other sailors have tried out this method, but it is certainly extremely simple and quick.

In a heavy sea I would, of course, be careful not to drive my boat close-hauled with the booms projecting on either side, for that would increase the top hamper. But with the wind on the beam, even in a heavy sea, there is no difficulty: you have only to haul on the lift and raise the end of the booms to ensure that their extremities do not dip into the sea when you roll. If they do, look out for breakages.

February 25th. We have covered 150 miles on the chart during the last twenty-four hours. *Marie-Thérèse II* has the bit between her teeth. Well done. And thank you, Equatorial Current, for without you we would not have covered more than 130 miles.

Towards the end of the afernoon the wind backs to the east. Our speed increases, because I have been able to set the port staysail as well as the lower running sail, boomed out. The sheet of this sail must be held as far as possible outboard, using the spear-handle: rather a rough and ready contraption, but it works. I removed the spear from the handle, and its thinner end was fastened to the sheet by two round turns. Then the handle was pushed outboard (taking the sheet with it) and the end of this makeshift spar which

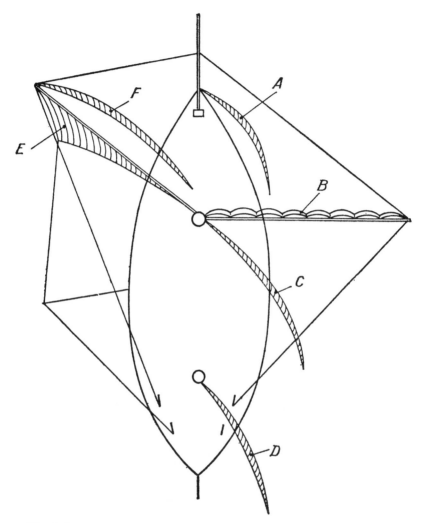

Fig. 8. Arrangement of sails in a quartering wind, in fine weather, when a following wind may be expected.

A. Working jib.
B. The starboard staysail is laced on the squared-off boom. If the wind shifts aft, it can readily be set and the mainsail and mizzen handed.
C. Mainsail.
D. Mizzen.
E. Lower port running sail.
F. Port staysail.

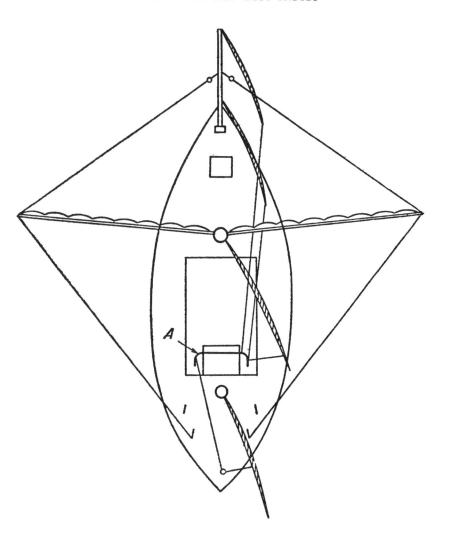

Fig. 9. In fine weather, when the wind is expected to come aft, the boom-guys are tautened to keep the booms from trailing in the water when the yacht rolls or heels. If a following wind is not expected for some time, the booms are swung forward, staysails still reefed, and secured against the bowsprit.

Note that all the sheets are secured on the horse A; they can be trimmed from the cabin.

was towards the boat was fixed in the angle made by the meeting of the handrail and bulwark. Finally, a length of line was lashed to the thicker end of the handle (on the boat side) and to the after chain-plate of the main-shroud. Thus, should this primitive device not prove as effective as I hoped, the handle of my spear would not be left in our wake. Nothing collapsed, but I decided to get a short spar, six feet or so, in Trinidad so that my weapon would not be immobilized just at the moment when a dorado appeared alongside.

In the morning the wind had finished backing, and veered back to the south-east. We proceeded under twin staysails and lower running sails, and covered 160 miles in twenty-four hours. If this continues, Trinidad should be in sight in eight or nine days.

The mouths of the Amazon are 250 miles to port. My boat will not be able to reproach me for risking her within flirting distance of this ill-famed part of the Brazilian coast. But I have no good reason for wishing to do so since it would divert me from my direct route; and a straight line, with favourable winds, is—at times— the shortest distance between two points.

There is nothing to do, except the cooking, which is quickly got through, and a few flicks with the duster when I am feeling particularly energetic.

Supposing I tried to write a little? It is possible that I might succeed today in carrying out the drunken promise I had made to *Marie-Thérèse II* before we sailed from Cape Town. This noble scheme had never, of course, produced a single line, on the few occasions when I made an attempt; for, miraculously, I immediately discovered that some extremely urgent work called for my presence elsewhere . . . anywhere except staring at a sheet of paper that remained obstinately blank.

It was when I was reading the account of *Moana* in Cape Town, that this promise of writing something every day, even if it was only a couple of lines, was solemnly made (in a low voice and without witnesses). After all, if Gorski had the courage and tenacity to put together during his voyage all the elements of so good a book, there was no reason why I should not manage to do so just as well (or, let's be modest, nearly as well).

True—but: there was a 'but' and after the 'but' there were many 'ifs'.

And today, as on other occasions, just as I sat down to write, I was possessed by a sudden dreadful worry about the boat. How was she maintaining her heading? Could not her sails be better set to take full advantage of the favourable wind that will not last for ever? And what about the spear-handle, and the broomstick that are holding out the sheets of the lower running sails? Could they not be pushed a little further outboard to increase the sail area?

And the fat notebook, still virgin, which, in an access of wild fancy, I had envisaged as a dark blur of close-written lines, was put back in the drawer.

February 28th. The trade wind is still in the south-east, but it has dropped for the last two days: average for today and yesterday, 120 miles.

We seem to have reached the doldrums, or rather the area of calm and variable winds that divides the north-east and south-east trades. We are creeping along over an almost dead calm sea under a sky heavy with large cumulus.

Nevertheless, none of the terrible squalls that have attacked me in the doldrums of the Indian Ocean has as yet shown its ugly face in the blessed zone in which we are now sailing. The most that happens is that the wind, still south-easterly, strengthens slightly as a cloudy mass passes over us. But there was to be no really dead calm, for *Marie-Thérèse II* is getting sufficient wind to keep the sails slightly bellied even during the calmest periods.

We have covered 130 miles in three days. The weather is still good, although the sun is off duty somewhere above the clouds. It is only occasionally that I can plot a position line, but as we are well out in the open sea that is sufficient for the time being.

Quite apart from the pretty disturbed meteorological conditions you can meet in the vicinity of the mouths of the Amazon, there is another serious hazard off that river and along the Guiana coast; floating trees which have been torn from the banks of the great river and carried out to sea, where they follow along the Guinana coast as far as Venezuela.

The danger of meeting one of these trunks, bristling with big branches, is particularly great during the rainy season, which produces severe floods in the Amazon basin. You get a violent current, which tears out the trees and washes veritable floating islands down to the Atlantic. Even though we are in the dry season, the danger is still present; and I have on board the South African Wightman's book on his Atlantic crossing from Cape Town to British Guiana to refresh my memory and instil caution. Wightman and his companion collided with a tree at five or six knots, but managed to reach Dutch Guiana and repair the leak.

A slight difference in angle, and a little bad luck, and their boat might have gone straight to the bottom.

It may perhaps have been as a consequence of such an accident that the great Slocum and his *Spray* set off together on their last voyage, over the eternally calm ocean of the seaman's Paradise, ever abounding in fish, where a Force 4 trade wind blows for ever under a flawless sky.

Today, however, one thing is certain: if *Marie-Thérèse II* were to hit a tree-trunk it would not be at the speed of a galloping horse. She would probably not even think it necessary to wake me from my dreams.

My spirits are high, because the current is making a good knot, and a letter from Cape Town is waiting for me to be called for at the post office in Trinidad.

Good news? Of course, because there is no such thing as bad news: you only have to look at it the other way round to see the good side. At the same time, let us hope that the news from Joyce is good, without it being necessary to look at it from the other side.

For three days, *Marie-Thérèse II* was to creep towards Trinidad with a wind of Force 1 to 2, just enough to keep the staysails slightly bellied and allow the self-steering gear to function.

The sky is still overcast, but in a way that does not worry me, because there is no rain. There has been a sharp rise in the temperature, but the forward hatch, which has been open night and day since Cape Town, provides excellent ventilation throughout the boat: the light breeze caught by the staysails runs down the sails, is funnelled into the hatch and escapes by the after hatch, after having passed through the whole length of the hull from stem to stern (and so preventing the damp, so constant and so unpleasant, which you meet during a long period with the wind after and a heavy sea).

In Durban we discussed—Jean Gau, Joseph Merlot, Bardiaux and I—the problem of whether it is better to allow yourself to be invaded by stagnant damp inside an unventilated cabin, or calmly to open a hatch wide even though some scores of gallons of water must inevitably enter from time to time.

After much argument on both sides, a compromise was unanimously accepted: to make a small ventilator, with an opening four inches wide, and place it on a shroud six feet from the deck, out of the spray, fitting to it a flexible pipe which runs down the shroud and across the deck.

There are, of course, ventilators which admit air but not water, but their cost put them out of our reach. In the end I adopted a slightly different principle in Cape Town, which gives satisfactory results.

Two small ventilators, made from curved joints for galvanized water-pipes, were placed at each end of the boat, on deck. Their external diameter was not more than two inches. They could be rotated, and were extremely strong. These ventilators were pointed in opposite directions, and worked by sucking up air from the cabin and expelling it outside.

Henry, who witnessed my deep cogitations about the practical application of this elementary principle, shook his head incredulously.

'In theory,' he said, 'this contraption ought to work; but in practice its output will be practically nil.'

'Slight or not,' I retorted, 'in spite of your sarcasm, there will be a slow but constant supply of fresh air.'

We carried out trials the next week, when my mini-ventilators had been bolted into place. The cabin hatch was open, and the smoke from a cigarette did in fact find its way down to both ends of the boat. Not quickly, it is true, but it did get there in the end. And so the whole boat would permanently enjoy the advantages of fresh air, both at sea and in habour.

*

Today was March 1st.

Marie-Thérèse II had been pressing on since two in the morning over a choppy sea. Sheets of water were sweeping the deck, and the cabin was lashed by spray. We were sailing close-hauled, full and by, the hatches closed; the twin staysails were furled on the squared-off booms, ready to be set as soon as the wind was in the right quarter.

This deterioration in the weather was sudden and without warning—it was just a simple call to order to remind me that winds are not always favourable and that fine weather never lasts for ever. As always when I am obliged to move about on deck at night in a squall of rain, I came out from the cabin swearing that God's providence is a myth.

But, again as always, my readapting was instantaneous and, with my work peacefully finished, the Primus was lit under the percolator: one mug, two mugs, three mugs, and that's the pot empty. And I was no longer sleepy. I switched on the radio. Surely everyone must be asleep now? Ah! I was forgetting the time-zones.

Dawn found me washing on deck, unlike the bad habits I acquired in the Atlantic (I am referring to getting up in the morning, not to washing). I suddenly understood the reason for the liveliness of the sea. It had lost its dark blue colour and had become a dirty grey with a tinge of green. The water of the Amazon—120 miles off the coast of Guiana? It suggested considerable floods on terra firma.

A group of doradoes appeared alongside soon after noon, and I got out the harpoon. Alas, this expensive weapon did not live up to my expectations. The first dorado, over a yard in length, simply somersaulted and escaped even though the point went well home. A second one did the same without any difficulty. In spite of its considerable size, this trident is not much use with such big fish.

I then brought out my home-made Cape Town harpoon: this time a magnificent dorado was beautifully harpooned, hoisted on deck without difficulty and dropped into the cabin through the entry hatchway, because I was afraid that, struggling so furiously, he might get away: and I only just had time to kill him with the hammer before he smashed all my cooking utensils, which were being sent flying up to the deckhead. This fish, four feet long, was incredibly strong; and, as Jean Gau told me when he called at Durban, such fish have an equally incredible vitality. Gau used often to catch them with a very short line baited with a white or red rag which he made flutter alongside, to give the dorado the illusion of a flying fish.

The doradoes followed *Atom* for some weeks and Gau did not like warmed-up fish—so one day when he wanted some fish for lunch he neatly cut a fillet from the side of a big dorado he had hooked and then threw the fish back, its purpose served, into the sea: only to find it the next day swiming alongside. And there it continued the next day, again, and on the following days.

We had covered 130 miles since yesterday, in a deluge of spray and over a choppy broken sea, traversed by unpredictable turbulences, the result of a fresh breeze blowing dead or nearly dead against the current.

Then, towards evening, the wind began to shift towards the

east. There is no doubt but that the north-east and south-east trades have declared war in a dispute over an area that normally belongs to the doldrums. Well, I would rather have it so.

The starboard staysail was set at sundown and the sheets of the other sails eased off for sailing with the wind on the quarter. The weather seemed to want to improve, and the moon, almost full, enabled me to see the horizon between the cloud masses. It would be full again when I made my landfall in the West Indies. That is in line with what I normally reckon for: I try to make my landfall coincide, so far as I can, with full moon when I work out the approximate length of my passage. (Rather showing off, perhaps?) It worked out exactly right for my arrival at Durban and it should do the same for Trinidad.

In coastal navigation, on the other hand, I like to start before the moon is full so that I can have the benefit and consolation of the kindly goddess for as long as possible. Nothing, of course, is perfect, since in the full-moon period the tides are stronger. But without any moon at all, they are no less so.

March 3rd. Another 150 miles to add to yesterday's total.

The wind is still backing and freshening. With the wind almost astern, the mizzen is beginning to blanket the mainsail too much. The second staysail is set, followed by the two running sails. And *Marie-Thérèse II* sails on with a bone in her teeth.

The racing mania, suppressed for some days, emerges again. Once again I shift weight forward, set the jib behind the empty triangle between the twin staysails and the spare mizzen at an angle, to raise the stern: and the result the next day is 165 miles at my noon fix—the best run since *Marie-Thérèse II* entered the water. However, without wishing to upset her, I should add that the current has been some help. It is now only 300 miles to Trinidad.

For the last three days a small sea-bird resembling in shape and size the white sea-swallow you find in the Indian Ocean has been visiting us at dusk and during the night. It sometimes settles on the boom of the port staysail, tucks its head under its wing and has an hour or two's sleep before flying away again.

At once tame and wild, it comes very close but keeps out of range of any expression of the sympathy I feel for it, well away from my hands, which are anxious to pick it up so that I can let it warm up in the cabin; but it is wrong to mistrust me, because I would never treat it like a common Durban pigeon.

Those Durban pigeons were lucky to escape. As they were too cautious to come within catapult range, Henry and I had tried to put into practice a Machiavellian scheme to transport them from the quay into our pressure cookers. This consisted of grains of maize soaked for some days in cheap brandy. These were scattered lavishly where the pigeons used to gather while we waited a short distance away until the alcohol should take effect.

It seemed to work, but the pigeons took to flight and went to sleep it off at home without waiting for me to get in a point-blank shot and the lightning snatch that Henry was deputed to effect.

March 5th. Another 150 miles at noon. If Allah so wills, Trinidad will be in sight tomorrow morning.

Since yesterday afternoon the sea has become blue again. We were then sailing through a dirty, broken sea, whose motion, in spite of the steady wind astern, was irregular. Then a line of foam, as straight as though it had been drawn with a ruler, appeared some hundreds of yards ahead, to vanish into the distance. And in the space of five minutes we crossed this mysterious frontier into blue water, with a regular and restful motion.

It was only afterwards that I thought of what I had forgotten. I ought to have dipped a foot into the sea, before crossing the line that divided the two sorts of water, and again after doing so, to check whether it was simply a difference of colour due to the Amazon or whether the temperature had something to do with the phenomenon. Eric de Bischop, I am sure, would have turned back, in spite of Tatibouet's bored protests.

The moon is full, and *Marie-Thérèse II* is travelling at nearly five knots through the clear night, under a trade-wind sky dotted with fine-weather cumulus. For the north-east trade has now set in and the boat is under normal working sail, with the twin staysails furled on their projecting booms.

My sea-swallow-like bird comes and settles, for the last time, I presume, for tomorrow I shall be a harbour-bird. But, I beg your pardon, Allah—I forgot to add, 'If such be your will.'

*

A clear night, and a sleepless night: because now I have to stay awake. An accursed reef at sea-level runs out from Trinidad thirty miles to the east. Moreover, the moon will have moved into the west when we are in the vicinity of the island and when the moon is behind such a reef, it becomes practically impossible to distinguish the latter. Our heading should take us twenty miles north of it but, particularly in the full moon period, you can never be certain of the currents.

Conditions would be ideal tonight for a star-fix. It is a pity, or rather it is idiotic of me, not to have got down earlier to learning how to make this very simple calculation. My friends in *Jeanne d'Arc* and *La Grandière* were only too ready to explain it to me, but I refused. And why? Because I had not the time to bother my head with it just then. I would leave it until another time, on Martinique, for instance. How foolish can one be?

Meanwhile, I am going to have a sleepless night, with lots of coffee to get me through it.

A school of dolphins has been escorting us for the last half-hour or more, threatening to leave forthwith if I persist in teasing them with the electric torch: when I shine it on them they are terrified— it may amuse me, but they take a very different view.

At nine in the morning, Trinidad is in sight, followed by the island of Tobago, to the north, while we head for the channel between the two. Good navigation, with or without star-sights.

And yet—a divinity of the second rank whispers in my ear that something is not quite as it should be: with Tobago also in sight, Trinidad should be bigger.

A position line, taken just as a matter of principle, places me on a line which runs almost through Tobago, and directly through Trinidad. I work out a second position line. I am a little less cocksure, because I get the same answer.

And then at last I see daylight, and I am rather cross. The big island I can see is Tobago, and the smaller one is an island some miles to the north.

I should, however, have foreseen that when the Equatorial Current is diverted by the large island of Trinidad it would turn north in these parts. A glance at the chart would have made me realize this.

At noon, we round Tobago to the north and follow its western coast under twin staysails over a completely flat sea.

Night overtakes us to the south of the island, and, still under staysails, we hold on for Trinidad, the riding-light swaying in the shrouds; every five minutes I am on deck, because a great deal of shipping uses this channel. Another sleepless night.

Thank God for the inventor of coffee: and thank you, too,

Neptune, for spoiling me with flying fish. Eighteen have landed on deck during the night, more than I have ever seen at one time.

At noon on the 7th, we turned gently into the second channel which leads into the gulf of Paria, with the wind astern. Then followed hours of light head-winds and finally a strong breeze dead ahead that obliged me to close the forward hatch for the sea was climbing gaily over the deck: extremely short, broken, seas, which I would never have expected in this large enclosed bay.

At about ten in the evening, I dropped anchor half a mile from the Yacht Club, beside a ship which was unloading bauxite. It was not possible to get closer in. The breeze had dropped completely, and all I was interested in was sleep.

In the morning, I hoisted the anchor again and dropped it some hours later in the schooner basin, opposite the Customs house. *Wanda* had come in an hour earlier.

'Well, Bernard, your old tub was left behind again?'

'Sorry but *Marie-Thérèse II* anchored yesterday evening at ten off the Yacht Club. That's where I expected to meet you. So, Henry, we're all square—or are you going to argue about it?'

'Did you really arrive yesterday evening?'

'Indeed I did, and we even went for a tour north of Tobago, just to check up on the geography.'

'No kidding? It was the current that put you up there. You kept clear of the Darien Rock, I presume? I thought it better to come into Trinidad from the south. There was a desperate sea in the Serpent's Mouth. Anyway, you've won this time and we're all square, as agreed.'

'You look about finished, Henry. Come and have breakfast here, and then you can take a nap while I go to the post office.'

'Say, have you had a look at yourself in the mirror? You must be in a mighty hurry to get your mail, not to be asleep at this hour!'

CHAPTER 14

Trinidad to Martinique:
250 miles

Trinidad is the largest of the southern Antilles, and the richest; although that, I should add, is a relative term. But it is nonetheless rich, because everything is relative and we are in the southern Antilles.

The chief crops are sugar-cane, citrus fruits, maize and coconuts. The oil extracted from underground in numerous wells on land and from rigs in the gulf of Paria, is carried by pipe-lines to huge tanks and then transferred to tankers of every nationality.

Another precious possession, less mundane than oil and sugar-cane, but infinitely valuable, distinguishes Trinidad from its near kin and raises it to the rank of artistic capital of the southern Antilles—music. It is a music made up of melodies but above all of rhythm, in which you find the naked soul of Africa beating on the skin tom-toms.

Today, however, the ancient drums have been replaced by steel bands, and from these emerges all the passion released by these erstwhile slaves.

As soon as we had assembled our dinghies, we went on shore, where we were speedily and courteously dealt with by Customs, Immigration and Harbour-master. In half an hour our papers were in order, without too much questioning.

The formalities were not of very much importance for me, because the Franco-British agreement entitles a French citizen to stay three months on British territory without a visa (and the consequent inconveniences). British citizens may do the same on French territory. (I learnt something, at any rate, at the French Consulate on Mauritius.)

On the other hand, a shattering experience might have befallen Henry. The Immigration authorities were entitled to demand from him a deposit of a thousand dollars, should he stay longer than two or three weeks (or it may have been a month, I forget which).

And yet Trinidad is included in the British Commonwealth, and Henry has a British passport.

The Trinidadians, however, can land in England without a penny, and stay as long as they please: how that is explained, I cannot imagine.

When asked how long he proposed staying, Henry answered evasively: he wasn't quite sure ... he didn't like staying in the same place too long ... *Wanda* would have to be hauled up onto the slip sometime ... probably at Martinique—and so on.

However, these awkward questions came to an end; for, after all, Henry did not look a pirate, and the hot sun of the tropics almost always tempers administrative regulations; the people of Trinidad are on the whole good sorts and have learnt, in their sun-drenched country, not to take things too seriously.

The post office was only a few steps from where this took place; our mail was soon collected, and we went off to find a cool and quiet corner in which to read our letters in peace.

'Hotel de Paris—let's see what that's like.'

Crossing the hall, we stepped into a shady courtyard, with round tables and elegant chairs, decorated with picturesque paintings. There was a bar, and at the back a dais for a steel-band group. Very tropical, cool, and inviting; and so we sat down.

It was then that the panthers, as I christened them, appeared, to ask us what we ... would like. We had evidently walked straight into a seamen's dive.

Rather maliciously, we enquired about the tariff—that's permissible, surely?—and then ordered a coke and a little peace in which to read our mail and answer it.

'Fine girls,' was Henry's comment. 'Not too persistent, not vindictive, and not expensive ... and wonderfully balanced under sail.'

'With your fertile imagination, Henry, haven't you thought that there may be the solution right here to a troublesome problem: take one of them on board, cart her round the West Indies and she'll earn her living, and yours too.'

'We might even go into it together, both of us, and start a pretty good business: you could be the manager: it would suit you perfectly.'

There was good news for me in my mail, but I should have to be patient. The only way by sea from Cape Town to the West Indies is by passenger-carrying cargo vessel, and passages are booked up a long time in advance. Joyce had put her name down as soon as she received my cable from St. Helena, but she would have to wait her turn. Meanwhile she would be saving up (an excellent idea) and would keep me informed every week about her sailing. At the moment the agency could give her no definite date.

We sent off letters and telegrams (while we were at it, we might as well do it thoroughly). But the first letter I wrote that day was to my chance acquaintance, D. F. Dorward, the ornithologist on Ascension. I passed on to him my observations about the places where I had seen his precious sea-birds. I had noted for him:

February 9th. Between Ascension and Fernando, three hundred miles from Ascension, wideawakes and bo'sun-birds.

February 13th. Six hundred miles from Ascension and five hundred from Fernando, saw a large group of wideawakes, with many juveniles among them. The juveniles were easily recognizable by the spotted wings (which disappear in the adults).

*

Wanda and *Marie-Thérèse II* had to have their bottoms scraped, and after a few weeks we made ready to sail to Santa Lucia, two hundred miles away, where we understood there was a shipyard with a good slip, which was not easy to find on Trinidad.

In any case, we were getting restless.

Henry was the first to sail: 'See you in hell, you French bastard!'

'If it's warm there, you English tramp!'

I was going to stay another week at anchor, because the Alliance Française had organized a little meeting under the patronage of the French consul at which I was going to give a talk about my voyages to the members of the Trinidad branch.

I had already experienced the horrors of stage-fright, but never so badly nor so persistently as on that day. Why here, I wondered, and not on Mauritius? Indigestion? The position of the moon in the sky? I have no idea, but of one thing I was certain, that I was not cut out for the no doubt respectable profession of lecturer. To thank (and reward) me for my heroic bumblings, the secretary of the Alliance handed me a cheque for fifty dollars: that was extremely kind and welcome, because I had not much left with which to go on the town in the Caribbean.

Let's hope, anyway, that Joyce has something tucked away....

And speaking of Joyce, her letters still had no certain news about the date of her sailing. She had her name down, that was all, and it might be in a week, or it might be six.

Since the bottom-scraping was indispensable, I decided to have it done on Santa Lucia, and then to come back immediately to Trinidad and wait for her. I sent a cable to Cape Town, 'Off tomorrow to careen Santa Lucia. Send mail poste restante. Stop. Meet you Trinidad when you leave Cape Town.' Long for a cable, but when you're an established lecturer and have fifty dollars in your pocket....

So that was all fixed. It had in fact been settled for a long time, by letter, that Joyce would cable as soon as she knew her sailing date, and would send me a second cable, just before leaving Cape Town, giving me the date of the arrival of her ship in Trinidad. There would be no danger, then, of our rushing round the West Indies trying to find one another and always being just too late.

*

You have only to look at a chart of the southern Antilles to decide that they must be a sailor's paradise. The islands are carefully arranged along a line running almost due north-south from Trinidad to Martinique, from which a graceful curve continues to the north-west. The long arrows that indicate the trade winds cut across it at almost a right angle. Wonderful—because whatever your destination you have a wind either on or forward of the beam.

There are other, smaller, arrows that you do not notice so soon. These indicate currents, or rather, I should say, the current, which is obstinately westward.

If you look closer, you will see notes in the margin which give the navigator fuller information. For example 'the current is generally strong in the channel between Trinidad and Grenada, where it sometimes makes seventy miles in twenty-four hours'. (The channel itself is about eighty miles.)

In the other channels, the current is generally not so strong, even though it is seldom less than one knot. In other words, wherever you are sailing along this girdle of islands you will be close-hauled, because you have to allow for the strong drift produced by the permanent current in the Caribbean.

On the other hand, the chart, being designed for shipping, does not include another important piece of information which concerns the state of the sea to leeward of the islands. An old schooner skipper told me about this.

'At first sight you might well hope to find a fairly calm sea in the lee of the islands. That is true if you are not more than three or four miles offshore. Further than that, it is not so. The reason is that the big wave masses of the Atlantic pass through the channels between the islands, curl round them and meet again some miles to leeward in waves that come from two directions almost at right angles, and this produces a very turbulent sea.

'With the wind steady, this would not be too bad; but in fact, even at over ten miles to leeward of the islands, the wind is generally variable and always lighter than to windward, so that the boat will not always be able to beat to windward. This is not always the case, but it is a good general rule.'

He concluded with the following advice, the fruit of a long experience of that area: 'Keep close under the lee of each island, even if at times you lose the wind entirely. There will always be a breath you can take advantage of, and you will have a completely calm sea with no westerly current.

'In the channels between the islands, you will meet the normal trade-wind swell, and a westerly current which greatly increases your drift. So you will have to hug the wind as close as possible. But if you have the misfortune to miss the first island (Grenada, as it happens) then I am sorry for you, for the wind may be very light and the sea very broken. You will have a good chance of missing the lot, one after the other, before you land up in the neighbourhood of Guadeloupe, as has happened to me.'

*

On March 26th, 1958, the anchor was stowed on deck, the sails hoisted and *Marie-Thérèse II* set out towards the 'boccas' which open out into the sea opposite Grenada, the first stage of our way to Santa Lucia.

This time I had a young Argentinian with me, Adolfo. He, too, was possessed by the demon of restlessness and he had been captivated by tales of boats ever since lending me a hand as a shipwright. He was even thinking of building his own boat himself as soon as he could get the money together. Until that great day, Adolfo, who had never set foot on a sailing vessel, was pining to be initiated into the sea and learn as much as he could as quickly as possible.

It is against my principles to have a companion at sea, though God knows that I am not a man of principle. But once does not make a habit, and I had real sympathy with this excellent comrade, who might well one day swell our scattered family of sea vagabonds, accepting the joys and woes that go with the instability of our manner of life.

Moreover, it was better that Adolfo should have the chance of getting some idea of the real thing, before committing himself finally and devoting all his energies to building his boat.

So it was, jump on board, Adolfo, and we shall soon be at Santa Lucia. But hold! I had forgotten to add the sacred formula, prudent and respectful, 'If Allah, who is great, wills.'

And similarly I had forgotten to make it clear that we were sailing 'towards' and not 'to' Santa Lucia—but anyway, what's two hundred miles?

At out first call, Adolfo would go back to Trinidad in one of the many schooners which trade among the islands.

We entered the 'boccas' just before sunset.

With the self-steering gear in action, we started on the first leg of the crossing at night. That was already my first silly mistake. In the southern Antilles, the trade tends to back some degrees north during the night. Ordinary common sense would therefore have suggested anchoring in the shelter of one of the islands which enclose the 'boccas' and waiting until, with the coming of day, we could have the benefit of a wind not so much ahead. But, unhappily, I was in a hurry to make Santa Lucia.

There was a fresh blow outside, and *Marie-Thérèse II* was pressing on, hugging the wind as close as she could, that is to say without much conviction because of her foul bottom. That was a second silly mistake. A foul bottom slows a boat down enormously, particularly on the wind. And yet it is not difficult to scrub the hull under water when you are moored, before sailing. I have done it on a number of occasions, the day before anti-fouling. Doing this enabled me to save a lot of time the next day when the bottom-scraping had to be done by grounding the boat at low water: in the tropics, I need hardly add.

The fact is that the day and even the hour of our sailing had been fixed too hastily (which was already silly enough) and then kept to (which was the height of folly).

The time to sail is when you are ready, without bothering about the day or hour. And it is better still to sail when you have an indefinable feeling that the right time has come.

At sunrise we looked for Grenada, which was late on parade. After some hours it finally emerged from its veil of mist, some fifteen miles to windward.

At noon we went about, because we had at all costs to make Grenada and then stick to the girdle of islands until we came to Santa Lucia.

And that was our third mistake: because the westerly current is generally stronger between Trinidad and Grenada than it is further north.

And, sure enough, another tack during the night brought us back to exactly the same place the next day, thankful that we were not still further offshore.

Net result: twenty-four hours wasted from having tried to sail close-hauled against the current with a foul bottom and an under-canvassed boat.

I then turned to the best (or rather the least bad) solution: to head due north as close to the wind as possible. But as the old schooner skipper had told me, the trades were no longer so steady and the broken sea reduced our speed, and so increased the drift. Two days later, which was four day after leaving Trinidad, St. Vincent was in sight and we reached it that night. We had only to cross the channel separating it from Santa Lucia and we would be home.

Sailing alone, I would no doubt have anchored to have a breather; but with Adolfo on board I had had only one idea in my head almost from the outset, to make Santa Lucia and get rid as soon as possible of the alien presence which, without knowing it, was destroying the mysterious balance that united my boat and me.

I believe I silently hated the unfortunate Adolfo, whom I had nothing against except that he was a witness of my poor performance, or rather the poor performance of my boat. Yet how could *Marie-Thérèse II* have had a sufficient sail area, seeing that I had not bothered to replace her mainmast as soon as I arrived in Trinidad? How could she make way against this broken sea with her foul bottom? I might at least have scrubbed her at anchor before sailing—alone.

Fortunately, peace would return on board as soon as we crossed the channel between St. Vincent and Santa Lucia.

Some hours later, Santa Lucia lay fifteen miles—to windward. Then twenty miles, still to windward, the next morning, in spite of a good breeze which had enabled me to go about and make three knots due east. In that particular place, unfortunately, the current was running at more than three knots.

We had therefore, to do what I ought to have done long before and get down to scrubbing the bottom. The time already wasted could not be helped, and we would make up for it very largely later. We hove to and I went overboard with goggles and a scraper, to find myself once again alone with my boat, under water.

The barnacles were scraped off and the hull freed from the growth that covered it. The time went quickly; I thought I had been under water barely twenty minutes, but in fact I had been working on the hull for over an hour.

I then headed north, and it would be just too bad if we made land in Guadeloupe or the devil knows where.

The next morning, six days out from Trinidad, I dropped anchor in three fathoms, off Martinique. Ouf!

CHAPTER 15

In the Caribbean

Wanda was at anchor!

Henry, summoned from his cabin by our delighted cries, issued in tones which were as sonorous as they were colourful (I only hope the onlookers did not understand English) told us that there had never been a haulage slip on Santa Lucia, apart from one vaguely projected. 'The only slip in the whole of the southern Antilles is on Martinique, according to what appears to be reliable information.'

All in all, Allah had not arranged things too badly. In the first place he had taught me that a single-handed sailor is not always a sufficiently social being to be able to carry a passenger of his own sex on board. And secondly, he had brought me to the only place where *Marie-Thérèse II* could be careened. So all was for the best. (In the whole of the southern Antilles the tides are too small to permit careening at low water. The local schooners are careened in the very sheltered bay of Bequia Island, south of St. Vincent, but the ballast keel of a yacht makes this operation impossible.)

I immediately sent a cable to Joyce telling her of my change of address, and another to the postmaster at Santa Lucia asking him to forward my mail to Fort-de-France; so that was all arranged, and I hoped soon to have news of my crew.

Henry had been in the roadstead of Fort-de-France for ten days and had made arrangements for hauling *Wanda* up the slip, but he still had to wait until they had finished with the boat then occupying it. I got in touch with the owner of the slip and explained how much he would be obliging me if he allowed me to use the slip at the same time as *Wanda* or immediately after her. This would enable me to get back to Trinidad as soon as possible, and to be in time. He promised to do as I asked.

The time I spent on Martinique was one of the most depressing periods in my life. There was no news from Cape Town, and none from Santa Lucia, in spite of my cable to the postmaster. I became more edgy every day and in the end I was really anxious and worried.

After a week, I sent Joyce a second cable, and I also wrote to a close friend of hers begging for news. No answer. What could be the matter?

Had Joyce already left Cape Town? In that case, she would have cabled to me at Santa Lucia and the message would have been forwarded to Martinique. So what? Had she given up the idea? I really must know how I stand, I felt, and then the man-boat unit can regain its equilibrium.

Marie-Thérèse II had just been hauled up, when a letter came from Cape Town, from Joyce's friend. It told me that Joyce had left Cape Town in the cargo vessel *Betwa*, on the day that I had left Trinidad: and so our cables had crossed.

Joyce's friend told me also that she had herself cabled to *Betwa* a repeat of the cable I had sent Joyce when I arrived at Martinique. I was in a fine state, I can tell you!

I hurried to the post office and sent a radio message to Joyce: 'Urgent you inform me date and port of arrival.' Her answer came a few hours later: 'Arrive Trinidad in four days.'

The anti-fouling was soon applied, *Marie-Thérèse II* was returned to the water, and the sails hoisted. Mr. Grant, owner of the slip, would not hear of payment for the use of the slip and its facilities: 'Keep your money; you need it more than I do. And take it easy, Bernard; it worries me to see you leaving so nervous and tired.'

I must, of course, I realized, calm down. But at the same time it was essential to reach Trinidad as quickly as possible, because Joyce was not sponsored, and might well be refused permission to wait for me ashore, when *Betwa* had unloaded and sailed again.

I had four days in which to make the crossing, without an engine. If Heaven did not smile on me, I should have insufficient wind in the channel between Grenada and Trinidad, and then the current would cook my goose. Normally, a small sailing vessel without engine waits at Grenada if the wind is light and does not attempt the crossing until there is sufficient wind. It has often happened to sailing vessels to find themselves off the windless coast of Venezuela through not having observed this precaution.

As the afternoon ended, the Diamond Rock (south-east of Martinique) was left to port. The wind was easterly, Force 3. We made good progress during the night and the Port Castries light (on Santa Lucia) came in sight. I had not slept the day before, because of the mosquitos which had invaded the cabin during the last night high and dry on the slip.

In the morning Port Castries was astern, and we were running down the west coast of Santa Lucia until we were blanketed south of the island.

I entered the next channel at sunset. We had drifted a long way west: wind light, current strong. With the coming of night, the wind strengthened to Force 3 to 4, from the east. And *Marie-Thérèse II* held her course again, sailing close-hauled. No light on the northern point of the next island, St. Vincent.

My third sleepless night was coming up—not that that mattered. I wondered whether the most sensible thing to do would not be to anchor at Grenada, which I should make the coming evening or the one after—if the powers above were with me.

From Grenada I could cable Joyce asking her to join me, telephone M. Agostini, the head of the Trinidad Immigration office, explain our position to him, and ask him to be so kind as to facilitate things for my future crew-girl. I am sure that he would tell one of his staff to take Joyce to the schooner harbour and fix her passage to come over and join me.

I would think about this when it was light. But my decision would depend primarily on the wind strength and direction when Grenada was on the horizon.

And then I fell asleep. In spite of the warmth of the tropical night, I felt cold in my bones: no doubt because all the fuss and bother had prevented me from having a proper meal for some days. Very silly of me.

At about ten o'clock the sky clouded over. During the night there was a succession of squalls: nothing vicious, and no need to reduce sail, which in any case was out of the question. The night was black as ink.

Coffee, and then more coffee, to help me to keep awake. Ah! Why had I never decided to keep a tin of Maxiton in the medicine chest on board?

In the end, I made a final adjustment to the self-steering gear, slackened the sheets a trifle, and wound up the alarm. This would wake me every half hour if I fell asleep—and was I sleepy!

I

At one in the morning there was still nothing in sight. That was what one would expect with the current I had already met in this channel during my last crossing. We were probably then about ten miles to leeward of St. Vincent, to judge from the less disturbed water through which we were sailing.

The squalls died away, but the sky was still overcast: the night was pitch black and it was impossible to see a single thing.

*

How long had I been asleep? Impossible to say; less than an hour, anyway, but more than half an hour, because I set the alarm for half-past one and it did not succeed in waking me.

It was then almost two o'clock. A violent crash woke me. I jumped on deck and removed the brass U-bolt that jammed the wheel, and tried to gybe.

A second crash shook the boat. And then suddenly another one, accompanied by a dreadful cracking of tortured wood, while *Marie-Thérèse II*, swinging on a rock, saw her deck and cabin swept by a sea.

The rudder, too, had struck. It had just been torn from its pintles and was trailing in the sea from the wire ropes that attached it to the wheel.

All this had happened in a matter of seconds.

A third sea then struck us and laid us over with the deck under water, before driving us towards the coast. We had passed over a group of rocks, just offshore.

I was clinging to the mainmast, at the foot of which the anchor, chain and nylon warp were lashed, ready for anchoring.

The next moment, the anchor went overboard, while *Marie-Thérèse II*, now in deep water, was moving irresistibly towards the line of foam which marked where the sea was breaking on the shore, some twenty yards distant.

The C.Q.R. had not held on the rocky bottom. It was too late, in any case, because there was not enough room to swing safely, so close to this steep-to coast, where the bottom drops suddenly to ten fathoms.

It was the end. I came out of it without a scratch, as usual, for vermin are hard to kill. But the death-knell was already sounding for my innocent boat; the terrible blows that thundered on her hull flung her again and again on the rocks.

Every impact as she struck the rock, went straight to my heart and tore at my innards. And there I remained, paralyzed, clinging to the mainmast and clasping for the last time what had been my boat: the most beautiful boat in the world.

CHAPTER 16

The Dream Boat

Marie-Thérèse II was built by eye. Not to try to be clever, but simply from lack of money. I had had to adapt myself to the local conditions on Mauritius, where curved timbers for the shaped frames are difficult to come by. To have had a design made, specially adapted to the materials available on Mauritius, would have been very expensive.

It might have been possible to hunt through nautical periodicals and dig out a plan that would more or less meet my requirements; but in that case the hull section would have had a double curve (bilge and bottom) and it would inevitably have been impossible for me to find the necessary timber. In any case, too, I must admit that I like improvising; and if you improvise when you are working from a plan you will get into difficulties. You must either follow the plan faithfully or never set eyes on it.

All things considered, in spite of her great beam in proportion to her length (the ratio was 2·65), *Marie-Thérèse II* was not so slow a boat as you might imagine. Why, however, the extreme beam?

Because I wanted a boat that was comparatively small and yet livable-in. Small, because of the cost of construction and replacements, and also because the smaller the boat the less time you have to spend in maintenance. Livable, because she was to be my home, in the full sense of the word, and not simply an instrument for a circumnavigation of the globe.

I had therefore to accept a compromise. It was extremely difficult to achieve this successfully, and I must admit that I failed. *Marie-Thérèse II* was big enough for me alone, even though there was not sufficient height below the deck-head beams (5ft. 4in.), apart from the after section (6ft. 1in.). But I was proposing to remedy this by changing the coach-roof, on the lines of *Les Quatre-Vents,* which would have given me a height of six feet inside the whole of the cabin. Even so, it was somewhat cramped for two (and some day there would perhaps be two of us): 27ft. 10in. is still only 27ft. 10in. even with a good beam. Still, even if it was not perfect, it seemed to me at least reasonable.

On the other hand, there was a serious problem which made this compromise a complete failure: the problem of maintenance. For, let me say it again, it was not for me a matter of having an instrument for sailing round the world, but a floating home that I could take wherever I pleased, without being enslaved to it. But in fact, that is just what I became, the slave of this boat, built hastily, and, so far as the planking was concerned, from materials of doubtful quality.

Yet even if *Marie-Thérèse II* had been built by a first-rate boat-yard, with prime materials, she would not have remained for long the ideal boat *for me*—and that, even had she been three feet longer. The maintenance problems would have been the same: painting, scraping, re-painting and re-scraping, protection against borers, and so on, one thing after another. For all wooden boats call for constant care and maintenance; it is a matter of necessity, whether the boat is old or new. You have to prevent a new boat from becoming old, and an old boat from giving up the ghost.

But, you will retort to the sailor, since you chose this life, why do you not put up with its demands: we have to do so on land.

That may well be: but let us have a closer look at it together. You live in a house, do you not? Concrete or wood? Concrete, no doubt. And may I enquire why you chose concrete? Because concrete, or stone or brick, needs hardly any maintenance, of course. Whereas wood calls for constant attention to preserve it from rot, from wood-worm, from fire and any number of other hazards. There is even a tendency, more and more marked, to do away with fragile tiles, held on wooden battens, and replace them by flat roofs of reinforced concrete. Is that because the flat roof is prettier? Certainly not: simply because it is stronger, more logical, and needs less maintenance than a nice tiled or slated roof.

It has taken generations of engineers to arrive at an approximate solution to the problem which a large part of mankind is up against: the development of practical dwellings, which release men from so many unavoidable duties and allow them to have more leisure for themselves.

Sailing for pleasure as we know it is no more than sixty years old. Even in that short time boat designers have been able to give the hull of a small sailing vessel an astonishing strength and lines that are often entrancing. That, unfortunately, is not enough. You can build a beautiful timber house almost as strong as a concrete or stone house; but its maintenance will be expensive and that entails a form of slavery. After all, it is much more pleasant and reasonable to spend your leisure listening to music or doing photography or making a film, or talking with one's friends, or taking it easy, than putting in overtime in order to pay for the paint and the workmen you employ to maintain the house.

What both town and country people feel about their houses, the sailor feels about his boat.

'We may admit,' you will answer, 'that you are right in one way. Nevertheless it is still true that those who live on land deserve to own the house of their dreams, because they work for the development and strengthening of society. They serve mankind, through the medium of agriculture, of industry, of trade, of any of the many activities that contribute to progress. Whereas you, Bernard, want to give yourself princely holidays, but do not want to pay a bean. I do not say this with the intention of offending you, but I like to put things bluntly.'

'So do I. But do you not leave singers in peace, and musicians and painters and jugglers? And what contribution do they make to this thing you call progress, with a capital P? As for my princely holidays, I often wonder what induced me to take up this sort of existence. It is true, I have had some princely holidays, as you say: but you make take my word for it, I have certainly paid for them.'

'So, your life has not always been a bed of roses? Then why have you twice gone back to it? How could you consider starting it again?'

'Do I ask you why you remain ashore, where life is equally far from being a bed of roses, and how you can live in the same dump until the end of your days, while our planet is one huge garden? Everyone to his own taste.'

'True, though I am not sure that that is a very sound principle. Even so, it is still a fact that there is no solution to your problem, is there?'

'I do not believe that it is insoluble. You always find an acceptable solution if you think about the problem long enough. Difficult, I grant you, very difficult. There are, in fact two problems, which makes things still more complicated.

'1. The construction of a boat that will be very strong, comfortable, with shallow draught so that it can enter channels that are difficult of access, and that in addition will require practically no maintenance. That last qualification is, in my view, a *sine qua non*.

'2. The finding of a source of income sufficient for this type of life, and allowing one to dismiss the nagging problem of obtaining ones' daily bread.

' "The first aspect of this problem," you will comment, "the boat herself, should, I imagine, not be difficult to solve, in spite of what you say. Modern technology should give you the answer to that. If man is envisaging holidays on the moon in the not too distant fututre, it should not be difficult to build a boat with the characteristics you want."

'True, but what about the cost? and what about the cost of experience? Perhaps you do not know just what I mean by the last sentence? Let me give you a couple of concrete examples which will explain it. Le Toumelin had *Tonnerre* built, and it was lost during the war as a result of enemy action. Then he had *Kurun* built on the lines he wanted, with an extra seven feet of length compared with his earlier boat, which he found too small. With the ıxperience gained during his circumnavigation, Le Toumelin decided he would now prefer a boat seven feet longer than *Kurun* in turn.

'Alain Gerbault had his second boat built to his plans after his circumnavigation in *Firecrest*, which had not suited him. And Gerbault later regretted that he had not had a 27-foot boat built instead of *Alain Gerbault*'s 33-foot.

'In the course of our conversations, Bardiaux assured me that his next boat would be very different from *Les Quatre-Vents:* some twenty feet longer, built of stainless steel or in light alloy, in order to avoid the countless unending tasks that force themselves on the owner of a wooden or iron boat. For Bardiaux the 'slavery' aspect was of prime importance.

'Jean Gau said to me of his first boat *Onda,* that she was much too big (some forty feet, I think). His second, *Atom,* thirty-two feet, required too much mtainenance. "If I had to start again," he told me at Durban, "my boat would not be more than 25 to 28 feet. In any case, I shall have to sell *Atom* when I retire to Tahiti."

'Henry Wakelam finds *Wanda* a little too small. "Starting again, my boat would not be so long as *Wanda,* but I should have more room below by making her wider and altering the shape."

'The Van der Wieles write, "If we started again, we would choose a stout wooden hull with a copper skin," instead of *Omoo*'s hull which required cripplingly expensive maintenance. (Each time they slipped her they scraped her wide bottom right down to the metal.)

'The Merlots were satisfied with *Korrigan:* but then, Bridgitte was growing and *Korrigan* (thirty feet) became too small. They had to resign themselves to selling her.

'Rex King tried to sell his *Jeanne-Mathilde* (forty-two feet) in every port at which he put in because that big boat was a real slave-driver. "If I started again, my boat would be of the same tonnage as *Marie-Thérèse II.* I think her dimensions are ideal," he told me in Cape Town.

'For my own part, I think *Marie-Thérèse II* had the ideal dimensions, *for my own particular purpose,* but not absolutely speaking. And, apart from her dimensions, she was *not by any means* the sort of boat that suited me. She was my third, and I still had not found the right one.'

After these various experiences, not to mention many other more ill-fated ones, one can perhaps understand that a single man or a couple who decided to buy or build their first boat for the great venture, would have very little chance of finding the right boat first time. There are two reasons for this. The first is lack of experience: the most capable sailor in the world cannot, without having lived it, know what the life awaiting him *really* consists in. He will nearly always put most emphasis on the boat's sailing qualities: speed, windward ability, or, on the other hand, comfort at sea at the expense of the other qualities. And his boat will probably be a success in the open sea. But a boat does not spend all her time sailing.

Take a few books about sailing round the world and count up the months spent at sea and the months spent at anchor. You will find that most such passages last from three to five years, with ten to twelve months, seldom more, actually at sea: not to mention the time spent on board before starting and after finishing.

The majority of long-cruise sailors will agree that at sea a boat can never be too big. The magnificent *Omoo,* for example, could be handled by a single person. Bernicot completed a successful single-handed circumnavigation in spite of the size of *Anahita,* a forty-foot sloop.

At anchor, however, when you have to struggle with a heavy anchor and a huge chain, and to pay for paint, new halyards, change the shrouds, cut out and sew new sails, clean the hull, burn off the old paint, apply anti-fouling—then you may well find your boat rather too big and too heavy, and feel that you are rather too enslaved to her—this 'dear and lovely source of worry', as Madeleine Merlot said of *Korrigan*, which after all, was only thirty-feet overall.

And the second reason is this, that man evolves; his ideas can change, and that is an imponderable that you cannot allow for. Take the Merlots, for example. *Korrigan* suited them perfectly, and then little Brigitte arrived.

There are, of course, exceptions. Harry Pidgeon, although he had never sailed before, succeeded first time in producing a boat that was perfect—for him—in which he was to spend many long years. I have even heard that *Islander* was lost after his circumnavigation and that Pidgeon built another boat which was an exact copy, and that the great seaman ended his days in her at over seventy years of age. Another example is that of Frank Wightman. He was a South African, and built a boat in Cape Town like Pidgeon's *Islander* in every respect, in which he twice crossed the Atlantic. Later, when he was in his fifties, he lived permanently in his boat at Saldona Bay, north of Cape Town.

Such examples, however, are exceptional, and it should be remembered that Harry Pidgeon and Frank Wightman remained on their own, which to some extent freed them from the too familiar 'imponderables'.

On the other hand, if the purpose of the boat is to sail round the world and leave it at that, there is no reason why a careful man who has made good use of his reading and can think things out, should not be able to build an excellent boat that suits him and above all suits his pocket. His boat will seldom, no doubt, be the 'ideal boat', but seeing that his adventure is only going to last a few years, does that matter? The trouble is that when he has completed his circumnavigation there is not much chance of his being able to settle down again to his previous way of living. He will probably want to continue his vagabond existence. However, there it is: three or four years of a boat that is not really adapted to his needs may not be too uncomfortable. Longer than that and it becomes impossible. You generally come home as broke as when you started with the added misery of having had the continual worry of wondering where your next meal is to come from, and of asking yourself some rather awkward questions about the future.

Of course, anyone who is already familiar with this sort of life (providing he has enough money) has a better chance of making a success of his next boat; for, besides the technical experience backed by years of practical application, he will have a much more exact idea than a beginner of the real problems involved. These problems, one must never forget, are strictly individual; Le Toumelin's experience is of no use to Bardiaux or Henry Wakelam or Merlot, any more than Bardiaux' is to any other man. The choice of the next boat will depend primarily on the personality of the man who is going to sail in it, and very little on technical considerations.

*

If one had to start again... but what is the use of talking about it, since when you are dealing with boats any ideas that may be put forward make sense only for the man who is explaining them? Still, to do so will help me to clarify my own ideas.

If, then, I had to start again, I would try (at least I hope I would try) to concentrate on the following points.

I would try to have a Marconi ketch designed to my specifications by one of our best designers.

The whole construction will be of good quality timber, previously treated against rot; and the structure will be almost exaggeratedly stout, in order to get the utmost strength and reduce as much as possible the effect of torsion in a strong wind and heavy sea. I would want to be sure that there was no danger of this cracking the fibreglass skin; for hull, deck, and cabin will be completely sheated in fibreglass. It will be expensive, but it will put an end to painting, the danger of borers, the necessity for bottom scraping and the endless slavery I have known with my earlier boats.

The keel will be very long: not to increase stability under way (for with self-steering gear that is no longer a problem) but to increase the strength of the hull when at sea and, still more, when slipped, or accidentally run aground.

The draught will be as small as possible, and I shall probably ask the designer to add bilge keels on each side of the central keel, to increase drift resistance and enable me to slip the boat at low water without having to support her against a quay or to use legs, which are always awkward and often dangerous. From the point of view of the overall strength, it is true that bilge keels raise difficult problems. But, *if the solution to this can be found*, I would not hesitate to add them, because they enable you greatly to reduce the draught, to ground the boat without difficulty, to come closer inshore and to enter channels that are barred to other boats. The friction would certainly reduce the speed a little, but one cannot expect to have everything.

She will be a ketch, because I prefer a divided rig as being easier to handle in heavy weather, even though I realize that a cutter can make better use of a good breeze. It is simply a matter of taste. One thing is certain, my boat will have an ample sail area, enabling her to sail well in light winds and close-hauled. You can always reduce sail, but you cannot lengthen your masts if you want to increase your sail area. A tall mast can be just as strong as a short one; all you need is stout shrouds. *Anahita,* you may remember, did not lose her mast when she turned turtle. Moreover, a tall mast enables you to set plenty of sail in a following or quartering wind, if you use Henry Wakelam's system of extra running sails.

I shall keep the *Omoo* staysails, as improved by Wakelam (see Fig. 4, p. 130). You will have heard plenty about these already in this book, so I shall say no more about them.

If I still have enough money after building the hull, my working sails will be terylene. They are strong, hard-wearing and need no maintenance, because terylene does not rot. Moreover they will be made by a proper sail-maker. If terylene sails prove too expensive, I shall use good cotton, not too heavy (because a heavy sail wears out more quickly in fact than one of medium weight); and I shall treat them myself against rot with *black* 'canvos' as Henry Wakelam did. Does the idea of black sails horrify you? Nevertheless there is a lot to be said for it.

Have you ever seen the reinforced parts of an old sail rot?—at the tack or clew? If you have, you must have been surprised to notice that the small triangles of canvas inside the reinforced patch are still intact, or practically so: and yet it is just these thicker parts which absorb and retain the most moisture and should logically be the first to rot. The reason why they last so remarkably well would appear to be, without much doubt, that they are protected from the light. Fresh water, in fact, is not the only cause of rot in a sail; light plays a large part. That at least is the conclusion Henry Wakelam and I arrived at after a close examination of a large number of rotted sails that had been slung onto the rubbish heap in the yard of the Cape Town Yacht Club.

Sails treated with black 'canvos' would accordingly be impervious both to water and to light, and so doubly protected from rot. You may think they would not be pretty, but you get accustomed to them (just as you do to flat concrete roofs). And if you have to set sail under cover of night for some personal reasons—well, you see my point?

I would like my next boat to be as small as possible, say 28 to 32 feet overall length. The coach-roof would be based on that of *Les Quatre-Vents*, giving full height inside the cabin, with no sharp angles, and so offering little resistance to wind and sea.

The width will be generous, to ensure the maximum space (and accordingly comfort) below: bold canoe stern, external rudder, the mizzen mast stepped on deck, with reinforcement for the beams. The mainmast itself might be stepped on deck, which would greatly increase the space below; but that would call for a good deal of thought, even though with good shrouds there should be no difficulty. There are plenty of sailing vessels so masted and they find it perfectly satisfactory. It might make one a little nervous at first but one would soon get used to it.

Shrouds and chain-plates would have to be stainless steel, of course, and the sheets nylon. But before buying my running rigging I would try samples from different sources and compare their resistance to friction, by trying to cut through a metal rod. I would then find (without surprise, because I have done this before) that a nylon line offered for sale by one dealer proves ten times more resistant to friction than one exactly the same in every respect offered by another dealer at the same price. Of course, if there were any friendly whalers about, my approach to the problem of rigging would be very different.

I need hardly say that this boat will include a down-below steering position in the cabin, as in *Marie-Thérèse II*. Quite apart from the comfort of the arrangement, you have also to take into account the help provided by the saving of energy. With the down-below steering position, there are no more compulsory spells on deck in rainy or even merely unpleasant weather, particularly at night. Moreover, using the down-below position considerably increases the safety of the crew, whether single or multiple. One should remember, for example, the terrifying night spent by the single-handed English sailor, Edward Allcard, in *Temptress*. *Temptress* could no longer heave to in safety in the conventional way, and he was pooped several times by breaking seas when he was running practically under bare poles, in a raging sea off the Azores. *Temptress* had her mizzen mast carried away by a breaking sea during that gale. There was that other big yacht, too, off the Cape of Good Hope, whose helmsman disappeared, carried away by a breaking sea which had torn away all the sails furled on the spars. Such tragic cases are fortunately rare, but they would become practically non-existent with a down-below steering position, enabling one to steer in the wildest weather, comparatively dry and warm, saving strength and calories, and at the same time with a perfect view of the sea from the scuttles around the steering position.

But such a boat, I shall be told, will cost a small fortune. True enough. At the same time, I look at it rather differently. A boat does not cost a thousand, or two thousand, or five or ten thousand. It costs *everything* you possess, and then some more.

So, when I do start again, I shall try to produce something really good.

One question, I know, must be on the tip of your tongue: 'Will this dream boat of yours be an end in itself or a means to obtain some distant and still nebulous end?

'If it is an end, then I fail to understand you, for to spend one's life roaming the oceans like the wandering Jew cannot be a very enviable end. But if, on the other hand, your real intention is to find some ideal spot on which to pitch your tent, why burden yourself with such an expensive boat when you will have to get rid of it in a few years' time? A second-hand boat, wood or steel, would do just as well. And you can get one cheaply enough.'

It is a reasonable question—but look at it from my point of view.

To me, the boat I dream of is both an end in itself and a way of finding, *without looking for it*, the place that really suits me: a corner of the world where the word 'to live' is not synonymous with 'to fight', and where the money-god, with his tribe of clamorous hirelings, is forced to share his empire with other gods, with sun and nature and peace and simplicity of life.

'But why, then,' you may ask, 'a boat that is built to last for ever, if, as I now realize, in a few years time you will have become a landsman?'

'Because,' my answer is, 'I do not believe that it will be possible for me to become completely a landsman. And a boat built to last will allow me, when I so please, to sail away again from my ideal corner, later, if need be to return to it.'

And so, by the help of God, perhaps it will turn out after all that freedom and my boat can, just possibly, be synonymous.

AUTHOR'S POSTSCRIPT
TO THIS EDITION

Since I returned to Europe to write this book and build myself a new boat, much water has flowed over the dam. In the last chapter I visualized my next boat; I saw her as moulded, of wood or fibreglass. I saw her, too, with a maximum length of 30 feet.

Well, *Joshua*, my new boat, which was built only three years after the wreck of *Marie-Thérèse II*, is 38 feet long, steel-built, without a single piece of wood outside, apart from the masts.

Why 38 feet rather than my 30-foot maximum? The fact is I could easily give five or six excellent reasons for such a difference: greater comfort, faster passages, the chance of making a little extra money by using the yacht for charter-cruises or a sailing-school—a 38-foot boat can accommodate twice as many people as a thirty-footer. (With my new boat I ran a sailing-school for three seasons as a result of which I had adequate finances when I set out on my cruise.) But I could give five or six equally good reasons to convince myself that I should have done better to build a smaller boat, no bigger than 30 feet. A 30-foot boat would have cost less in upkeep—but then it would have earned me less when I ran sailing courses. It would have been less trouble to haul out a 30-foot boat, or to weigh anchor—but it would not have given me as much satisfaction in the open sea. *Joshua* rounded the Cape of Good Hope twice, Cape Leeuwen twice, Cape Horn twice. It could doubtless have done as much had it measured only 30 feet, but it certainly wouldn't have performed as well.

Why steel? Because I no longer believe in wood (rot, leaks, borers). And because I do not yet believe in fibreglass and probably never shall entirely—think of a fibreglass boat stranded on the rocks, especially one 38 feet long. And yet fibreglass has a decided advantage for my type of life: it takes little maintenance. But fibreglass lacks the solidity of steel.

Is not a steel-built boat too difficult to maintain? I say no.

As I write these lines *Joshua* is eight years old. She went to Tahiti and returned to Europe round Cape Horn. She left again for a round-the-world non-stop voyage by the three Capes and went on to anchor in Polynesia after completing her circumnavigation. She never sustained any damage, however small. And her hull is as sound as the day of her launching, eight years ago. Her deck is absolutely watertight, her lockers are absolutely dry, a broom has replaced the bilge-pump, and she is protected from electrolysis by zinc anodes soldered on to the hull. I could if I wanted leave her for years in harbour without seeing to her bottom. At this moment I am in Tahiti. Next to *Joshua* lies another steel-built boat, whose owner is at present working on shore to get together a nest-egg before setting sail. He has only slipped twice in five years since he left France. The zinc anodes fixed to the hull protect it most effectively.

People who buy books on yachting often look in them for the author's views on boats in general. My opinion now is that a steel-built boat will give no trouble if the hull is treated sensibly. To any-one thinking of buying a steel-built boat I should therefore be inclined to offer the following advice:

A. Have the hull sand-blasted to one foot above the waterline. Or, better still, sand-blast the entire hull, deck, and coach-roof, if you have the money.

B. Immediately after sand-blasting, apply two coats of zinc silicate. (This solution can be found in Britain under the trade-mark, *Dox-Anode*. In France it is supplied by O.M.E.X.I.M., 1 rue Lord Byron, Paris.)

C. The next day (or several days later) spray all the surfaces to which *Dox-Anode* has been applied with a solution of one part phosphoric acid to fifty parts water. This operation serves to stabilize the zinc layer, so that the coats applied to the hull and keel will hold fast. Without this stabilization, the other paints might not hold properly.

D. Apply priming and finishing coats recommended by a manu-facturer of marine paints, *ensuring that they are right for a steel-built boat.* It is important that the manufacturer should know that they are for a steel-built boat: certain brands of anti-fouling can provoke electrolysis on a steel hull in spite of intermediate isolating coats.

E. Solder three or four small zinc anodes on either side of the keel, distributed fore and aft. Anti-corrosion engineers are not all unanimous as to the usefulness of these zinc anodes if the hull has been treated with *Dox-Anode*. In my view they provide an additional precaution. But the anodes must be soldered, not bolted as is too often the case. (The anodes approved by the French Navy, and probably by every other navy, are extremely effective thanks to the purity of the zinc of which they are made, and they are fixed to a galvanized iron shoe which allows them to be soldered onto the hull.) In France one of the manufacturers approved by the Navy is Zinc and Alliages, 34 rue Collanges at Levallois Perret (Seine).

One final word of advice. Give the inside of the boat six or seven coats of paint and you will have no further worries. As for the outside (hull above the water, deck, coach-roof) a quick go-over with sandpaper and two coats of paint a year should do the trick. After ten uninterrupted months at sea *Joshua* showed no signs of wear. She had had no coat of paint for a year, and only the hull had been treated with *Dox-Anode*. *Ophélie*, a 38-foot steel-built ketch moored alongside *Joshua* at present shows no trace of rust. *Dox-Anode* had been applied all over at the outset.

Bernard Moitessier
Tahiti. March 1970

K. ADLARD COLES

Heavy-Weather Sailing

Bernard Moitessier is one of the great deep-water voyagers and few small-boat sailors have greater experience of the moods of the ocean. In this book he writes of his voyage in *Marie-Thérèse II*, which was made before his passage in the much larger steel-hulled *Joshua* which led to his entry in the Single-Handed Race round the world.

In view of the author's knowledge of the behaviour of yachts in heavy weather, it is with diffidence that I venture to add these notes as, although I made research in the subject of wind forces and the state of the sea for my book *Heavy-Weather Sailing,* my own practical experience has been limited to North European seas and the Atlantic Ocean.

Before commenting on what Moitessier tells us in his book it may be useful to recapitulate the standard methods adopted by yachts to cope with gales, which are: Heaving to, lying a-hull (drifting under bare poles), lying to a sea-anchor, running under bare poles while towing warps to steady the yacht before the seas. In addition there is a fifth method, first practised by Vito Dumas in *Lehg II* and more recently by Moitessier himself and others, which is to run before a storm with plenty of steerage way taking the following seas at about fifteen degrees on the quarter. This technique, which remains controversial, should only be resorted to if the more conventional methods fail, as may occur in hurricanes or fully developed ocean storms with the exceptional seas.

Moitessier was not involved in such a 'survival' storm during the voyages which he describes in this book, although he encountered one such in his next yacht *Joshua*. The first major gale which he met in *Marie-Thérèse II* occurred in the Mozambique Channel between Madagascar and South Africa on passage to Durban. This is a dangerous area of sea, especially in southerly gales setting against the Mozambique Current. Conditions can then become as bad as in a northerly gale in the Gulf Stream.

This gale must have been severe because even after it had

moderated Moitessier states that the wind was Force 7 or 8, gusting violently at times. *Marie-Thérèse II* hove to under mizzen
alone swinging between forty-five and zero degrees to the wind.
This puzzles me as, although it is possible to heave to under
various combinations of sail, the conventional method is to heave to
with a storm jib aback and the mizzen or trisail sheeted hard in.
The aim is to keep the yacht heading close to the wind and fore-
reaching sufficiently to maintain steerage way, position and sail
balance. Under mizzen alone I would expect a yacht to gather stern
way at times with risk of damaging her rudder or tiller and causing
her to fall off beam to the seas. Furthermore, I have found that at
Force 10 (confirmed by a near meteorological station) even a tiny
storm jib will shake the whole yacht like a terrier to a rat. I am
surprised that a mizzen can stand up to the strain for long,
especially in the ocean where a small yacht is alternatively in the
trough under the partial lee of a wave and then exposed on the
crest of the full blast of the wind. However, the proof of the
pudding is in the eating and this is the tactic which was successfully
adopted by Moitessier in many gales. What he emphasizes is the
reliance he places on creating what he terms 'dead-water' between
the yacht and the approaching seas by drifting and giving way thus
making lee-way leaving a sheltering belt of smooth, bubble-ridden
water which he says acts in much the same way as a film of oil.

Marie-Thérèse II weathered the gale successfully and there was
no trouble until the worst was over and the wind had moderated to
Force 5. She was then struck by a huge sea which swept her from
stem to stern and delivered a knock-down blow so violent that she
heeled over until her keel was above the horizontal. Moitessier
describes this as 'one of those isolated waves which come from a
great distance, strike with extreme force and, when they had moved
on, leave behind an impression of comparative calm'. What better
description than this of what is commonly called a 'freak' wave?
Such waves are not scientifically freaks as they are phenomena
caused by the synchronization of differing wave trains, augmented
sometimes by local conditions such as wind shifts, shallow water or
perhaps in this case by the contrary current. This is the third
example I have heard of where a freak wave has occurred after the
gale was over, the other two being in the North Sea and the Mediterranean respectively. Happily such incidents are rare but there is
no doubt that they can occur.

The wave caused chaos below in *Marie-Thérèse II* but more serious was the loss of the hatch cover. Moitessier immediately went forward on deck to pay out his anchor on all his chain and a warp. He tells us that this proved more effective than a sea-anchor in keeping the boat head to the seas. He then lashed the helm amidships to avoid damage to the rudder through stern way.

Despite Captain Voss's demonstrations of sea-anchors, the general opinion today is that they are of little use to deep-keeled yachts except to prevent drifting towards a lee shore. Evidently Moitessier shares this opinion but nevertheless found his trick of letting go his bower anchor (note that it was a C.Q.R., which creates more resistance in the water than an anchor of fisherman type) was sometimes a help. A conventional sea-anchor of adequate size would be difficult to stow in so small a yacht as *Marie-Thérèse II*, but Moitessier devised and describes a substitute made of canvas on rollers which would roll up like a blind and seems to me to provide a useful gadget. In passing I would add that when a boat is lying head to wind in this fashion I would not call her hove to under mizzen but lying to what in effect is a sea-anchor with the mizzen set as a riding sail to help in keeping head to wind, but this is only a matter of idiom.

Another point which the author makes is that for ocean cruising the cabin structure of a small yacht should be low, which is obviously correct as it is dog-houses and high coach-roofs which are the first to suffer if the vessel receives a knock down. More original, however, is the interior position he constructed in *Marie-Thérèse II* whereby he could steer from inside the cabin, completely sheltered from the seas which inevitably invade the cockpit from time to time. He obtained a view aloft through a perspex hatch cover and all round through slits covered with plexiglass. The same principle of giving shelter to the helmsman and avoiding exposure in bad weather was adopted by another great single-handed boat sailor. H. G. Hasler had an interior steering position in his Folkboat *Jester* in the first Single-handed Transatlantic Race.

Moitessier soon had the opportunity to try out the interior steering position he had constructed. 'I now had to remain constantly at the helm,' he writes. He found that 'in the shelter of the cabin this was no hardship, even should a wave break over the stern and sweep the deck.'

During the night he hung a powerful pressure paraffin lamp

(250 candle-power) in the main rigging. This ensured that he would be seen by passing ships which is preferable to being run down under regulation lights which, if as poor as they are usually are, may not be identified in big seas and poor visibility. The pressure lamp proved a success in more ways than one. Besides illuminating the mainsails and jib it shone on the sea 'particularly the slope of the wave towards my side, which I could see clearly through my little windows aft in the reflection of the light on the spume. . . .' 'I managed to estimate their height, present the stern of the boat dead on them and then return to my slightly south-easterly bearing.'

The reader seeking guidance on heaving to and sea-anchors will enjoy the account of the meeting in the cabin of Joseph Merlot's cutter *Korrigan* in the yacht basin at Durban of three famous French single-handers—Jean Gau of *Atom*, Marcel Bardiaux of *Les Quatres-Vents* and the author. It will be noticed that these men use the term 'heaving to' in its broadest sense to mean bringing a yacht to a standstill whether by various methods under sail or bare poles. Their conversation evidently became a little acrimonious at times which is understandable since single-handers tend by nature to be great individualists centred on their own boats and their own experiences. Nevertheless, they had points of agreement as, for example, in the value they placed on drift to leeward to create a belt of dead-water between the approaching seas and the yacht. They shared a common dislike of sea-anchors but occasionally used an ordinary anchor and chain for the same purpose. Jean Gau regarded lying beam-on to the seas under bare poles as dangerous. He considered that a yacht without sail will not drift enough in this position to provide a protective belt of relatively smooth dead-water on which he evidently places great reliance. Lying a-hull is a practical tactic in ordinary gales and the ordinary seas which accompany them, but most experienced yachtsmen agree with Jean Gau that it can be dangerous in severe gales. There is plenty of evidence of knock downs and damage to yachts when lying a-hull if struck beam on by a dangerous 'freak' sea.

Boats differ in type, size, ability and condition, so do their skippers and not least the seas which they encounter. Thus there can be no hard and fast rules about what must be done in exceptionally heavy weather.

K. Adlard Coles

MICHAEL RICHEY

A Note on
Self-Steering Devices

Bernard Moitessier's account of the development of his self-steering
gear is of great interest and it may be useful now to try and see it
within the wider context of later developments, largely inspired by
the three single-handed transatlantic races of 1960, 1964 and 1968,
and of course by the recent crop of circumnavigations.

Marin Marie (Durand) seems to have been the first yachtsman to
have produced a seaworthy wind-vane gear which would hold the
boat's head at a constant angle to the apparent wind (the resultant
of the ship's velocity and the velocity of the wind), although of course
model yachts have been steered in this fashion since the thirties.
The disadvantage of this simple concept, of which Chichester's
Miranda is perhaps the best-known example on a full-sized yacht,
where the helm or rudder is directly controlled by a vane which
simply stays downwind of the apparent wind is that, particularly in
light airs, there is generally insufficient force exerted to steer the
boat properly in any but the most favourable conditions. Some form
of servo-blade either attached to the rudder, as described by
Moitessier, or independent of it as in Hasler's 'pendulum' gear, is
thus used to harness the much greater force of the water moving
past the boat to turn the rudder. In this type of system, the wind-
vane is turned by the servo-blade which in its turn alters the rudder
angle.

Wind-vane steering will normally produce a better course than
the average helmsman, since the gear reacts immediately to every
momentary shift of wind velocity. It cannot, however, anticipate and
in heavy weather off the wind where there is a danger of a broach
a good helmsman might do better. On the other hand Hasler recom-
mends that the gear should not be unshipped for severe weather
even when hove to. No doubt this will depend to some extent on

what tactics are adopted and survival storms or freak seas are of course no more a fair test of self-steering gear than they are of helmsmen. Certainly I have quite happily run *Jester* before a full gale in the North Atlantic with no thought of touching the helm. At the other end of the scale, a sensitive wind-vane gear will steer the boat with light airs scarcely perceptible on deck.

Since the apparent wind is a function of the boat's velocity, a change of speed will produce a change of heading. In conventional boats where the range of speeds is small this effect is absorbed for the most part by the far greater effect of the strength of wind on the triangle of forces. Multi-hulls however have a far greater range of speeds and are subject to rapid accelerations which makes wind-vane steering much less satisfactory.

The angle of the apparent wind alters more quickly for a given alteration of course with the wind aft than with it ahead and thus whilst it is comparatively easy to devise a system that will steer the boat on the wind, it is much more difficult to produce one that will steer her on all points of sailing and notably when running. Furthermore, the engineering tolerances are very small. For example, the effects of friction and inertia are far from linear and it will require a much greater force to alter the vane and tab from rest than to go on turning it once it has started. Or again, the force exerted by the wind on one side of the vane will diminish as the vane turns, as will consequently the force exerted on the servo-blade or rudder. The design of a successful self-steering system is thus a matter of considerable complexity, for all the simplicity of the principles.

Self-steering gears are now commonplace for cruising yachts on this side of the ocean. Ten years ago they were virtually unknown. This development has been very largely the work of H. G. Hasler who started designing vane gears in 1953 and still maintains a commanding lead. In 1960 and again in 1964 he took *Jester* across the ocean and back in the *Observer* single-handed transatlantic race (of which he was the originator), a distance of some 12,000 nautical miles during which he estimates the boat was steered by hand for less than 50 miles. I, too, have raced and cruised the boat some 10,000 miles using the same gear with similarly impressive results.

Self-steering has thus emerged from the experimental stage at which Moitessier describes it here and is on the way to becoming standard equipment for a certain type of yacht. In the main, this equipment is used for short-handed rather than single-handed sailing: to enable, for example, a man and his wife to cruise extensively without any particular hardship. This is not the least of the benefits which the sailing community as a whole derives from the ingenuity and resourcefulness of the great single-handed sailors, amongst whom Bernard Moitessier's splendid exploits rank him so highly.

Michael Richey

INDEX